"I spent almost 15 years at RCA Records. You really can sell a hell of a lot less records and make a hell of a lot more money doing it independently. And you don't have to fight with somebody over fuzzy accounting. I feel great. It's liberating. Independence worked for America. Why not for the artist?"

— CLINT BLACK, popular country artist who began his own record label, Equity Music Group

"Why should someone with a good fan base sign to a record company, where they retain ownership of the master tape of our recordings in perpetuity, as we experienced with RCA and Capitol? It seems criminal that the label merely lends you money to make the record, recoups before you see a dime, and then gets to keep your work for the rest of your life. We've been around the block a few times and know how the game was being played. We want control of the product."

— PAT DINIZIO, lead singer and guitarist for the Smithereens

"Being independent gives you the opportunity to really have vision for your art and what you you're trying to accomplish and to realize how to reach your fans, which is the most important thing that you're doing."

— SPEECH, of the hip-hop group Arrested Development

"The main revolution that I'd like to start is just getting people to play their own music."

— MICHELLE SHOCKED, successful solo artist who started her own label, Mighty Sound

I DON'T NEED A RECORD DEAL!

Your Survival Guide for the Indie Music Revolution

DAYLLE DEANNA SCHWARTZ

BILLBOARD BOOKS

an imprint of Watson-Guptill Publications/New York

Executive Editor: Bob Nirkind
Project Editor: Amy Dorta
Production Manager: Ellen Greene
Cover design by Cooley Design Lab
Interior design by Sivan Earnest

First published in 2005 by Billboard Books,
An imprint of Watson-Guptill Publications,

Crown Publishing Group, a division of Random House, Inc, New York

www.crownpublishing.com
www.wgpub.com

Library of Congress Cataloging-in-Publication Data
The CIP data for this title is on file with the Library of Congress
Library of Congress Control Number: 2001012345
ISBN: 0-8230-7948-1

Every effort has been made to obtain permission for the material in this book. The author, editors, and publisher sincerely apologize for any inadvertent errors or omissions and will be happy to correct them in future editions.

Printed in the United States

First printing, 2005

2 3 4 5 6 7 8 9 / 13 12 11 10 09

Dedication

This book is dedicated to all of the many independent artists who are working so hard to stay true to their souls and create the best music available today. The DIY spirit is soaring to new heights. I thank each and every one of you for your perseverance and determination to rock the world of music. You inspire me with the creativity in your music and your fortitude in marketing it. May independent music continue to prosper and prove that an artist can survive and thrive without a record deal!

Contents

Acknowledgments

First, I want to thank God for all of my blessings. I wouldn't be where I am today without my faith. This book wouldn't have reached its fruition without the support of many people. I'd like to acknowledge everyone who helped me. I consider all of the folks below part of my blessings!

Thank you Bob Nirkind, Executive Editor at Billboard Books, for your sustained faith in me and your consistent support. The wonderful relationship I have with you continues to be a BIG blessing! Thank you – thank you – thank you – to my project editor, Amy Dorta. Your ability to understand my writing style, immerse yourself into indie music, and help me bring this book to fruition so well is a tribute to your expert skills as an editor. And your friendly and supportive demeanor made it a total pleasure to work with you! A VERY big thanks to Kyle Barton, the best intern I could hope to have! You have been a lifesaver, taking care of so many important details for me and doing it so well, with your cheerful nature that made it fun to have you around.

This book was a labor of love. I became more inspired each day by the people I talked to. A great big, jumbo thanks to all of the artists who made time to share their knowledge and experience with my readers. Independent music is finally making a big mark on the music industry and you are part of it! I sincerely appreciate and respect your efforts to bring great music to consumers, and I applaud your work ethics and the creative ways you've made inroads. Thank you a million times to (in alphabetical order):

Gregory Abbott, Matt Allison, Robby Baier, George Baum, Clint Black, Canjoe John, Cari Cole, Clare Cooper, Jennie DeVoe, Pat DiNizio, Danielle Egnew, Kyler England, Lorraine Ferro, MC Forge, Mary Gauthier, Marly Hornik, Tor Hyams, David Ippolito, Michael Johnathon, Christine Kane, Eric Kaye, Justin Lassen, Jennifer Marks, Daniel Lee Martin, Corky McClerkin, DJ Minx, Ezina Moore, Zak Morgan, Lisa O'Kane, Dorothy Potter, Preech-Man, Hamish Richardson, Adam Richman, Evan R. Saffer, Rachael Sage, Anton Sanko, Dean Seltzer, Michelle Shocked, Speech, Howie Statland, Suzanne Teng, Pete Tong, Barbara Tucker, Visual Poet, Michael Whalen, Jonathan Williams, Beth Wood, Mark Wood, Alex Woodard,

I've said it before and I'll continue to say it: The music industry is known for its cutthroat reputation, yet the pros who took time to share their experience and knowledge prove how many wonderful people are in this business. You're all terrific! Thank you to all the people I interviewed for sharing your knowledge and experience with me. You were all such a pleasure to talk to and added to my ability to provide my readers with the best education possible. Thank you a million times to (in alphabetical order):

Dalis Allen (Kerrville Folk Festival), Audrey Arbeeny (AudioBrain),

Alexei Auld, Esq. (Volunteer Lawyers for the Arts), Phyllis Barney (Folk Alliance), Michael Baur (Edel Music AG Germany), Michelle Bayer (Shelly Bay Music & Sugaroo!), Danny Benair (Natural Energy Lab), Gerald Berke, MD (UCLA Center for Voice and Medicine in the Arts), Katja Bittner (Popkomm), Jim Black (ClearSongs), Rob Blesma (Joan Records), Jason Blume (6 *Steps to Songwriting Success*), Bobby Borg (*The Musician's Handbook*), Todd Brabac (ASCAP), Jessica Brandon (USA Songwriting Competition), Tina Broad (BROTHER), Andy Burhenne (Metal Blade Records), Keith Cahoon (Hotwire, Inc.), Brian Caplan, Esq. (Goodkind Labaton Rudoff & Sucharow LLP), Glen Caplin (I-Cue), Jose "Chilitos" Valenzuela (AudioGraph International), Wallace Collins, Esq. (Serling, Rooks & Ferrara, LLP), Mitch Coodley (Metro Music Productions), Paul Corbin (BMI), Julie Coulter (MusicPro Insurance), Zhang Dajiang (China Record Corporation), Jeanne DaSilva (Vault Music), Thomas Degn (NiceandFirm Records), Eric Dimenstein (Ground Control Touring), Nick DiMinno (Three Tree Productions), Bernie Drayton (Three Tree Productions), Dan Evans Farkas, Ricardo Ferro (Zona Music), Rey Flemings (Memphis and Shelby County Music Commission), Kim Frankiewicz (Universal Music Publishing Group, UK), Mathew Fritch (*MAGNET* Magazine), Dick Gabriel (American Federation of Musicians), Michael Gilboe (Copperheadz Productions), Nic Harcourt (KCRW, Santa Monica), Johan Hendrickx (2 Brains Entertainment Group), Bart Herbison (Nashville Songwriters Association International), Clive Hodson (ABC Music), Steve Horowitz (Nickelodeon Online), Kevin Joy (Joy Productions), the late Larry Kamm (YES Network), Kevin Kinyon (Gigmasters), JJ Koczan (*East Coast Rocker/Aquarian*), Jodi Krangle (The Muse's Muse), Jan Kubicki (Magic Records), Amy Kurland (Bluebird Café), Eric Lambert (Association for the Promotion of Campus Activities), Alex Lasmarias (Discmedia International Records), Henri Lessing (Media Records Benelux), Mario Limongelli (NAR International Records), Borje Lindquist (Liphone Sweden), Alex Luke (iTunes), Tom Luteran (EMI Publishing), Sarah Mann (The Music Garden), Steve McClure (*Billboard*), Jim McGuinn (WPLY 100.3 [Y100] FM, Philadelphia), Iain McNay (Cherry Red Records), Jim Merlis (Big Hassle Media), Gregor Minnig (ZYX Music), Martha Moore (So Much Moore Media), Rev. MOOSE (The Syndicate), Nancy Oeswein (Auburn Moon Agency), Carl Parker (ToCo Asia LTD), Kathy Peck (H.E.A.R.), Gena Penney (Whisky A Go-Go), Christopher Porter (*Jazztimes*), Martin Pursey (Bonaire Media), Steve Richards (Hot 107 in Memphis), Jorma Ristila (Stupido Records), Jorge Rojas (FreedomZone), Lillie Rosenthal, D.O. Physical Medicine and Rehabilitation (Kathryn and Gilbert Miller Health Care Institute for Performing Artists), David Ross (*Music Row*), Joseph Saba (Video Helper), Ken Schlager (*Billboard*), Mara Schwartz (Bug Music),

Michael Sweet (AudioBrain), Ted Suh (9 Squared, Inc.), Yuko Suzuki (Avex Inc.), Tony Talbot (Northern Ireland Music Industry Commission), John Taylor (Tootsies Orchid Lounge), Jim Tremayne (*DJ Times*), Phil Tripp (IMMEDIA), Israel Vasquetelle (Insomniac), Billy Joe Walker (Marathon Productions/ Marathon Key Music), Brian Austin Whitney (Just Plain Folks), Matthias Winckelman (Enja Records), Stewart Winter (VideoHelper), Peter Wohelski (Studio Distribution), Jose "Chilitos" Valenzuela (AudioGraph), Sun Xiangyan (Logistix), Rick Zeiler (Jägermeister).

A special thanks to the people at MIDEM for allowing me to experience their wonderful yearly event, and to the city of Nashville for welcoming me when I went there to interview people and learn about its music scene. A special thanks to everyone at The Silver Spoon diner on First Avenue in New York City—where I regularly take my laptop out for a yummy meal with terrific service and lots of refills on my coffee. I wrote a lot of this book there!

The music industry has shown me lots of friendship. After writing this book, I'm thrilled to have experienced a lot more. I want to thank all of my industry friends for helping me find some of the people I interviewed. You know who you are! I feel very blessed to have had the privilege of getting to know so many supportive industry people! Thank you all once again!

Introduction

The music industry is changing dramatically. Since I wrote my first book, *The Real Deal: How to Get Signed to a Record Label from A to Z*, the allure of a record deal has dimmed. Musicians are waking up to the realization that record deals don't automatically create careers. Too many signed artists are poor. Many don't go on to a second or third album. Major labels only promote a small handful of their artists. A career in the major label system can die before it's born. But in your search for a music career, you don't have to be eaten up and spit out by the major-label machine. This book will show you that you have choices. There are many different ways to make money with music. I interviewed 47 successful independent artists and over 100 industry pros. You'll see the many sides to the picture of being an indie musician.

There are more opportunities than ever to develop a career independently. My revised edition of *The Real Deal* encourages artists to stop chasing record deals and start putting all their energy into making money from music. Once you have developed a thriving career, labels will want you more—IF you still want a deal. With the resources available today, I'm a bigger advocate than ever of controlling your own career. When you put the destiny of your music into someone else's hands, your chances of achieving a long-term career diminish greatly. This book takes *The Real Deal* to the next level.

I'm not against taking a record deal. But I want you to be selective. Major labels sign many artists, but few of them truly benefit. When you develop a career first, you're in a win/win situation—you can take a deal that gives you what you need to get to the next level, or you can continue earning an indie living if the deal sucks. I also write relationship books to encourage creating an autonomous, satisfying life if you want to find a romantic partner who makes you happy. Then you can stay in the relationship if you're happy—a winning situation. Or, when you know you have a good life on your own, you can walk away from an unsatisfying relationship—also a winning situation. A satisfying life gives you control and prevents desperation from allowing you to be with someone not good for you. It's the same with a record deal.

Working hard and generating a buzz for your music—one that allows you to earn a living—enables you to walk away from a bad deal or one that won't advance your career. Just like in romance, any deal isn't better than no deal. Labels will take advantage of artists whenever they can. Give yourself the clout to leverage a deal that works for you by developing a career that doesn't depend on a record deal. Then you have choices. Win/win. Being able to say *no* to a bad offer is the sweetest position to be in! The artists I interviewed for this book have been offered many deals, but they turn most down. As I wrote this book, a few accepted deals on their own terms. In

Chapter 2, you'll see that most artists are open to the possibility of working with a record label. But it will be on their terms—or they'll continue earning a living independently.

Win/win. When a label wants you more than you need them, you call more of the shots! Win/win. The leverage of success as an independent allows you to partner up with a label instead of taking whatever deal they offer. If you do consider affiliating with a label, think in terms of a partnership. Labels now give artist development deals to artists they want, and work with some as partners. These artists have more control over their creativity and marketing strategies. Win/win. Refusing to take a deal unless it adds fuel to the career you've already established is the only way to go if you want longevity and satisfaction. Don't be scared to turn a bad deal down. If a label wants you, there will be more offers as your career grows. Artists who wait will get more in the end. Fear makes us jump at things that aren't good for us. If you're convinced you need a label deal to survive as a musician, you probably won't have a career. People get abused in relationships that they enter out of desperation, both in romance and in business. Be prepared to walk!

Declare your independence! Stop looking to others to give you a career. Why be one of those musicians who whine about how no one has discovered them when you can be happily paying bills from music-related income? Why spend time and money sending packages to record labels when you can be answering fan letters and booking gigs that pay? Put all your energy into creating income-earning situations for your music. Throughout this book, I will elaborate on many different ways to do this. It doesn't matter what your genre is: If your music is great, you can use the tools in this book to make a living from it.

Successful indie artists are resourceful and create many revenue streams at once. CD sales alone might not pay bills, but you can try licensing your music to film, TV, advertising, or foreign labels; playing in venues that pay; selling music-related merchandise; winning songwriting contests; touring Europe or other foreign markets; and finding many other alternative venues. Successful indies prove that this adds up to a decent income. It can take time to develop revenue streams. Independents need sources of backup income at first. This book provides options. While you'd rather perform your original music in front of adoring fans, performing for 200 people at a wedding or playing covers at a local club pays the bills and keeps your chops active. Most indies say it's better than having a day job not related to music. I have found lots of ways to increase your income, and I will share them with you in this book.

I highly recommend that you read my other books to complement the info in this one. I'm not saying this to make more money. I've tried not to repeat much here—there was plenty more info that I wanted to share, so no need to reinvent the wheel! *Start & Run Your Own Record Label* has more details on the business end and specific directions on how to market and distribute your CD. *The Real Deal* teaches more important basic info, including specifics on creating a press kit and developing as an artist. This book—*I Don't Need a Record Deal!*—has new details and new resources for musicians who are ready to commit to a career in music without depending on a record deal.

Since I also write about and teach personal growth topics, I've included some of that, too, but geared towards musicians. The industry can eat you up and spit you out. I want you to persevere until you have a sustainable career! Chapter 6 has details on how to hang in there when things aren't going well and tools to build the confidence needed to succeed. The music industry isn't just about the music. You need to sell yourself, which can be hard. Asking for things is even harder. And believing in yourself enough to push for the higher-paying gigs can be the most difficult thing of all. This book has many ways to get over yourself and develop the confidence to go after the success your music deserves. Since this is a survival guide, Chapter 8 has details on caring for your physical health throughout this process.

I entered the music biz when I was teaching school and my students dared me to make a rap record. They said a white woman couldn't rap, but I proved them wrong! After the industry ripped me off, I opened Revenge Records. I wanted to teach the kids how to use the energy behind anger to do something good. I released two rap records, got nicknamed "The Rappin' Teach," wrote songs that made it on the radio, and experienced being an indie. Then I signed other artists. I got label deals for several of them and learned the industry hands-on. After teaching workshops on starting a record label and artist development, I began writing books. I interview the best pros I can find to give you many perspectives and tools for succeeding. Then it's up to you to do the work.

The hardest workers and the biggest hustlers make the most money. Accidents rarely happen in this biz! You may think someone is lucky because he or she has more opportunities. Not true! People create their own luck. The more you play live, the more people hear your music. Make your music's wings strong enough to soar high and catch the eyes of people who can make you the lucky one! Throughout the book, I'll emphasize the importance of doing whatever you can to be THAT GOOD. You must have THE GOODS before putting your music out into the world. Then you can get out and network. The more people you meet, the more contacts you have. Everyone knows someone. We're all within six degrees of separation, and in the music industry it can actually be no more than two or three degrees. So put on your best smile, and get out there and meet folks!

The music industry is tough but it can be conquered. It's time that musicians establish a personal declaration of independence for creating a music career that sustains their livelihood. I had no trouble finding indie musicians to interview. They may not be household names, but they're happily earning a living without a day job. YOU CAN, TOO. Allow me to guide you in developing a satisfying career that you control! Prepare to declare your musical independence!

● ● ● ● **CHAPTER I** ● ● ● ●

Meet the Players

I interviewed about 150 industry people for this book. This chapter has short profiles of each of them, in alphabetical order, as a reference. I've quoted people throughout the book, some in many different chapters. Rather than repeat their pertinent info, you can look up anyone you want and their website right here.

GREGORY ABBOTT (profile on page 37) is a platinum-selling recording artist, song-writer, and producer who was signed to Columbia Records and then chose instead to be independent (www.gregoryabbott.com).

DALIS ALLEN is the producer for the renowned Kerrville Folk Festival (www.kerrvillefolkfestival.com).

MATT ALLISON (profile on page 171) is an independent folk/pop artist who owns and runs Upside Down Records, a label out of Cape Town, South Africa (www.matt-allison.com).

AUDREY ARBEENY began in a band and is now the executive producer of AudioBrain. She was Senior Producer/On-site Music Supervisor for the 1996 Atlanta and 2000 Sydney Olympic Games and has produced music for many sports programs. Arbeeny is developing AudioBrain's sports music library (www.audiobrain.com).

ALEXEI AULD, ESQ., is Director of Education and Senior Staff Attorney for VLA (Volunteer Lawyers for the Arts; www.vlany.org).

ROBBY BAIER (profile on page 93) was previously signed to BMG Ariola in Germany and is now independent, both solo and with his band, Melodrome (www.melodrome.net).

PHYLLIS BARNEY is President of Folk Alliance (www.folk.org).

GEORGE BAUM (profile on page 167) is half of the Christian duo Lost And Found (with Michael Bridges). They released their first album in 1980 and have been performing together ever since (www.speedwood.com).

MICHAEL BAUR was formerly Chief Operating Officer and Chief Financial Officer of Edel Music AG Germany, considered the major label of Europe (www.edel.com).

MICHELLE BAYER owns Shelly Bay Music, works in music publishing administration and music supervision, and places songs in TV and film through her partner's company, Sugaroo! (www.shellybay.com, www.sugaroo.com).

DANNY BENAIR is the founder of Natural Energy Lab, a music marketing company that represents labels and artists for film/TV and advertising. He was Vice President of the Film & Television Department at Polygram Music Publishing for eight years (www.naturalenergylab.com).

GERALD BERKE, MD, is an ear, nose, and throat specialist, mainly a voice doctor for the last 15 years, and Program Director for the UCLA Center for Voice and Medicine in the Arts (www.surgery.medsch.ucla.edu/headandneck).

KATJA BITTNER is Director of Popkomm, an international music conference held in Berlin (www.popkomm.de).

CLINT BLACK (profile on page 41) was signed to RCA Records for almost 15 years. His path is now independent with his own label, Equity Music Group (www.clintblack.com).

JIM BLACK began as a jazz saxophonist and is now a music supervisor for studio and independent films (www.clearsongs.com).

ROB BLESMA is the export manager for Joan Records, a classical music label in the Netherlands (www.joanrecords.com).

JASON BLUME has written songs for many artists, including Britney Spears, the Oak Ridge Boys, and the Backstreet Boys. Some have appeared on Grammy-nominated albums. He also teaches songwriting workshops and is the author of 6 *Steps to Songwriting Success* (www.jasonblume.com).

BOBBY BORG was drummer for Beggars and Thieves, which was signed to Atlantic Records. He played with the rock band Warrant, and he also wrote *The Musician's Handbook* (www.bobbyborg.com).

TODD BRABEC is Executive Vice President of Membership for ASCAP in Los Angeles and author of *Music, Money and Success* (www.ascap.com).

JESSICA BRANDON heads Artists Relations for the USA Songwriting Competition (www.songwriting.net).

TINA BROAD is Manager for the independent band BROTHER (www.brother music.com).

ANDY BURHENNE is Marketing Manager for Metal Blade Records in Germany (www.metalblade.de).

KEITH CAHOON is CEO of Hotwire, Inc.®, a music publishing company based in Tokyo. He was head of Tower Records® in Japan for 18 years (www.hotwirejapan.com).

CANJOE JOHN (profile on page 240) builds, sells, and plays the canjoe, a one-stringed musical instrument with one tuner key, ten frets, and the string pulled through a 12-ounce beverage can as the resonator (www.canjoe.com).

BRIAN CAPLAN, ESQ., is an attorney specializing in entertainment law with Goodkind Labaton Rudoff & Sucharow LLP (www.glrslaw.com).

GLEN CAPLIN is an independent film and television music supervisor and consult-ant (www.i-cue.tv).

CARI COLE (profile on page 103) is an independent artist and voice teacher (www.caricolevoicestudios.com).

WALLACE COLLINS, ESQ., is a music attorney in private practice. He is also currently "of counsel" with the firm of Serling, Rooks & Ferrara, LLP, specializing in Entertainment Law & Intellectual Property matters (www.wallacecollins.com).

MITCH COODLEY started as a freelance guitarist and is now President of Metro Music Productions, providing foreground and background music to the film, broadcast, advertising, and corporate audiovisual industries. He also has an extensive music library (www.metromusicinc.com).

CLARE COOPER (profile on page 176) is a singer/songwriter who has found many ways to use her musical talents as a full-time independent artist (www.clarecooper.com).

PAUL CORBIN is Vice President of Writer/Publisher Relations for BMI in Nashville, Tennessee (www.bmi.com).

JULIE COULTER is Vice President of MusicPro Insurance (www.musicpro insurance.com).

ZHANG DAJIANG is General Manager of China Record Corporation in China.

JEANNE DASILVA has been involved with rights clearances and catalogue promotion as President of Vault Music Services and currently does music supervision full-time (www.vaultmusic.com).

THOMAS DEGN is Label & Product Manager of NiceandFirm Records (Bonnier Amigo Music Group) in Denmark (www.bonnieramigo.com).

JENNIE DEVOE (profile on page 157) is a full-time singer/songwriter who has run her own Rubin the Cat Records since 1998 (www.jenniedevoe.com).

ERIC DIMENSTEIN is a booking agent with Ground Control Touring (www.ground controltouring.com).

NICK DIMINNO is a partner in Three Tree Productions, a music production company. He began as a working musician, has produced major label artists, and now creates music for advertisers (www.3tree.com).

PAT DINIZIO (profile on page 235) has been lead singer/guitarist for the Smithereens for more than 25 years and now tours extensively through the Living Room Concert series he developed (www.patdinizio.com).

BERNIE DRAYTON is a partner in Three Tree Productions. His advertising credits include Burger King™, Sprite™, Nissan™, and many more (www.3tree.com).

DANIELLE EGNEW (profile on page 154) is a solo artist who is also the front woman for indie band Pope Jane (www.danielleegnew.com).

KYLER ENGLAND (profile on page 195) is a full-time singer/songwriter who tours and often opens for top acts (www.kylerengland.com).

DAN EVANS FARKAS is a music editor for film and television.

LORRAINE FERRO (profile on page 189) is a singer/songwriter signed to EMI for her songwriting but still performing independently in a variety of venues and situations (www.lorraineferro.com).

RICARDO FERRO heads A&R at Zona Music in Portugal (www.zonamusica.pt).

REY FLEMINGS is President of the Memphis and Shelby County Music Commission (www.memphismusic.org).

MC FORGE (profile on page 224) tours colleges and festivals as part of the hip-hop group Little Egypt (www.littleegypt-ny.com).

KIM FRANKIEWICZ is Vice President of International at Universal Music Publishing Group, UK (www.umusic.com).

MATHEW FRITCH is the senior editor of *MAGNET* magazine (www.magnet magazine.com).

DICK GABRIEL is Assistant to the President of the AFM (American Federation of Musicians; www.afm.org).

MARY GAUTHIER (profile on page 246) is a singer/songwriter who tours the world. Her music is licensed internationally (www.marygauthier.com).

MICHAEL GILBOE is producer, engineer, songwriter, drum programmer, and keyboardist of Copperheadz Productions (www.copperheadz.com).

NIC HARCOURT is Music Director for KCRW in Santa Monica and also DJs the very popular show "Morning Becomes Eclectic" (www.kcrw.org).

JOHAN HENDRICKX is Managing Director for 2 Brains Entertainment Group, a record label, management company, and booking agency in Belgium (www.2brains.be).

BART HERBISON is Executive Director of NSAI (Nashville Songwriters Association International; www.nashvillesongwriters.com).

CLIVE HODSON heads ABC Music, a record label connected with the ABC network in Australia (www.ABCmusic.com.au).

MARLY HORNIK (profile on page 255) is a pop/rock singer/songwriter who tours the country and sells her CDs (www.marlyhornik.com).

STEVE HOROWITZ is a composer/sound designer currently running the Audio Department at Nickelodeon Online. He also composes for video games.

TOR HYAMS (profile on page 208) is a singer/songwriter who found his niche in composing for film and television (www.tor.net).

DAVID IPPOLITO (profile on page 128) is known as "That Guitar Man from Central Park" after playing his music in the same spot since 1992—and making a full-time living from it (www.thatguitarman.com).

MICHAEL JOHNATHON (profile on page 59) is an acoustic folk singer who's earned a full-time living from his music since 1985. He is also the founder of "WoodSongs," an internationally syndicated radio show (www.woodsongs.com).

KEVIN JOY is President of Joy Productions, a high-tech music house. He has won numerous awards, including the Clio, ADDY, Mobius, and International Film Festival Awards, in more than 20 years as a composer, producer, and advertising executive.

LARRY KAMM, recently deceased, was the creative consultant to the YES Network (the New York Yankees TV station) after being its coordinating director for years (www.yesnetwork.com).

CHRISTINE KANE (profile on page 34) is a singer/songwriter who has toured the country and sold her CDs since 1995 (www.christinekane.com).

ERIC KAYE (profile on page 213) is Creative Director/Executive Producer for The Lodge, a music production, design, advertising, and licensing group. He is also a songwriter and is part of the band the Shrines (www.thelodge.com).

KEVIN KINYON founded and is President of Gigmasters, an online booking service for a variety of gigs covering many genres (www.gigmasters.com).

JJ KOCZAN Editor of *East Coast Rocker/Aquarian* online and print magazine (www.theaquarian.com).

JODI KRANGLE created and maintains The Muse's Muse, an organization/website for songwriters since 1995 (www.musesmuse.com).

JAN KUBICKI is head of A&R for Magic Records in Poland (www.magicrecords.pl).

AMY KURLAND is the founder and owner of the legendary Bluebird Café in Nashville (www.bluebirdcafe.com).

ERIC LAMBERT is Executive Director of APCA (Association for the Promotion of Campus Activities; www.apca.com).

ALEX LASMARIAS is International Assistant for Discmedia International Records in Spain (www.discmedi.com).

JUSTIN LASSEN (profile on page 182) sees himself as a digital symphonist/composer in classical/pop/rock/alternative/electronic music who also sings, remixes, and produces (www.justinlassen.com).

HENRI LESSING is Managing Director for Media Records Benelux in Holland (www.mediarec.nl).

MARIO LIMONGELLI is General Manager for NAR International Records in Italy (www.narinternational.com).

BORJE LINDQUIST is President of the record label Liphone Sweden (www.liphone.com).

ALEX LUKE is Director of Music Programming and Label Relations for iTunes (www.apple.com/itunes).

TOM LUTERAN is the creative director at EMI Publishing (www.emi musicpub.com).

SARAH MANN is a booking agent with The Music Garden (www.music garden.net).

JENNIFER MARKS (profile on page 197) is a solo artist who put out her first CD in 1998 (www.jennifermarks.com).

DANIEL LEE MARTIN (profile on page 149) is a country music singer. His records are released on ChinMusic, a label whose founders/investors are Major League baseball players who believe in Martin (www.danielleemartin.com).

CORKY McCLERKIN (profile on page 00) is a full-time pianist who plays hard bebop, soul jazz, and contemporary jazz (www.corkymcclerkin.com).

STEVE McCLURE is Asian Bureau Chief for *Billboard* magazine (www.bill board.com).

JIM McGUINN is Program Director for WPLY 100.3 FM radio (Y100) in Philadelphia (www.y100.com).

IAIN McNAY is Chairman of Cherry Red Records in London. (www.cherry red.co.uk).

JIM MERLIS is President of Big Hassle Media in New York City (www.big hassle.com).

GREGOR MINNIG is Director of A&R/Vice President of ZYX Music in Germany (www.zyx.de, www.zyxmusic.com).

DJ MINX (profile on page 160) founded Women On Wax with a group of other female DJs. They hold events in Detroit to showcase up-and-coming female talent. Minx has also performed all over the world (www.womenonwax.com).

EZINA MOORE (profile on page 144) is a rock/R&B artist who has sold more than 15,000 CDs and toured around the world (www.ezinamoore.com).

MARTHA MOORE is President of So Much Moore Media in Nashville (www.somuchmoore.com).

REV. MOOSE does college radio promotions and more through The Syndicate (www.musicsyndicate.com).

ZAK MORGAN (profile on page 48) writes, records, and performs children's music and was nominated for a Grammy in 2004 (www.zakmorgan.com).

NANCY OESWEIN is President of Auburn Moon Agency, a booking agency that specializes in the college market (www.auburnmoonagency.com).

LISA O'KANE (profile on page 274) is a country artist who has established an independent touring and recording career in Europe (www.lisaokane.com).

CARL PARKER is General Manager of ToCo Asia LTD, a record company in Hong Kong that licenses music for Asian markets (www.toco-international.com).

KATHY PECK was a recording artist with The Contractions, a national Punk/ New Wave band, before she cofounded H.E.A.R., an organization with resources for helping prevent hearing problems among musicians (www.hearnet.com).

GENA PENNEY books bands for the legendary Whisky A Go-Go in L.A. (www.whiskyagogo.com).

CHRISTOPHER PORTER is Editor of *Jazztimes* magazine (www.jazztimes.com).

DOROTHY POTTER (profile on page 280) is a guitarist, composer, and songwriter who began making music professionally in 1990 and made it a full-time living in 2002 (www.dorothypotter.com).

PREECH-MAN (profile on page 125) started rhyming for money when he was 16 years old and has opened for many artists, including DMX.

MARTIN PURSEY heads Bonaire Media, a publishing company in the U.K. (www.bonairemedia.co.uk).

STEVE RICHARDS is Operations Manager for Hot 107 in Memphis (www.hot 1071.com).

HAMISH RICHARDSON (profile on page 75) is lead singer of the Australian band BROTHER, which began in the U.S. by busking and now tours extensively, having sold more than 200,000 records (www.brothermusic.com).

ADAM RICHMAN (profile on page 230) is a singer/songwriter who broke in through the college market by doing 100 to 150 gigs a year (www.adamrichman.com).

JORMA RISTILA is Managing Director of Stupido Records in Finland (www.stupido.fi).

JORGE ROJAS is Executive Vice President of FreedomZone, a company that brings musicians together with Mountain Dew and AMP Energy Drink for promotions and support (www.freedomzone.com).

LILLIE ROSENTHAL, D.O. PHYSICAL MEDICINE AND REHABILITATION is a board-certified physiatrist specializing in the treatment of musculoskeletal conditions including repetitive strain injuries at the Kathryn and Gilbert Miller Health Care Institute for Performing Artists (www.millerinstitue.org).

DAVID ROSS is Publisher of *Music Row*, the industry magazine of the Nashville music scene (www.musicrow.com).

JOSEPH SABA (profile on page 218) is President and the cofounder of VideoHelper (also see Stewart Winter). He was keyboardist for Fabulon on EMI Records in 1993 and is now happier writing for and running his music library (www.videohelper.com).

EVAN R. SAFFER (profile on page 109) is lead singer of FIXER, which formed in 2000 and now tours extensively (www.fixermusic.com).

RACHAEL SAGE (profile on page 55) is a singer/songwriter with a full-time label manager and three part-timers to back up her national and international touring and CD sales—about 35,000 so far (www.rachelsage.com).

ANTON SANKO (profile on page 180) was one of the first musicians to master sampling technology and became a highly sought after keyboard player and programmer. He now provides scores for film and TV (www.antonsanko.com).

KEN SCHLAGER is Executive Editor of *Billboard* magazine (www.billboard.com).

MARA SCHWARTZ is Director of Film, Television & New Media for Bug Music, a publishing company that collects mechanical royalties (www.bugmusic.com).

DEAN SELTZER (profile on page 251) left his day job in 1996 and continues to tour the country and market his CD (www.deanseltzer.com).

MICHELLE SHOCKED (profile on page 135) left Mercury Records and has kept her recording and touring career going independently through her own label, Mighty Sound Records (www.michelleshocked.com).

SPEECH (profile on page 186) is in the hip-hop group Arrested Development, which was signed to EMI Records in the '90s. Since EMI closed, he has developed a solo career while continuing to record and tour with the group (www.speechmusic.com).

HOWIE STATLAND (profile on page 259) is a singer/songwriter who made three records for RCA and now records and tours independently full-time (www.soundarte.com).

TED SUH is Chief Marketing Officer of 9 Squared, Inc., a company that licenses music for many uses, including ringtones (www.9squared.com).

YUKO SUZUKI is Manager of Business Affairs for Avex Inc., a record label in Japan (www.avexnet.or.jp).

MICHAEL SWEET is Creative Director of AudioBrain. His specialty is creating music for video games (www.audiobrain.com).

TONY TALBOT is former Chief Executive Officer for the Northern Ireland Music Industry Commission (www.nimusic.com).

JOHN TAYLOR is Entertainment Director at the World Famous Tootsies Orchid Lounge in Nashville (www.tootsies.net).

SUZANNE TENG (profile on page 116) is a New Age music artist with a specialty in the flute (www.suzanneteng.com).

PETE TONG is a top internationally recognized dance music DJ and producer based in the U.K. He also has one of the most popular dance music shows on BBC Radio 1—it's broadcast internationally.

JIM TREMAYNE is Editor of *DJ Times* magazine (www.djtimes.com).

PHIL TRIPP is the founder of IMMEDIA!, an entertainment company in Australia that has many online music resources and publishes a directory of the Australasian music industry (www.immedia.com.au).

BARBARA TUCKER (profile on page 72) is a singer and dancer who had dance hits with Strictly Rhythm. She now executive produces her own projects and has promoted the Underground Network (www.barbaratucker.com).

JOSE "CHILITOS" VALENZUELA is the founder of AudioGraph International and author of *The Complete Pro Tools Handbook* (www.audiographintlstore.com).

ISRAEL VASQUETELLE is Publisher of *Insomniac Magazine* and also has his own independent hip-hop act (www.insomniacmagazine.com).

VISUAL POET (profile on page 224) is part of the hip-hop group Little Egypt (also see MC Forge).

BILLY JOE WALKER is the owner of Marathon Productions/Marathon Key Music. He produces top artists, including Travis Tritt.

MICHAEL WHALEN is an award-winning composer for TV, advertising, and films. His Emmy Award–winning music can be heard on more than 350 television and film projects as well as thousands of national advertisements, including the theme for ABC's "Good Morning America" (www.michaelwhalen.com).

BRIAN AUSTIN WHITNEY is the founder of Just Plain Folks, an organization of artists and industry professionals (www.jpfolks.com).

JONATHAN WILLIAMS (profile on page 136) is in the U.K. hip-hop act Hoodz Underground, which has received consistent high-profile media coverage. Williams also runs Trackshicker Records, the label that releases the group's music (www.trackshickerrecords.com).

MATTHIAS WINCKELMAN is Managing Director of Enja Records, a jazz label and publishing company in Germany (www.enjamusic.com).

STEWART WINTER is a composer and the cofounder of VideoHelper, a boutique production music library. VideoHelper's music is heard in dozens of movies and many significant TV spots on all networks and cable channels, including the theme music for "20/20" (www.videohelper.com).

PETER WOHELSKI is Project Manager for Studio Distribution, a national and international distributor (www.studiodistribution.com).

BETH WOOD (profile on page 82) is a singer/songwriter who tours all over the country and has performed with top artists (www.bethwoodmusic.com).

MARK WOOD (profile on page 201) is an electric violinist who has achieved platinum and gold records. He now composes for television and has a music library of his original compositions (www.markwoodmusic.com).

ALEX WOODARD (profile on page 51) is a singer/songwriter who has earned a full-time living for years by putting out his CDs and performing in a variety of venues (www.alexwoodard.com).

SUN XIANGYAN is General Manager of Logistix, a marketing and promotions company in China (www.logistix.com.cn).

RICK ZEILER is Director of Marketing & Brand Development at Jägermeister (www.jagermeister.com).

● ● ● ● **CHAPTER 2** ● ● ● ●

Why Be Independent?

I believe that independence breeds happiness, and happiness breeds creativity. Too many artists are unhappy with their label deals. Many don't have the creative freedom that leads to their best work. Indie artist David Ippolito (profile on page 128), also know as That Guitar Man from Central Park, says, "I love being independent—in every way. It gives me freedom and a platform. I feel like independent artists are in the front covered wagon in a whole new frontier. No one knows where we're going yet. I love the word independent and everything that goes along with it."

After being signed to EMI for years, indie artist Speech (profile on page 86) of the hip-hop act Arrested Development has been independent since 1995, and loves it. He explains, "It gives you the opportunity to really have a vision for your art and what you're trying to accomplish. You decide how much your product is going to cost them, what you're going to give them. It allows you to have a firsthand relationship with the fans." When you achieve indie success, it's exhilarating! DJ Minx (profile on page 160) adds, "I feel I'm exactly where I need to be. I have the power to make happen *what* I want to happen and *when*. I love being my own boss!"

Indies may not get as much recognition as the most successful signed artists, but everything is possible. Being indie didn't prevent children's artist Zak Morgan (profile on page 48) from being nominated for a Grammy in 2004. He explains:

It's not easy to get nominated, but it's not impossible. There's not some club that won't let you in if you're independent. It can be done, especially if it's outside of the big major pop categories. There are 105 categories. Ninety percent of the Grammys are people you've never heard of. It's a great opportunity because that word "Grammy" opens doors galore.

Doors of opportunity are opening wider, and indie artists are walking through. Consumers are fed up with the music coming from major labels. They're realizing that the newest, most innovative music comes from indies. Independent music is thriving in today's markets. When I wrote my first book in 1997, not many unsigned artists had a CD. Now, it's common. New technology makes it much cheaper to record. Manufacturing costs are down considerably, so more independent music gets exposure. Each CD released might not get a huge market share like the blessed few on a major, but indies need to sell MANY fewer CDs to make a decent living.

There are more avenues than ever for indies to make money. In this chapter, many of the indies I interviewed explain why they chose this route. Indie artist Christine Kane (profile on page 34) is very proud of being independent. She says:

It's a great time to be an independent artist. Music fans are hungry for something real. And they're seeking out alternatives to TV and commercial radio. I'm blown away by how many great artists I know who are doing this independently, and doing it well. It is a challenge, yes. And it's tempting to get whiney or victimy about it. But I believe it's where the future of art is headed.

Ken Schlager, Executive Editor of *Billboard*, says that independent labels are more important and more viable than they've been in many, many years because of consolidation at the major label level. While he's referring to established indie labels, much of the explanation can apply to indie artists, too. It can be very hard to compete with the marketing dollars that majors have, but that's softened somewhat because major label budgets are tighter. Schlager explains, "At the same time, the Internet has leveled the playing field a lot because it's a very inexpensive and effective way to reach a target audience—specific consumers. An independent label can do that as easily as a major label, and perhaps even better. An independent artist, even without a label, can do that, too."

YOU CAN!

Yes, you can make a living as an independent! The proof is in the artists I've interviewed for this book. Some of them made a conscious choice to be independent, while others developed their careers independently out of necessity. Indie artist Hamish Richardson of the Australian band BROTHER, which has sold more than 200,000 CDs independently (profile on page 75), says:

> We were busking (street performing) in Los Angeles when we first arrived, just to survive. We'd get big crowds and good tips but were constantly being asked where people could get recordings. As fresh-faced kids almost straight off the farm in Oz, we never contemplated the possibility of making our own records. We were biding time until we landed a big record deal and lived happily ever after. Then, suddenly, we decided, "Lets just record our own." There we were, sitting in a production line between sets on the street, cutting and pasting artwork to have enough cassettes for the next show. We broke the 1,000 mark before moving into mass production. Suddenly, we're an "indie success story," with our own label, catalogue, and lifestyle brand. What the hell's going on?

The happiest musicians tend to be those who, like BROTHER, control their careers. Indie musicians are lovin' it! They create music THEIR way and they choose their own paths. Indie artist Kyler England (profile on page 195) says, "I'm a do-er. I wasn't interested in waiting around. The reality these days is that you have to be willing to build a career for yourself, so it was in part necessity. There's no point in waiting for a record deal to find you, especially when there are so many amazing resources available to get a career started yourself." Successful indies find all sorts of ways to make money, because those ways really do exist. They know if they get an offer they can't refuse from a label, they may end up accepting it. But if they don't get one that provides great support with distribution, touring, and promotion, they CAN earn a living without one. Indie artist Canjoe John (profile on page 240) says, "It is hard to convince anyone that good music can come from a stick with a string and a can. I chose to prove that success starts with hard work and perseverance, and that the music business *is* business." Indie artist Dean Seltzer (profile on page 251) began with the intention of having fun by playing music but found out where that could lead. He explains:

> *I planned to do solo acoustic shows, sitting on a porch at Chili's® playing Jimmy Buffett tunes. The idea was to have a good time. It snowballed into the band. The highlight of my career was when we opened a show for Dwight Yoakham with about 5,000 people. The club gave us 200 tickets to give away, instead of paying us. I gave them to diehard fans. When the announcer asked if there were any Dean Seltzer fans, I thought people would boo. Our fans, and others, rushed to the stage. We sold out of merchandise. It was a real good show of support.*

Indie artist Alex Woodard (profile on page 51) says, "Getting signed was a big goal when I started. I wanted what most songwriters want—to write, record, and play songs that people connect to. I thought the only road was getting signed. That changed quickly. I didn't have a choice. If no one else would take a chance on me, I had to take a chance on myself." Woodard did just that, and now he's happily earning a full-time living both performing live and selling CDs. He says he'd take a record deal that would give his career more fuel, but he's not waiting around—win/win. It feels so good when you're not desperate to find a record deal! Indie artist Lorraine Ferro (profile on page 189) says:

> *I had to experience hard knocks before going the independent route. When I began, I wanted to be a rock star and get the big deal. I came close many times, all the way from the showcase to the paperwork. But the deal always fell through. A company can pass on you because they feel like they already have a "you" at their label and don't need another one. I was passed on once because although they loved my sound. . . they said I sounded like a "real rock chick" but why didn't I smoke, do drugs, have a bottle of Jack on me at all times. Why wasn't I the "real deal"? Hmmmm. . . . Okay, sign me and I promise to be a junkie? I don't think so.*

When you support yourself independently through your music, you can wait for the *right* deal. Or, if a deal won't allow you to do music your way, you can remain independent. Indie artist George Baum, half of the Christian band Lost And Found (profile on page 167), says:

> *Initially, we were independent because we had no real aspirations to play music for a living. Over time, we remained independent because no label*

would have been interested in a band with our sparse instrumentation or unique sound. These days, we remain independent by choice, since signing with a label seems to be the kiss of death for most bands. We had some interest from a label, but fortunately that did not work out, since all their other bands have dried up and disappeared.

Successful indie artists have gotten over the fantasy that an A&R fairy will drop dust on them and whisk them off to the Rock Star Ball. They focus more on a desire to make a living from their music and to create their own reality rather than try fitting into some glass slipper that makes them a star. Indie artist Jennie DeVoe (profile on page 157) says:

My goals when I began were to never work behind a desk. I wanted to make a living by singing. After graduating from college, I took a job at a music studio pouring coffee, getting doughnuts, and singing an occasional jingle. A huge superstore liked a demo and contracted me for five years of commercial voice-over and singing work. It was an awesome gift because it allowed me freedom to travel around, do music, and build up my fan base. People frequently ask about the path I chose and how I got going independently. I'd be lying if I said it was a "plan" per se. It sprouted out of a passion for writing and a love of performing.

Indie musicians tend to have more passion and seem happier. Indie dance artist Barbara Tucker (profile on page 72) says, "I haven't worked in about 20 years on a nine-to-five." She was signed for years and chose to leave and become an indie. Indie artist Clare Cooper (profile on page 176), who has been independent since 1997, says "It's not financially stable, but I don't have to get up at 7:00 A.M., knowing I'll spend the entire day doing something I'm not interested in. It's been scary at times, but I hope I never have to go back!"

I won't delude you: It's a lot of HARD WORK to get a music career going. There's lots of competition and plenty of road blocks. DeVoe explains:

It is rewarding to be a performer with a loyal audience, some radio play, and nice record sales under my belt. I am proud of what I've accomplished. The aggravating part of being independent is not ever being on an equal playing field with major label artists in the public's, radio's, or a booking agent's eyes, even if you are a better artist/songwriter. The truth is there are lots of walls you can't climb over if you're not on a major, and that totally sucks. But if you're good enough, you have a shot at getting heard. I have a song that is good enough to be voted the best pop song in a world song contest put on by the Billboard *folks; that tells me I have something special. On top of that, I've licensed songs to major television shows.*

Yet DeVoe admits, "It is hard to keep totally and utterly positive when some of what you need is just not offered to you unless you are on a label other than your own." Indie artist Beth Wood (profile on page 82) agrees that there are times when being independent is very hard: "Competition is fierce, money is tight, and pep talks are few. But an indie artist is free to protect and nourish his or her vision, and that is important above all else. No one will tell me what set list to play, how to dress, or how long to spend on the StairMaster™. Those are my decisions, as they should be."

Throughout this book I'll give you tools to use for earning a living—IF you have THE GOODS. I'll also give you resources and personal tips for hanging in there to create independent success. It's not always going to be easy. Indie artist Daniel Lee Martin (profile on page 149) says, "I love being independent one minute and hate it the next. It is ten times the work that being with a label would be. It's also ten times as fulfilling. There are quite a few downs, but there are a lot more ups. The ups mean so much more, because you know that they are a result of your labor, hard work, and your belief in what you do." *You* will have to decide if you have it in you to go the indie route. Jazz artist Corky McClerkin (profile on page 64) did more than 20 years ago. He explains:

Despite limited exposure and limited success after three years, I realized major jazz labels might never come knocking at my door. One early lesson was that versatility as an artist was sometimes perceived as a disadvantage to both radio stations and record labels. My first recording reflected music of many different genres (hard bebop jazz, gospel vocals, rhythm and blues). Fortunately, I developed relationships with DJs and media personnel to receive airplay consistently with targeted stations. A close friend told me, "If you truly want success, learn how to make it happen for yourself." I started my own label, WinCor Records, and produced my first album.

PROFILE
....
Gregory Abbott is a platinum recording artist, songwriter, and producer who was signed to Columbia Records. He has reached No. 1 on charts around the world and has won two Soul Train music awards. Abbott's songs have been placed in film, television, commercials, and interactive projects. His remastered hits from Columbia are licensed in the U.S. and abroad. He has also done numerous public service spots (Bands to Beat AIDS, Rock Against Drugs) and appeared in singing roles in film and television.

McClerkin has put out his own records and has been performing ever since.

There's nothing wrong with being signed to a label—IF it pushes your music. Succeeding independently *first* puts you in the driver's seat when you negotiate your contract with a record label. Zak Morgan understands the deal with labels: "Initially I had no choice but to do it independently. A record company is a business and wants to make money. You have to demonstrate that you can earn someone else money before anyone will want to work with you." But you CAN earn good money independently—IF you have the talent and the drive to market it. Indie artist Mary Gauthier (profile on page 246) worked hard and now reaps the rewards. She says, "I'm really proud of what I've put together in the last five years. Nobody handed me anything. I went out and got it." Nobody will hand it to you either.

TAKING CONTROL

Being independent means *not being dependent*. Signed artists put their careers in the hands of record labels. While many A&R people are passionate about music, they often can't help artists who don't sell in large quantities. Too many signed artists wait around for their label to develop their career—dependent! Artists usually have to give over control of the master, yet if the label does nothing, the artist can't use it—dependent! Waiting for a label to discover you is the surest way *not* to develop your career—dependent! A record deal probably won't magically "give" you a career if you don't already have one. Mary Gauthier says:

> I think musicians get told this great lie that someone's going to discover you and make it happen for you. It puts you in a position of powerlessness—if that doesn't happen, you get burnt out and feel defeated. I look at it the complete opposite way. You have to make it happen for yourself—pick up the phone, start booking yourself, play shows, make CDs, go around the country. I've been going around the world and selling to whoever would buy it. You have to just do it.

Being independent gives you control over your career. That doesn't mean you'll succeed, but it's an opportunity. Major labels rarely do artist development these days, so promotion, tour support, and publicity aren't guaranteed if you're signed. Pat DiNizio, lead singer and guitarist for the Smithereens, agrees: "The labels never did a good job of promoting. When we were with Capitol, our single 'A Girl Like You' was making its way up the charts to the Top 40, and they gave up on it. We had to pay for radio promotions based on revenues from being on the road." Signed artists quickly lose the stars in their eyes. South African indie artist Matt Allison (profile on page 171) says he originally wanted to sign a major deal. Not anymore!

Over the years I stopped trying to be a rock star and started to enjoy making music independently of labels, the feeling of sharing it with others and being in control of my own career. I love the flexibility and freedom I have in creating my art and career. I also love not being in huge debt, waiting to sell 500,000 units before I see my first paycheck, if you pay back your advance by then! Being indie, within the first few hundred to a thousand I start seeing profits.

Developing yourself as an independent artist gives you a much better shot at a career than chasing labels does—not a *sure* shot, but a better shot. So much of it is up to you: You can sit on your butt, or you can work it as hard as possible. Kyler England says, "I like being in charge of my career and my future. These years of handling all aspects of my career taught me a lot about the business, which gives me confidence in choosing my team of people to help build my career." Indie success begins with talent. If you're not THAT GOOD, work on your skills first. Without THE GOODS it's hard to generate a buzz. But if the talent is there, being an indie can be exhilarating. Former RCA artist Howie Statland (profile on page 259) says, "I love being independent. I hope that I can continue to do it because it's not easy. To me, it's worth it because I'm more in touch with the end product when it's independent, which is really beneficial."

Acts such as Dave Matthews, Hootie and the Blowfish, Nickelback, and Godsmack developed their careers, selling many thousands of records before they had label interest. Indie success gave them the leverage in their deals that put them into the win/win situation I talked about. Indie artist Danielle Egnew (profile on page 154), solo artist and front woman for the band Pope Jane, loves being independent. She says:

There is artistic and creative freedom, but also the burden of making things happen yourself, which is fulfilling but can be very tiring. But if I want to crack out a meditation CD, and then crack out some industrial stuff, I don't have some producer breathing down my throat about finishing one project before I move on to the next. I tend to be very prolific, and recording, for me, is like doodling.

Being independent allows Egnew to "doodle" and still sell lots of CDs—over 75,000 with Pope Jane as of our interview. Platinum artist Gregory Abbott (profile on page 37) was signed to Columbia Records. He now loves his freedom:

With the ever-shrinking list of major record labels, being independent takes on a new meaning. The number of independent labels has grown dramatically. So much so that it has become the new paradigm of the music business and no longer the exception to the rule. Major labels now function more in the capacity of distributor and promoter, as opposed to producers of records and developers of talent. Discovering new talent and generating new styles has become the playground of the independent labels, and this I like. The independent music-buying public are always open to new music and choose for themselves what they like. Bravo! I like this independent thinking. . . making my own decisions and living with the consequences. This is when I'm at my best. It doesn't mean I'm always right, but in making decisions, I learn and grow. And when I am right, hallelujah!

When you're independent, you control what goes on in your career without label people breathing down your neck. Of course, there's no label to bankroll you, but being creative in the music marketing biz can pay off with indie success. Electric violinist Mark Wood (profile on page 201) earned a super living for years as an indie:

Why wait for a company to tell me when and when not to record? To tell me that I'm valid or not valid, or that I'm not going to sell records if I play that music? That helps one realize they must create their own business ventures. I started to get paid to write music and realized there is an income pipeline that I needed to tap into, and I needed to stay away from record companies and managers—the pipeline stops with them. They decide how much you get after taking their percentages. Once I realized I could talk directly to directors, music people, producers—and could get paid directly from clients—everything changed. I manufacture all my merchandise and products. The ultimate for me is that the money I generate is specifically given to me for what I produce. I truly believe that it is possible to make a living without a record deal.

Wood is now in a band signed to Interscope, but he mentions it casually, because this isn't the main part of his career or his main source of income. *Control* is the major factor in deciding to be an independent. Indie artist Ezina Moore (profile on page 144) agrees:

I LOVE IT! There is nothing more rewarding than being your own boss and creating the life you imagined. My dreams come true everyday. I left a $50,000 salary to do music full-time in 1998. My goal was to replace my income completely in one year, and I did that. My salary has increased every year since I quit my full-time job. I now have the courage to dream even bigger than ever before because I have seen the light.

MAJOR LABEL EXODUS

More than ever, acts on major labels are not renewing their contracts. Well-known recording artists are leaving record labels to pursue independent careers. Barbara Tucker, signed for more than six years to Strictly Rhythm, says, "They did not release me. It was a choice that I had to make. As a businesswoman, I wanted to go to the next level. A man would keep promising to do this and this but never showed faith. So I said, 'Honey, it's time for me to find a new man.' It's a good feeling. I'm not helpless." After almost 15 years with RCA Records, followed by a five-year break, recording artist Clint Black had several offers to choose from while he worked on his latest album. Soon it was time to decide which deal to take. Black says:

> I started to get depressed and realized that I didn't want to take any deal. Early on we had talked about the possibility of starting a label, but there was nobody to run it. When I had to decide on a deal, I told my manager I wasn't going to sign any of them. I would finish my CD and we could talk about it again. Mike Kraski became available and my manager knew he was like-minded. So we began to put the label business model together. Once that began, I had no trepidation. I feel great. It's liberating. I was away for five years. I think no matter where I had been, we'd be coming back from being gone. You go away for five years and it's a campaign to get back up, get your slots, and remind people why they'll like your new record. The reception has been good. We expected a climb after five years out of the business.

Natalie Merchant left Elektra to put her songs out on her own label, Myth America. The Eagles started Eagles Recording Company II. Jimmy Buffett's *Far Side of the World* album on Mailboat debuted at No. 5 on the *Billboard* 200 Album Chart. After leaving Epic Records, Pearl Jam now distributes their music independently on the Internet. Gregory Abbott changed his relationship with record labels to his advantage:

PROFILE

Clint Black was signed to RCA Records for almost 15 years. After taking five years off, he chose to pass on the major label deals he was offered. Instead, he put his music out through Equity Music Group, a record label he founded that also signs other artists. Black wanted to start something that would impact the industry's way of doing business and also dispel common industry myths that a record company can't survive if it pays its artists, and that there's no way to account for record sales as you go.

I enjoy the freedom and control over my work and career that the independent scene affords me. I also like to record more frequently than what's usually required under most major label deals. Since I write and produce my own material, it's more appropriate for me that I relate to a major label as a production company, as opposed to a direct signing. I believe it's important to own your master recordings. Now, if I release something through a major, I license it, since I no longer need their financing to produce CDs. I have used Sony/Columbia in this way. This frees me to release records independently, through a major, or a combination of both. The independent scene has grown exponentially, as has its credibility. And with the Internet, the sky's the limit.

In 1987, indie artist Michelle Shocked signed an unusual deal with Polygram. In exchange for no advance, the master rights reverted to Shocked ten years after release. But after her third album, she was told that this label wouldn't be able to properly promote her because she had too good a deal. Shocked refused to renegotiate and got stuck in major-label hell. She now says:

For five years I couldn't release records, which then didn't allow me the benefit of having promoters want to book me on the strength of a new record. I had to play on the strength of my live shows. At a certain point in that process I began selling my own bootlegs at shows. I was not allowed legally to distribute them at retail outlets. I had to treat them like merchandise. I sustained and supported myself as an artist for five years that way.

Shocked found a lawyer to free her from this unfair deal in 1996, and she retained the rights to her masters. She says it took her about five years to find the emotional maturity to accept the whole endeavor and start her own label. She released an album on her label, Mighty Sound, in 2002 and is still going strong.

Would You Take a Label Deal? Maybe . . .

Most artists in this book have been offered record deals. Few find them acceptable, but they keep their options open. Zak Morgan says, "Being independent is a source of pride. You've done it on your own. But it is a business. I probably won't sign with a label, but it's worth investigating. I would like to stay independent: I'm selling thirty to forty CDs a day on Amazon to people I don't know. I like owning my product, but if someone can do things I can't in terms of getting my product out there nationally, I'll investigate it."

Indie artist MC Forge (profile on page 224) of the hip-hop act Little Egypt says, "If the label deal were *right*, we would take it. We've done enough that we have leverage to negotiate. But we're not starving and don't *need* a deal." Visual Poet, also of Little Egypt, adds: "We're trying to get into a position where we can pick and choose the right deal." Being independent extends your control to a better position for negotiating with a label. Daniel Lee Martin is open to the *right* deal, but he can wait. He's had many offers from major labels, but as he explains, "The opportunities that came along weren't where I *needed* to be. Some labels wanted me to change my style, and it wasn't right for me."

Hip-hop indie artist Preech-Man (profile on page 125) says labels have no say on his style: "A major label would have to talk a lot of zeroes, because I've never had to answer to anybody about what I write. If they want input, it's going to cost." Few indies want a straight, standard artist deal. When you've developed a career, you're in a better bargaining position for a deal you benefit from. Kyler England says, "Long-term, I'm very interested in partnering with a label, be it independent or major. Frankly, I want to spend a lot more time writing and making music and less time making phone calls and standing in line at the post office!" But few indies will rush into anything. Indie artist Rachael Sage (profile on page 55) never says never, but she is wary:

> I've seen many peer artists get signed to major labels, spend a million dollars, make a record, and get dropped. Or not get dropped and have no way to put out their own work. That would kill me. I've been offered record deals in the past, but the closer I looked at the deal being offered, the more I appreciated being independent and the luxury of all the mistakes I can make and learn from. For me, it's about winding the circle, finding like-minded people, connecting and reaching out.

Successful indies would only accept an offer that provides many benefits to help expand an already thriving career. Indie artist Jennifer Marks (profile on page 197) just accepted one. She explains, "I had been busting my butt as an indie artist, and the president of Bardic kept seeing my name pop up. I wasn't actively seeking a deal but I put it out that I was ready for help to take my career to the next level." A majority of the artists I interviewed say they are open to a record deal—IF it's the right one for advancing their career. Mary Gauthier signed with Lost Highway Records (Universal) after our interview. Her hard work as an indie put her in a good position for a deal worth taking.

Smart indies think in terms of "partnering up" with a label, not putting their career into a label's hands and at its mercy. Speech is talking to record labels and may even be signed again by now—IF he gets the right partnership. He says, "We don't want to sell ourselves one hundred percent to anyone. We've been there, and we see many benefits in not having to do it that way. For us, it *must* be a business *partnership*. The label would be involved with marketing or distribution, but we'd still be in control." Arrested Development is in a position to be selective because the group makes enough money independently. Speech's solo indie album sold 120,000 copies, and the group's sold 200,000 copies—just in Japan! Make it work for you, if you choose a label route. You CAN, if you develop your independent career first. Tina Broad, manager for BROTHER, says:

> Never say never. We'd look at any proposal. The bottom line is that a label or distributor has to be able to demonstrate to us that they'll add value to us—that their value to us will be greater than the cost to us in having them in the mix. In a way, the industry revolution has meant there are many, many more creative ways to structure win/win relationships between artists and labels. We're not rushing into anything, and we're happy to continue to asset-build ourselves, but I think sooner or later we'll need to find a bedmate.

Matt Allison agrees:

> After I put out my first band EP, a major re-recorded a single for a showcase CD. From then on, I knew I wanted to do this myself. Corporate politics and the treatment I received while working with them was nothing short of abysmal. All I got out of the deal was debt. When I needed a hand up, I got a ragtag hand out. If I found the right deal and label, I'd consider it, preferably a larger indie—they give their roster more time and are more in tune with how to market their artists. They have more money for promotion than I do, and normally a great distribution chain to take my music to more people. As an acoustic singer/songwriter, I feel a smaller label that knows its niche is a better bet. I've yet to hook up with one I feel meets my needs and whose needs I meet, so for now I'm happy where I am.

Would You Take a Label Deal? No!

Many artists have no desire for a record deal. David Ippolito says, "I want to do exactly what I'm doing now, but [for more people]. That's the only difference. I don't want anything else in my life to change—just the zeroes after the one in the check. If I took anything, it would have to be a distribution deal." Like Ippolito, some artists are adamant about staying independent. Indie artist Michael Johnathon (profile on page 59) is staunch in his belief that independent is the only way to go. Once signed to Capitol Records and now grateful to be out of the deal, he explains his view of signing with a label:

> They give you $150,000 and you think you're rich. Then you realize you have to pay for the album, the music video, the producer and musicians. If

the label sells 150,000 albums, they make more than half a million dollars profit—and you make nothing. Then when you pay off your advance, you still own nothing. When a bank loans you money for a house, when you're done paying them, you own the house. With a record deal you do not own the master or the work that you slaved over. I learned fast that a major label deal was not what I wanted. I started Poetman Records. The formula is simple: Unless you're going to sell more albums in the store than at live gigs, you do not need a record company. Even if you sign with a really good independent label, they're not going to get you on the racks. They sign artists who will sell five to ten thousand copies at gigs. If you sell ten thousand copies at gigs, that's $150,000. Why give half of it away when they only gave you a ten to fifteen thousand dollar budget to record the album to begin with?

Clint Black agrees: "The record companies don't pay for the recordings. The artists do. If I pay to record the product, the idea that then *they* own it does not make any sense." Pat DiNizio adds, "Why should someone with a good fan base sign to a record company where they retain ownership of the master tape of your recordings in perpetuity, as we did with RCA and Capitol. It seems criminal that the label merely lends you the money to make the record, recoups before you see a dime, and they get to keep your work for the rest of your life."

George Baum sees no point in taking a deal. He feels being independent is like breathing: "Though we've tried to think up a record deal that would be an improvement over what we have, we can't even envision it. Any arrangement (with the possible exception of distribution) involving a label means making less money and having less control over our lives. We can't even imagine any record deal that would benefit us." Ezina Moore has been offered record deals but has turned them down. She says, "I have friends on labels who sold millions of CDs but can't afford to eat at McDonald's® and can't look at themselves in the mirror. Being on a label means that I have absolutely no faith in my abilities to make it happen on my own. I am worth more. We are all worth more."

CHAPTER 3

Do You Have What It Takes to Be Independent?

N ot everyone is cut out to be an independent musician. Before making the decision to go after an independent career, you—as a musician—must ask yourself:

- *Have you done everything you can to be as good as possible?*
- *Can you trade dreams of being a star for the reality of making a living from your music?*
- *Are you willing to bend with suggestions from others?*
- *How much time are you willing to devote to your music career, including touring?*
- *How big are your balls?*

The sections in this chapter will help you to ask these necessary questions. *Be honest.* If you're not prepared to take charge of your career, the independent route isn't for you. There are many tools and support systems to help you along the way, but it all starts and ends with you. Brian Austin Whitney, the founder of Just Plain Folks (see Chapter 9), says:

> *Indies should never assume anyone will do anything for them that they aren't willing and able to do for themselves. No one will ever care as much about*

your music and career success as you do. The only helping hand you can truly depend on is connected to the end of your arm. Don't expect others to do it better than you can do it yourself!

THAT GOOD!

Are you open to improvement? In order to make money, you must grow as an artist. The most important thing you can do for your music is to develop it. Your best chance at success comes when you hone your craft! Alex Woodard advises, "Be the absolute best you can be. When you are that good, get better. Don't waste time complaining about not being where you think you should be, or bitching about the bad music that's out, when it should be yours. There aren't many folks with absolutely amazing songs, that play them with everything they have. Spend your time being one of them." Do whatever it takes to become THAT GOOD. Practice as much as you can. Take vocal lessons. Recommit to your instrument and voice. Listen to CDs of great musicians. Play along and see if your playing holds up. Keep trying to surpass them. Your level of commitment will separate you from other musicians.

Play live at every opportunity, even without pay: It's free rehearsal space and a chance to improve before a live audience! If you can't cut it live, forget about succeeding. Robby Baier advises, "Get real feedback from people outside of your circle." Forge adds, "Look at your target audience and see where your strengths and weaknesses are—an *honest* assessment! Then play on your strengths. It's important to realize that not everyone will like your stuff. Getting an idea of exactly what they *don't* like helps me." Beth Wood says, "The most important thing I learned from touring is that it can only make you better. The only way to be a better performer is to perform more. You have to practice performing just like you practice guitar parts." Strive to play your instrument better. Take lessons with pros. Practice A LOT. However good you are, go beyond it.

Success begins with GREAT songs. Without them, all the talent in the world won't give you the best chance at success. Fans should want to sing along because the songs are meaningful. Mary Gauthier says:

The most important thing I did was to really study the craft. A songwriter has to be a great communicator. You need songs that people want to hear. A big part of the work is honing the craft of songwriting to the point where you have something to say that will shut up people in a bar. Powerful songs can do that. You don't have to shout or turn it up loud. If you write your song good enough, it's more interesting than what they're talking to each other about. It's hard to tell if you can make a living at this. If you can write a song good enough to shut a bar up, you're on your way.

Take songwriting workshops. Once you've got THE GOODS, hone your performance. Recording artist Evan R. Saffer (profile on page 109) of the band FIXER advises, "I've learned you are not as good as you think. Road test the songs. Beat and tweak them until they shine. Nothing gives you more power in this industry than devoted fans, which touring can provide. It also humbles you: There are great musicians and many empty clubs listening to them." Work on your live performance. Just because you record good tracks doesn't mean fans will love you live. Brian Austin Whitney says, "What most indies lack is how to truly entertain an audience at a live concert. It takes a lot more than sound and performance skills. To build your fan base, you need to be so entertaining that your existing fans want to show you off to their friends. That is one piece of the puzzle where artists are falling short across all genres and success levels."

FAME VS. EARNING A LIVING

Do you have realistic expectations of being independent? The reality is, you may not become a household name, but you *can* make a full-time living. Marly Hornik (profile on page 255) says, "If you want to make a living playing music, you can. Just make sure that your dream is not to be a rock star, because it's not likely." Danielle Egnew adds:

> It is not realistic for you to simply wait for the Opportunity Faeire to bonk you on the head with a wand containing a record contract or savvy booking agent. You should have pride in what you do, and the drive to book your own shows and produce your art, even if you are financing it. I believe that a musician's drive to really bring their art into the world in a tangible format is the difference between a musical artist and a musical hobbyist. The laid-back "hobby" energy isn't enough to propel a career in music forward.

Do you want a career or a hobby? Musicians often complain that business and practicality get in the way of their creative process. They just want to do

PROFILE
....

Zak Morgan quit his day job in 1999 to pursue a full-time career, from scratch, as a children's artist. He has performed many times across the country, doing about 200 gigs a year, and he sells CDs of his original songs. Libraries and schools are his biggest markets, but he plays theaters and other venues, too. Morgan achieved a big goal in 2004—a Grammy nomination!—proving that an indie can get the same kind of recognition as a major label artist. Don't be surprised if you see him someday on a kids' television show he's created—another of his goals.

their music and not deal with any of the business. If this is you, keep your day job and do music as a hobby; you're not really serious about an independent music career. Dean Seltzer is serious. His band opened every show for a week for top acts on San Padre Island. Then the producer asked if he had a day job. Seltzer recalls, "I said, 'I'm working on music all day and don't have time for a day job.' He hired me and said, 'If you have a day job, you're not taking it seriously,' and he didn't have time for hobbying musicians."

Are you passionate about your music, or do you follow a formula? As poet Robert Frost said, "Two roads diverged in a wood, and I—I took the one less traveled by, And that has made all the difference." Like being an indie, taking the road less traveled isn't as easy as taking the obvious, well-worn path along with many musicians trying to be "clones" of the rock stars. You may have to be more creative to make progress. But the rocky, less obvious path pushes you to greater levels of yourself. It also allows you to dig deeper to create songs that are unique to you. This is the best way to develop your talent to its fullest. Follow your passion, not a formula! That's the true indie way. Beth Wood says:

> If music is your calling, it's worth a try. We live in an amazing age where you can make a professional-quality CD for relatively cheap. The Internet is a powerful tool, so it's getting better for the little guy. If after a few years you decide to do something else, you can look back and know you gave lots of time and energy to your dream. To me, that is the definition of success.

Have the courage to follow the road that calls you, no matter how little it's been traveled. Someone must go first! Don't let people discourage you or push you to an unsatisfactory record deal. Kick back! Give yourself the pleasure of being true to you!

FLEXING YOUR INDIE MUSCLES

How flexible are you? To succeed as an independent musician, prepare to bend. You don't know it all, and you can't do everything your way. Try new things. You can always improve your music—and your game plan. Ego often makes you inflexible. Henri Lessing, Managing Director of Media Records Benelux in Holland, says, "Too many musicians think they know better than the world. If they're not open, they lose out." When musicians indignantly tell me, "I know what I'm doing," it often means "I'm too stubborn to be open to other possibilities." Beth Wood says:

> Being a touring musician may sound glamorous, and it definitely has its moments, but those moments come at great sacrifice. If I come to a point

where it is just too emotionally taxing, I'll reevaluate what I'm doing and make adjustments. Music is a calling for me and will always be part of my life. I imagine that as I grow and change, so will my path.

Determination doesn't mean being rigid! Stay open to new routes. When I began recording as the Rappin' Teach, I was SURE that "Teacher's Breaking Back" would put me on the map. Someone said *this* project might not fly, but one I wasn't expecting might hit big. I laughed. He implored me to keep my options open and not get fixated in one direction. I thought he was nuts—I was sure I had a hit record! But I thought about his words as I recorded "Girls Can Do," which I hadn't pursued since I was focused on the other rap: *That's* what launched my career! "Teacher's Breaking Back" was never even released. The advice stuck.

It's said that if you keep doing what you've always done, you'll continue to get what you've always gotten. This is true. Many musicians go in circles, playing the same clubs to mostly the same people. They ignore input, thinking they're already good enough and they already know it all. These musicians moan about not making money after one, three, or even five years. Remember, you may never get to the next level or make real money if you're won't take risks and try new things. Stay alert for interesting opportunities to make money with your music. They're out there!

The only one who limits you is YOU. Since I decided to go with the flow, I'm always ready to change course if I see a possibility anywhere else on my horizon. I've made good money in places I never thought would be lucrative. If asked about my goals, I say that I plan to live up to my potential. I have no idea where I'll be in one year, much less five. I'll probably be writing and speaking, because that's what I love. But it might be in an area I've never pursued, or I might find something satisfying I'd never thought of before. While writing this book I found many innovative ways that musicians are making money. Use these suggestions to open new doors. Mary Gauthier says, "Be able to repackage yourself in ways that work for the marketplace. You have to be flexible. All these years I've been on my own, I've played just about anywhere that will take me. The main thing is to *keep going no matter what.*"

Many musicians start out in one direction and end up successful in another, equally satisfying one. If you want to earn a living as a musician, you must be willing to try new avenues. I interviewed many artists who intended to be rock stars but landed in another music arena by taking different offers that came their way. Some produce; others pursue songwriting. Don't just take the main road: Less traveled roads offer opportunities you might love. Recording artist Dorothy Potter (profile on page 280) found many alternative avenues for making money from music. She says, "With my first CD on the market, it became clear that I needed to progress to the next stage—not playing at being an artist, but really living from it. That was in 2000." Potter found many small alternative venues that you'll read about in later chapters. They add up to a full-time living!

Flexibility also means being patient, and patience is key to success. You may want to rush to the next level but may not be ready yet. Have patience. Hone your craft until your music shines. Perform in front of a small group and slowly build a larger following. Don't approach managers, agents, etc., before you're ready. Appreciate each baby step on the road to a music career. Michelle Shocked says, "The music that I make has a real long gestation period. I set myself up to not play the obvious game of getting a quick hit tomorrow. Instead, I established a trail of breadcrumbs so that people can follow the trail and come across me at some point in the future." Please, don't rush your career. Be patient and develop it one step at a time. Getting each foot firmly down before taking another step is the best way to increase your chance of longevity. As Abe Lincoln said, "Nothing valuable can be lost by taking time."

GIVING IT YOUR ALL

In order to succeed as an independent, you must be willing to work hard. Be ready for long hours! Prepare yourself to endure doors closing and things going wrong. Indie artist Lisa O'Kane (profile on page 274) suggests:

> Be ready to work your ass off! It's a lot of work, but I've gained an education that perhaps I would not have if someone else did it. Besides, I have total control and can't blame anyone but myself if something doesn't go right or get done. People congratulate me on my success and say things like, "You must be making a lot of money." If I were in this for money, I'd quit. There are different measures of success. It's amazing that I've come this far in just over two years. My favorite saying is "I have problems of abundance." I wouldn't trade them for anything.

PROFILE

Alex Woodard quit his day job in 1997 to become a full-time artist, and he has been touring and putting out his own records ever since. Woodard's band has included players from other top acts, including the Posies and Fountains of Wayne; his latest album was recorded with Pete Droge. Woodard gets airplay on commercial and college radio stations in the U.S., his songs have been licensed to film and TV, and he also enjoys steady CD sales in Europe. Alex's latest album was released through a distribution partnership deal with 33rd Street Records.

Today is the first day of the rest of your life! Take the next step towards achieving your long-term goals. Success isn't just the big picture. Each little thing you accomplish that puts you a wee bit closer to your ultimate goal is success, too! If you only see success as making big money, playing huge venues, or selling 100,000 CDs, you're setting yourself up for disappointment. More importantly, you're selling yourself way short. Real success is appreciating anything you can do now that you hadn't done yesterday. All progress is success! If you appreciate every step you take, you'll feel less discouraged when the hard stuff happens.

Kyler England says, "As an independent musician, it's hard to know what the best next step is. Often you don't know where your next check is coming from, unlike when you're an employee of a company. You have to be willing to live with uncertainty, and most of all, to bust your ass seven days a week." When I finally accomplish the harder things, I feel great satisfaction—but I don't shrug off small achievements. There are always things still to be done. Every gig is progress, whether there are two or two thousand people. Everyone who buys your CD is a fan you may not have had before. Appreciate it all! Visual Poet (of Little Egypt) says, "It's about persistence. We started rhyming at open mics. Three years later we're doing shows at colleges and getting paid. You have to keep pushing and pushing, getting your name out as much as possible in a professional way, so people remember you. If you keep moving forward, everyone will come around."

Corky McClerkin advises, "Learn to be aggressive without being offensive in order to make this lifestyle work for you." Be ready for a less-than-glamorous life—quite the opposite of a rock star. Are you prepared to tour as much as possible, even on a tight budget? Canjoe John says:

> Being independent means no first-class buses and luxuries; sleeping in a van or on the ground in a tent at festivals; waking up to cold showers followed by sixteen to eighteen hours of intense public interaction. Those who want to make it in this business must learn what they are willing to endure and understand that living like a major idol is fantasyland for most of us. If you are unwilling to stay focused and driven, persevere, suffer, accept rejection, eat when and whatever you can, go the extra miles, take big risks, fail, and then do it again tomorrow—stay away from this business! But the rewards for those who love it and do succeed are immeasurable.

If you go the independent route, prepare to wear many hats. You'll probably do everything yourself for quite a while. If this ain't your thang, choose another route. It's hard work! But the harder you work, the "luckier" you get! Pat DiNizio recommends, "Devote yourself to your music to the exclusion of everything that you hold near and dear. The Smithereens devoted themselves to making a living through music. While everyone else went through college and prepared for their futures, we played nightclubs free for five years. You have to be completely devoted and work hard on every level." Zak Morgan adds: "If you love what you do, you'll be willing to make the calls you need to make, send stuff out, and follow up. Pound the pavement and do a lot of shows. Be willing to work harder than you would for someone else. I work harder now than when I was a sales rep. But it doesn't seem like work because it's my own baby."

Morgan says he took a day job for four years but couldn't stay away from music: "I quit my job and started doing it from scratch in 1999. Other artists are unwilling to do what you have to do to get busy, like sitting on your butt and making phone calls." Barbara Tucker says few house artists have her longevity. She believes her relationship with her music is key, explaining, "I give the people my soul. When I leave the stage, I need at least fifteen minutes of downtime because my spirit, soul, and emotions have just been pulled." Justin Lassen (profile on page 182) credits dedication for creating a reputation that keeps him busy, including remixing for top acts such as Linkin Park. He explains:

> When everyone else is out partying, I'm working in the studio. I go to trade shows in the music, film, and game industries year-round and generally get a lot of attention at those. Working hard gets me the best results. Nothing beats the proof to back up the hype. That is why I continue to make proof and work on music for me and me alone. The stuff I do for myself tends to be the most successful. Do what you love, and they will come. If you are meant to work in the business, your hard work will speak for itself. How did I get all this high-profile work? I do not have an agent, publicist, label, or manager. I have done every single thing up to this point with my own hard work, professionalism, and persistence.

Get off your butt—and your BUTs! If you sit home waiting to be signed, you'll become one of the bitter musicians who complain that with all their talent, no one's found them. Hello? Welcome to reality! No one looks for you. Matt Allison says, "Many artists sit around waiting for that elusive A&R person/booking agent/ manager to walk past their garage and sign them to a major deal. They don't want to put in the work required to launch your own career." Musicians complain they want a career BUT. . . . No more excuses! The only way to give yourself the best chance of a career in music is to get off your butts, stop your BUTs, and get busy. Dean Seltzer advises:

> Be realistic—use your head. Many musicians wait to be discovered. Some Mr. Big Guy is not going to pull up in a limousine and sign you to a major

label. Make things happen! If you want a band, put one together. If you want a gig, get one. If you want a record, make one. Stop making excuses! I know many musicians that are working as shopping cart wranglers at grocery stores instead of doing what they want to do. I hate when people say they've got bills to pay. What, mine are free? Use your head—put down on paper how you can make it work instead of waiting to be discovered.

You can complain that signed artists have more opportunities, or you can get out so people can see you. *Visibility attracts opportunities.* The more people see you, the more chances something good will come your way. David Ippolito, who gets tremendous exposure playing in Central Park, says, "I had a song played on NBC for the New York City Marathon. They came to the park and asked to use it." Don't make excuses for why you're not doing what it takes to get a career. Instead, *do what it takes.* Zak Morgan says:

A lot of people embrace victimhood and use that as an excuse rather than go out and plug away. There's a cliché that's true: Hard work doesn't guarantee success but it sure improves your chances. If you've got a good attitude about something, you can create your own good luck. It really does boil down to that. I thought it was true, and now I know it's true. You continue to work hard and it's amazing what happens.

Remember, he was nominated for a Grammy!

BALLS!

Can you handle risks? If you want to get ahead, you must develop heavy-duty balls so fear doesn't stop you from taking risks. It takes balls to accept a gig that's bigger than any you've done. It takes balls to ask for what you need. Rachael Sage proved she's got them: She sent Ani DiFranco a letter explaining how much she loved her music and that she'd written a song for her. Months later, Sage got an email asking her to open some shows for DiFranco. She wondered if it were a prank but got herself together when it proved real. She says:

I screamed. Then I realized I had to get myself together and figure out how to advance that type of gig. I didn't have an ounce of experience. The most people I had played for was one hundred. I got nervous. That helped me get to work on the press kit. I rehearsed and got a touring partner. We quickly put together what we thought was a tight twenty-five-minute set and printed up T-shirts and postcards. Somehow I got together a press list and did a big mailing. I was out touring for a few weeks.

If you keep doing what you want to be good at, you will become good at it. The worst that can happen if you try something and it doesn't work is that you learn something for next time. Feel good about taking risks, even if it doesn't work out. DJ Minx created Women On Wax because she felt that women weren't getting the exposure they deserved in this industry. When she started out, instead of complaining about how women were treated, she took a stand, explaining:

> I knew I wouldn't be alone if other women pursued this career. I got laughs and was shown no respect when I mentioned being a DJ. I had to prove myself. It wasn't right! I became the support for women who felt this is a male-dominated line of work and were afraid to go for it. The name "Women On Wax" created a buzz. People contacted me to find out what my company might do for them. A lot of folks look up to me for staying out there and being aggressive, for demanding what I want, since it was believed that this was "for the guys."

Ask and Ye Shall Receive

DJ Minx had the balls to go after what she wanted, and now she's in a position to help other independent artists. Many of you are uncomfortable asking for what you need. Get over it! I could never ask for anything, and so I got nothing to show for it. I remember yearning for many things but not feeling worthy enough to go after them. Well, that's changed! I'd never be where I am if I hadn't accepted that the worst thing that can happen is a "No" response, which I can handle. Indie artist Marly Hornik advises, "Never be afraid to ask for help or to accept help." It's really okay if people say no. As long as you're asking, there's a chance that at least one person

PROFILE

Rachael Sage is a full-time singer/songwriter who tours almost nonstop. She has played the Lilith Fair and opened for top acts, including Ani DiFranco. With a full-time label manager and three part-timers, her serious biz has secured distribution for her label, Mpress, in 1998 and has sold more than 35,000 CDs. She's released seven albums and has extensive play on both college and commercial radio. Sage plays at clubs, festivals, colleges, and other venues and is sponsored by Kurzweil. She has written jingles and won over a dozen songwriting contests. Sage also tours Europe regularly and sells many CDs there.

will acquiesce. Hornik adds, "I talk to everybody. I've gotten better about talking to the right people and asking the right questions. Not everyone will do things for you but if you keep opening your mouth, you'll learn who can help you. It's important to be a really nice person, too."

So much more comes to you by getting over the fear of asking for what you need. Asking puts us in a position of power; fear, in a position of lack. Which do you prefer? Here are some tips for asking with the best chance of receiving:

- *Know you deserve what you're asking for.* Accept that it's okay to ask and receive. Your attitude shouldn't reflect that you doubt whether you're worthy of asking. On a spiritual level, we get supported in return for what we put out. If you put doubt out there, you will get the rewards of doubt. If you put out a positive vibe, you'll be supported with a more positive response.

- *Expect to get what you need.* If you assume people will say *no*, you won't ask. Don't sabotage yourself by second-guessing others. Raise your expectations! Asking for only a little won't get you a lot.

- *Don't ask apologetically.* Begin by asking for what you need—*with conviction*. Why apologize for needing something? That makes the person expect you to ask for something that he or she won't want to give. Confidence makes a MUCH better impression than apologies. Ask in a positive way to make people more likely to acquiesce.

- *Be specific about what you need.* We often don't get what we want because we don't clearly articulate our needs. Figure out *exactly* what you need, and be specific when putting it out there.

- *Be polite.* When people help you, show appreciation. Manners and professionalism get you further. Thank people, whether they help you or not: If they can't do something now, they might help later if they remember you as a courteous person. "Please" and "thank you" go far in the music biz, because so many people don't use them. Stand out by showing courtesy and gratitude to everyone you approach. They'll be more likely to help. British indie artist Jonathan Williams (profile on page 136) learned this from one of my books and applied it:

  > Since not many musicians say "thank you," when you do people remember you for it. It makes them feel better that they helped you move forward. That goes a long way with people, especially if you're making noise. I experienced stores pushing my records more after we sent thank-you letters for stocking them. One

store manager called me back and said thanks for the letter because he was having a very bad day until he read it.

When you follow these tips on asking for what you need, you will find something positive in the experience. Mary Gauthier adds, "Be willing to put yourself out there and not take *no* for an answer. When a door shuts, find a window."

The Powerful "E" Word: Embellish

I'm an honest person. Honestly, I am! But getting the balls up to ask for that first one of anything can be the hardest. Sometimes a harmless "non-truth" makes it easier to ask for what you need. A little white musical lie can give you the courage and support to begin. People often don't want to be your first—club gig, song collaborator, radio interview, etc. So don't tell them! And if they ask about it, embellish and stretch what you can.

A synonym for embellish is "adorn." Careers get started by adorning them. Give me a crumb to work with and I can make it seem like a whole loaf! Embellishment is milking what you have to the max—truth with omission. Leave out the exact number of CDs you sell. Talk about the markets your CD is out in, even if only a few have sold—it sounds better. If hardly anyone shows for a gig, it's still a gig on paper. Leave out negative details. When asked how I'm doing, I give a big enthusiastic "Great!" And I am. But I wasn't always great. When I first began my label, I *always* said my record was selling. I had only sold three, but three meant it was selling! The music biz is about hype. You can create yours by taking what you have and building it into something bigger with carefully crafted words.

My debut TV appearance was an hour on a major prime-time talk show. When I first spoke to the producer, I acted confident, as if I'd done lots of TV. I was terrified but knew I had to grab this opportunity. They bought it, and that appearance opened many doors. If you *believe* you can do something well, let that confidence shine! This requires balls, but it's important. Getting your first opportunity can lead to more. Don't be afraid to embellish; it may just give you that shot to prove yourself. When someone asks if you can play to a festival audience, talk around it as if you have—as long as you believe in your ability to give a great live performance. Radio interviews? You *love* doing them (in your mind!). A corporate function for good bucks? Why not! When you're confident in your musical ability, you can lead people to believe that you're more experienced than you are. That's how to get the experience, and that's how to earn more money.

● ● ● ● **CHAPTER 4** ● ● ● ●

Me, Inc.

I f you want to earn a living from music, get down to business! Award-winning composer Michael Whalen says, "There is a balance between the fire in the belly of your artist side and taking care of your business." Kyler England says, "I conduct myself as a business, since I make my living from my music." Like it or not, you must treat your music as a business if you want to make money. If not, keep your day job and play for friends. Treat it like a real job, though, and there's a shot you'll earn a real living. Christine Kane does:

> Doing business stuff taught me every bit as much about myself and my voice as writing songs and performing. It made me stronger—more equipped to deal with any triumph or tribulation that comes my way. I encourage you to free up enough time and energy to do at least a little work each day towards your career. Even if you believe you stink at the business end, get over yourself about that! I began this career thinking I would be rescued or discovered— someone would do it for me. That didn't happen. [My career] didn't start happening until I truthfully, painfully assessed my situation and began taking tiny steps to make a real business grow. I used my long tours to read business books that I was embarrassed to tell other artists I was reading. I hired someone to help with things I hated doing, that were emotionally draining and time consuming. That slowly led to having a real office and full-time employees.

DO YOU WANNA MAKE $$$?

I relate to aversions to all things business. I'm with you! But I love to pay my rent and eat and shop, so I take myself seriously as a business to facilitate that. You must, too! Zak Morgan explains: "My artist friends think business is a bad word. That's hogwash! It's how you eat! When I'm not performing, I send out contracts and invoices and try to get press. I pay a few people to work for me. That's what a business is. You try to move products." Once you achieve some success, hire help. Until then—DIY! Canjoe says, "The music industry is not a giant talent show; it's business. Become a businessperson, not just another act." Let your passions and need to pay bills motivate you. Having bills to pay is a terrific catalyst for getting serious as a self-contained music business. Let reality inspire you to market like a biz. Michael Johnathon says, "You have to have one hand on a guitar case and one hand on a briefcase. I'm a folk singer with a staff. You don't find a lot of those. Poetman Records is an office in an office building. I make albums and go on the road." Matt Allison adds, "For any artist, art and commerce go hand in hand. I can't be naive enough to think that the art will sell itself."

Money is important! If you insist on idealistic thinking, keep your day job. Clint Black explains:

> It's not the well-established paradigm in our minds, so a lot of us think that operating a business is a big mystery and allow ourselves to be at the mercy of those who have an understanding of the business. It's not an art; it's a science. It's been thought through and figured out. Break it down. Too many musicians think that the music business world is something they can't understand. You can!

Accept that marketing music is like selling candy or cars. Christine Kane says, "Even a half hour a day can give you a tremendous sense of accomplishment."

PROFILE

Michael Johnathon is an acoustic folk singer—a full-time musician since 1985. Capitol Records signed him in 1993. He says he spent the next 18 months trying to get out of the contract, and then he began Poetman Records. Johnathon has a real business around his music, complete with an office and staff, and he tours nationally and internationally. His website sales are driven by "WoodSongs," his weekly radio show. The recording of his show is broadcast on radio shows around the world. He also wrote a book based on "WoodSongs," and WoodSongs cafés are developing across the country.

DJ Minx adds, "I *am* a business. Anyone wishing to get into this game needs to be ready to interact with individuals on all levels!"

Create a company name and use it when contacting people. Act like a business that belongs in the industry! Dorothy Potter says, "Becoming a working musician has meant growing up and taking responsibility for my life and my art. Being responsible and disciplined is even more important than being the 'best' musician if you want to work for a living." It's important to set up a formal business. A DBA (Doing Business As) certificate from your county clerk office allows you to open a business bank account to keep that money separate from your personal accounts. Little Egypt is incorporated. Visual explains why they created a company that owns the group: "Being incorporated is a degree of separation from myself. It helps keep the finances totally separate and forces you to stay organized." Jennie DeVoe incorporated herself as "Rubin the Cat Music." She says, "I was advised to have a separate business for record purposes." Talk to an accountant to decide your direction.

Brand your product. That's you! Consistency in image and music helps people to recognize your brand. DJ Minx advises, "Carry yourself as if you're constantly in the spotlight." You'll attract fans to your brand when your name and image are recognized all over. Ezina Moore explains, "When I go out, I look like the Ezina Moore brand. My company cannot afford less from me. I am its main representative. Everywhere I go, I introduce people to the Ezina Moore brand." Be conscious of your image. Mary Gauthier learned the hard way when she did her first press junket for a licensing deal in Europe: "I let every journalist take a different picture of me. I looked [awful]. I had no clue that I was building a brand and needed a consistent image. Letting every photographer take a different picture leads to [awful] pictures in the paper."

GIVING YOUR PRODUCT VALUE

Once your music is THAT GOOD and your performance reflects it, take your business seriously enough to expect compensation. Dorothy Potter says, "I don't do anything I don't get paid for anymore. I won't drag my amp, body, and 20 years of performing experience into a place and do it for free to make others feel good. [Some musicians] accept poverty. I won't do it anymore!" If you want a long-term career, value yourself. You may not get top dollars, but once you've polished your music and performance, you should get paid for your work. Ezina Moore says:

> *Never buy into the notion that you are supposed to be poor and perform for free. There is never a good reason to perform for free in a venue where they are making money because you are there, unless it is a charity event. You don't ask a doctor to treat you for free, or go to the grocery store and expect to take what you want and not pay.*

Because she holds on to these standards, Moore makes a good living from her music. Jennifer Marks adds, "Expect that people will pay for your product. For a long time I didn't believe I deserved to charge people for CDs, etc." When you value yourself, others will, too! Michael Whalen says, "The Internet has infused people with an attitude that music isn't worth anything. We've gone from one extreme, where music was overpriced, to music having no value."

Do you get hit up for freebies? Lorraine Ferro says she finally operates as a full-time business and can take money from friends for her music, explaining:

> I've always been squeamish about money around art. I don't know anyone who got onstage the first time who didn't feel at least a little surprised about getting cash after the gig. I've learned that God wants us to have abundance and make a living at what we love. Learn to separate business from friendship, no matter how uncomfortable it seems. You can be friends with people you love and admire, but if you work with them, know it's business.

Amen! If you don't believe that you should make money, you probably won't make any. People buy milk and clothes; they pay to get haircuts. You should also be paid for your product and services. Barbara Tucker says:

> This is the business of music. You have to know your worth. Don't just sing for every Tom, Dick, and Harry for free and let them use you. If that's your gift, and what God gave you to use, that's your business. A boss won't say, "Wait until we get some business, then I'll pay you." No. When it's payday, you get paid. Many artists feel used and say that people did certain things to them. No! You did it to yourself. You have to take care of the business first.

Giving value to your music is just a matter of working hard at it and knowing that your product deserves the appreciation—and the financial reward.

BEHAVING AS A PROFESSIONAL

Professionalism attracts people. Speak with authority, look confident, use manners, and be prepared. Mark Wood explains, "The way I come off as a person is essential. I get calls from musicians who are not as articulate and have not spent time developing more social skills. They are twice as talented as I am but don't get the gig." Return calls promptly. Thank people for their time. That's professional! Robby Baier advises, "Check your email and respond as quickly as possible." Beth Wood adds, "Dealing with clubs, radio stations, record stores, etc., on the phone can be very frustrating. Remember at all times that these folks are busy and trying to make a living.

Be respectful and concise." Aristotle said, "Quality is not an act. It is a habit." If you want a music career, create good habits, high standards, and a professional vibe around your music.

You can conduct yourself as a business without going broke. There are resources to help you cut corners. Don't avoid making all the necessary long distance calls in order to save money—visit www.onesuite.com and sign up for $10 worth of calls. Domestic calls are 2.5¢ per minute from a local phone, and long distance is almost as cheap. No fax machine? Signing up at www.efax.com allows you to get a free fax number. You can then receive 20 free faxes a month as an email attachment. They charge low fees to send faxes. This service comes in handy on the road. Those of you in other countries can have a free U.S. fax number!

Handling your business professionally is important. Making a good first impression leads to opportunities. Often we don't get a second chance to create an image that gets mileage. Be very conscious of the first impressions you give to potential fans and industry people. People who come into contact with you for the first time make judgments about you from:

- *Your phone presence*: An impression about you is conveyed by how you speak on the phone. Some people mutter or sound sleepy; I forget them when I hang up. I'm told I give "good phone" because I'm friendly and cheerful. Your tone of voice leaves an impact on someone who doesn't know you. Sounding positive and upbeat will make people want to talk to you again. Robby Baier advises, "Have a professional phone manner. Don't have a goofy answering machine message, or one that announces your gigs." If you call someone for press, radio play, or to book a gig, have a script in front of you if necessary. Sound confident and professional. Thank people for their time. Don't drag out the conversation!
- *Your personality*: People don't like bores or grumps. They like those who bring them up, not down. When you meet someone, build a rapport that can develop into a relationship. Keep abreast of interesting news, so you can add to discussions. Be interested, and you will be interesting. An energetic presence is contagious.
- *Your business card*: A plain, simple card just gives folks your information, but a well-designed one on nice paper sets you apart from many others. One that makes people say, "Nice card," also makes them think you're doing well. Writing contact info on a piece of paper shows you don't take your business seriously. Even when I wasn't making money, my impressive card said "successful." Before and after an event, people will only have your card to remember you by.

Packaging with Care

Industry pros emphasize how important packaging has become. Press, radio, music directors, and other industry pros are swamped with CDs, so packaging can set you apart from others. Packages that can compete with CDs from major labels are opened quicker. No one can listen to everything; attractive packaging often makes the crucial difference. Press, radio play, and other exposure hinge on having good music, but if no one hears your CD, the music won't matter. An appealing package entices people to hear what's inside. Look at CDs in stores and see how yours stand up.

Daniel Lee Martin has a marketing background and knows that having quality material sets him apart. He explains:

> Our marketing materials are top-notch. I make sure everything that goes out is as good as what a major label puts out. You are competing against guys with half-million-dollar budgets for marketing. I'm fortunate to have that kind of background. It's about quality—make sure you have a reputable printer and copywriter. I invested in one of the best digital photos around to be in line with what was happening in country music. I knew that for the first album, identity is key. Everything that leaves this office has to look top-notch. Every station we went to was impressed with our media kits.

Quality packaging provides a good first impression. If you don't show that you take your music seriously enough to dress it up nicely, it might not get heard. You want to be heard? Lure them with competitive packaging. Then your music can speak.

Keeping Records

Many musicians throw receipts into a big pile. Instead, find ways to organize from the get-go so it doesn't pile up. This end of the biz is tedious. Enlist the help of a friend or fan. Take an accounting class or hire an accountant to teach you the basics. Accurately keep track of sales, fees for performing and licensing, and ALL expenses. Also record how many people each venue draws and where you sell merchandise. It keeps you on top of your biz. Marly Hornik tracks every sale of every CD and every T-shirt in each size. She says, "From every tour, I keep track of every expense from every day, carefully. That information is important when planning a tour. My expenses for a ten-day tour are around $3,500. I have to know exactly where that money goes out and comes in."

Records are important at tax time. Keep all receipts related to music or running a business. Howie Statland says he keeps track of everything sold and everything spent. He advises, "If you're losing money, write that off on your tax returns. You can save money that way." If you have taxable income from a side gig or day job, use your expenses to offset how much you pay, or to get a refund. Lorraine Ferro advises, "Keep all receipts. Get an entertainment accountant. Mine understands what a musician or artist can and can't deduct. I've qualified for a tax refund almost every year—definitely due to good record-keeping." Every year when my accountant asks, "Do you want to come in now," I say "no." Paperwork is distasteful to me. I just want to write and speak, and do my thing. But I enter my accountant's office and take care of biz, since this is my livelihood. Keep good tax records, and find a good accountant!

CREATING A PLAN

Many musicians do what I see as "jack-in-the-box marketing": jumping without thinking or planning whenever someone suggests something. That burns you out fast. I used to jump whenever I saw a possible opportunity. If someone gave me a lead, I ran after it, zigzagging until I got dizzy but not getting very far. You need an organized plan. Create a long-term goal broken down into baby steps. Beth Wood suggests:

> Define your goals. Often. Figure out what they really are—be specific. Know what you want, and reassess it every few months. I know many musicians who changed the course of their careers because they grew to want different things. Be sure that you are okay without a set income every month. If you are uncomfortable with financial uncertainty, set a time limit. Know your boundaries. If you don't want to play for tips at a coffeehouse anymore, prepare to stick to that. Make sure you want to eat, sleep, live, and breathe music. Revisit your goals often.

Outline long- and short-term goals however it works for you. Corky McClerkin says, "I had no goals when I started playing professionally, except to perform for

PROFILE

Corky McClerkin is a pianist who plays hard bebop, soul jazz, and contemporary jazz, and has released several albums on his label, WinCor Records. A semifinalist in BET's search for Best Jazz Trio, he's done a three-month trio engagement at Singapore's Westin Hotel and was part of a resident trio at the Chicago Drake Hotel for eight years. McClerkin was musical director for the award-winning Chicago play *Sasha! Sings Dinah*, and gave a solo concert with the music of Duke Ellington at Chicago Orchestra Hall Annex. He also performs for weddings, parties, as a session player, and at other events.

an appreciative audience. Years later, I realized I needed a survival plan. My graduate studies in planning helped in clarifying my musical ambitions. I developed three- and five-year plans on what I wanted to accomplish." Put many details in the plan; acknowledge progress with each small achievement. What big picture do you eventually want to reach? Figure out the steps needed to achieve it.

Set reasonable goals. If your goal is to tour nationally, you probably won't feel progress for many years. Make a plan with smaller goals that lead to that. It's better to have mini bits of progress. People make plans for three, six, twelve months, etc.—those create pressure. It takes years to develop fully, and that's okay. Break down your goals into the minutest steps instead of months. Go from one to the next when the time is right. What media outlets can help you? What regions can you tour in? What clubs are there? Step by step, coordinate those steps in a logical sequence. Each step makes the next one easier.

Budget wisely. Don't just spend till you're broke. Estimate what your different revenue streams—CD and merch sales, payment for gigs, licensing music, etc.—will earn. Will they meet expenses? Jennifer Marks advises, "Make your budget and work within it. Know how many CDs you have to sell to make back your initial investment. Business plans are really helpful in terms of setting goals and achieving them."

GETTING LEGAL PROTECTION

Part of your business plan should always be to take care of the legal side of things. It's important to have a written agreement with anyone you work with. Beth Wood applies this to consignment deals with record stores, performance dates, or licensing songs. A simple agreement can work. She says, "It doesn't have to be a long-winded document full of legalese." But NEVER sign anything without an attorney looking it over. Alexei Auld, Esq., Director of Education and Senior Staff Attorney for the New York VLA (Volunteer Lawyers for the Arts), says, "A great deal of rights and responsibilities come with being creators of intellectual property. I see many situations in which people get hoodwinked. At least have an attorney look over what you're presented with in writing. Utilize our services for any question you have. We have inexpensive services with quality attorneys." Organizations such as VLA (see Chapter 9) exist around the country, so there's no excuse for not having a lawyer. It's important to use a *music or entertainment attorney*. Others won't understand the music biz. A contract that comes from your lawyer is best, but at least put everything in writing somehow. Lorraine Ferro says:

I have gotten burned many times because I didn't set boundaries that gave clients parameters to work within. Clients I trusted stabbed me in the back.

> When I am close to a client and don't sign contracts up front, I signal that they don't have to pay for my work—that I'm doing them a favor. Think about it: You pay the person who makes it clear that he expects to be paid at a specific time. When I'm not clear, in writing, about what I expect to be paid for my services, I'm underappreciating myself. The client does the same. The first thing I do now as a businessperson in the arts is get it in writing before doing any work with an artist. It's not a crime to ask to get paid well for high-caliber services, whether it's a friend or stranger. In fact, they respect you more. In turn, you take yourself more seriously as someone who deserves to be paid your worth. Contracts are good commitments. They allow both parties the freedom to be close and work hard, without fear that at any moment either party could leave the other in the lurch after the time and sweat invested. Otherwise, it's her word against mine.

Business names, logos, and names of recording artists and record labels can all be trademarked. If you want to use these symbols on merchandise (hats, T-shirts, etc.), get them registered from the get-go to protect against bootlegging when your acts become well-known. Check the U.S. Patent and Trademark Office's site (www.uspto.gov) for information on the ins and outs of trademarks. Wallace Collins, Esq., explains:

> Just as a copyright under the copyright law accrues to the creator when the work is fixed in a tangible medium, so trademark rights accrue to a person or entity based on "use" of a particular name or mark. I usually advise that an artist or band register the name as early as possible but not later than when they start distributing their recordings to third parties. Among other benefits, registration gives the artist the presumption of "first use" nationwide!

ARMING YOURSELF WITH KNOWLEDGE

In addition to taking advantage of legal resources, you have many other opportunities to get educated about the music biz. Ignorance is no excuse for taking a bad deal or getting ripped off. It's up to you to get educated! Visual says, "Once we did more shows, we pulled back and read up on the music industry to at least be in the same conversation with people. Take the time to learn the business." Reading *Billboard* will help keep you up-to-date. Executive Editor Ken Schlager says it tells you almost everything you need to know to function. The charts provide an understanding of what's happening in the marketplace. He explains:

> The magazine can be thought of as the textbook. A young player should use it to get information on how songs are marketed and how acts are signed.

We're the only publication that covers the industry in a horizontal way. We look at all the elements—from radio, retail marketing, the Internet, touring—all the different elements that add up to essentially a marketing program. Different pieces of the picture can play a larger role in the development of a specific act. Many acts are developed just because of touring; some acts just through radio; some largely on the basis of TV appearances. Other acts have a combination of all of those things working for them.

Go to every seminar possible. Gregory Abbott advises, "On the independent level, you have to be prepared to read and ask lots of questions. If you remain attentive to what artists like you are doing, you can better approximate a plan that will work for you." Justin Lassen says, "I listen to the news, specifically news in the entertainment world. I stay tuned for websites, newsletters and industry events, parties, etc., where things can happen, and insert myself as the catalyst in making sure things go down how I want them to go down." He says that staying informed about the industry gives him an edge. Beth Wood says, "Figure out how you can operate within (or without) the system. It is a big, complicated system mostly geared towards major labels, but independent labels and artists gain more power every day."

Read my books and others. Clint Black advises, "Read books about the business—lots of them. Get different points of view and from that develop your own perception. Read books on leadership, team building, management, marketing. Learn how businesses operate. Then if you decide that you're going to start a band, make a CD, and try to sell it, you can make it profitable pretty quickly." To break into the Nashville scene, check out *Music Row*, a monthly trade magazine that is an insider's guide to the Nashville music business scene. Subscribers also receive an email report full of great resources on Tuesdays and Fridays. Publisher David Ross says, "We put out our *In Charge* book once a year. It's like a Who's Who of all the movers and shakers, with their photos and contacts. An independent person should memorize that book if they're interested in the Nashville industry." Most print issues have some sort of directory included. Ross adds:

I look up to the Wall Street Journal and want to follow in its footsteps, having a much more national and global focus than it did in the past. We're like a community information exchange [with] subscribers all over the world. The challenge for an independent is to be as informed and knowledgeable as anybody on a major. Everybody wants you to believe that the playing field is not level. So in the quest to level it, you have get yourself UP to the field. Nobody is coming down to [you] or giving you a ladder—except us. Reading trade magazines is very important to learning about the industry—who the players are, what they're doing—and being able to recognize where opportunities might lie for you and your product.

INSURING YOUR BUSINESS

Please, think about getting at least *some* insurance. Julie Coulter, Vice President of MusicPro Insurance, says at the minimum, get gear insurance: "That is the biggest exposure an artist has, and their most valuable asset." Coulter says it's important to have the protection of tour insurance when you begin making money and acquiring assets. She explains, "One lawsuit against you can cost everything in the long run if you are not properly protected. More clubs require this type of coverage since the Station incident with Great White in Rhode Island." Tina Broad says BROTHER learned the hard way in 1999 about the cost of not being appropriately insured, when Hamish, Angus, and another band member were seriously injured on a road trip:

> *A smashed rental van, smashed equipment, critically injured band members and crew—every band's worst nightmare, and it happened. It derailed lives for months, ran up debts we're still paying off, and looked like that was the end of BROTHER. The message: Protect and insure yourself and your gear. If you're an employer, make sure your employees are covered while they're working for you. Shop for insurance and really make yourself understand the intricacies of the policy—what it does and doesn't cover.*

Coulter advises reading your policy carefully, no matter how boring it is. Broad advises insuring the band members and gear, adding, "If you're the bandleader, know what your obligations are to your employees or guest players from an insurance/legal point of view." Unfortunately, there are few ways to save on insurance. Coulter says, "MusicPro's musical equipment floater policy program is a perfect example of the 'strength in numbers' theory—a Master policy plan that is affordable because enough people have joined the mix to help keep the costs down." AFM (American Federation of Musicians) has good instrumental insurance, but it can be hard to get other kinds of insurance at affordable rates.

CHAPTER 5

Indie Teammates

Independent doesn't mean being alone. Creating a support system of like-minded people can help you to advance in the music industry. Learn to be a team player. You'll need support to succeed as an indie. That might sound contradictory, but it's not. Preech says, "You can be a one-man independent, but it helps to have a team behind you. You need people who believe in you."

NETWORKING 101

Networking is a valuable tool. The music industry is a people biz, so it's imperative to develop as many contacts as possible. When money is tight, your mouth and personality are free promotional tools. Barbara Tucker says, "No man is an island. If you think that as an artist you need to stand in a corner and not meet somebody, [you're wrong]. In order to find how people can help you and you can help them, *you have to meet people.*" Create excitement about your music! Network whenever you're near people. Talk about it to everyone; don't be selective. I've made more contacts by talking to random people who turned out to know someone than by singling out specific ones. Tell *everyone* what you need. Someone may know someone who knows someone.

Jennifer Marks' career started by networking. She says, "I met one person who knew another one, etc." Ezina Moore called everyone she knew and advises:

You cannot do this alone. Make a list of everyone you know. Call them, email, reach out. Tell them about a great new product—YOU. Be attractive, innovative, and imaginative. Tell everyone what you are doing—your dentist, hairstylist, veterinarian, stores you shop in. Be excited, positive, and energetic. You won't have to work as hard: People love positive people. I dug up old contacts. I got my high school class reunion roster and discovered that a guy I played with in a school band is the program director for the radio station in my hometown. He immediately added the record, called his program director friends, and helped me get it on more stations and in record stores. I say "hi" to anybody and meet people everywhere I go.

Moore asked everyone she knew at big companies to get names of those who promote annual events. She got booked to perform and to contribute songs for corporate presentations and auto, boat, and motorcycle shows. The more people, the more possibilities. Daniel Lee Martin agrees: "Networking is one of the most important things you'll do. You need to know everybody so they know who you are and why you're here. The guys I met opened many doors."

Start with a smile and a cheerful attitude; grumps won't get as far. Marks advises, "Be nice to everyone. . . . You will see the same people over and over." If you don't have a personality, develop one to get ahead. *Friendly* and *positive* are universal and make you feel good. Marly Hornik says, "My first priority is to be happy and connect with people. Music is my second. With that attitude, people are more likely to want to help. I have a big mouth. Having one is the most effective way to get what you want. Otherwise, how will they know?"

When drummer Bobby Borg, author of *The Musician's Handbook* (Billboard Books) lived in Boston, he would take a five-hour train ride to New York, and then the subway, to try for the opportunity to play in a jam session—sometimes just one song. As he recognized people with good energy, he formed relationships. Borg proved that meeting people and staying in touch works: Two guys he jammed with got a record deal and asked him to be the drummer. He went back to New York. The person he stayed with knew someone just signed to Atlantic who needed a drummer. Borg says, "I went from being a recent graduate to having two signed bands want me to be a member of the band. It took lots of groundwork."

Seek to develop relationships with people you meet, like Borg did. They could end up being the backbone of your career. Start by not being a pest. If you use too much of someone's time, they'll ignore you later. Catch their interest with something that's short and sweet enough to make a good impression. I talk to everyone I meet. Most top people begin at entry level, so be friendly to industry pros' assistants. Invite them to gigs. Ask them to critique your music. If they like you, someone higher up might hear about you. Show EVERYONE appreciation! Always be prepared in case someone shows interest. Alex Woodard says, "An industry pro told me to always have a record with me everywhere I go. You never know when an opportunity will come up."

Many creative types (me included) hate to follow up with people. Work against your nature if necessary to create good habits from the beginning. I keep my cards in one place and put other people's in another so they don't get mixed up. Be sure to note something about what they do or what you talked about on the back of their business card as a reference. Right after meeting people who might help later, send a friendly, personal email to say it was nice meeting them—and make it as short as possible. Mention something you discussed or that happened when you met to establish a personal connection.

Communicating for Success

Good communication greatly enhances your chance of achieving success, and it doesn't cost a dime. This skill makes networking more productive. What's the point of meeting people who can help you if you can't connect to them verbally? Here are some tips for better communication. They may seem obvious, but a surprising number of musicians don't follow them:

- *Listen to the other person.* Ask questions. Often when you meet someone in the industry, you bulldoze them with a pitch about your music. Yak, yak, yak. Don't assault people with words about what you're doing and your needs. Ask what *they* do. Listen carefully. Communication is two-way interaction. Connect with people by listening.
- *Speak slowly.* Motormouths get taken less seriously. When you explain yourself in a calm, confident, professional tone instead of rushing to get everything out that you can, people will pay more attention.
- *Make eye contact when you speak.* It shows you are confident, interested, sincere, and focused.
- *Display good manners.* Use "please" and "thank you." Many industry people forget. Thank people for their time and you'll stand out.
- *Be considerate of other peoples' time.* Don't just dive into your pitch. Show respect by asking if it's a good time to talk.
- *Think before you speak.* I hear it all the time: "I wish I could erase what I blurted out." Take a deep breath before responding to something important.
- *Monitor the pitch of your voice.* If you're nervous or excited, start an octave lower. Voices tend to get shrill if emotions kick in, so this allows leeway.
- *Smile.* People will like you more. A smile shows that you are a positive person. Friendliness and enthusiasm are infectious.

Creating Alliances

Accept that other artists are not competition. There's room for all good music. Go to places where you can meet other acts: clubs, industry workshops, etc. Develop friendships. Help other musicians. Share contacts. Invite them to open for you, and open for them. Support one another by going to gigs. Beth Wood adds, "Befriend other bands that play the same clubs as you do. Sharing information and resources with other musicians is invaluable. Other musicians are your greatest allies, so make an effort to be friendly."

Start your own support system. Find like-minded musicians to interact with regularly. Recruit five musicians on your level for regular meetings. Critique one another. Cross-promote. If indies work together and support one another, we can own tremendous power! Preech is friendly to everyone, explaining, "If two artists network, neither knows how far the other will go in the game. If you keep in contact all the time, they'll remember that. I met someone once and we started talking. A few months later I opened up for him—he had been signed to Ruff Ryders. You never know who's going to do what."

Once relationships are on solid ground, book group gigs with other acts. Ask venues for the whole night. Do a group mailing to everyone's fans. Advise them to stay for the whole show; you'll share fans and have a bigger crowd. Plus, it's nice to be part of something. Many indies are banding together on a business level to create a more powerful entity. Tina Broad (BROTHER's manager) says, "We're structuring an alliance with other indies we know and love so we can use our sites to refer and do crossover selling between us. We're excited by the potential in that."

Many indies are creating co-ops. They operate under one umbrella, sharing a distributor and the cost for a publicist, radio promoter, etc. Money for CD sales is often paid directly to each individual artist. They share expenses, which allows for things that one person couldn't afford. Everyone

---

PROFILE

Barbara Tucker is a singer and dancer who was signed to Strictly Rhythm as the longest act at that time signed to a house label—seven years. After many hit records, working with artists including the Eurythmics and the Pet Shop Boys, now Tucker executive produces her own projects and works with other artists. She also writes songs for several signed acts—one album went double platinum. Tucker was instrumental in promoting the Underground Network, an organization that promotes dance music parties. She still gigs regularly, both here and overseas, and does the voice of C&C Music Factory on their tour.

chips in equally, and often a small percentage of sales goes into the mutual pot (if you do this, have a written agreement from a lawyer). Creating an umbrella company to which each artist contributes gives you more options. When you unite with the right musicians, your clout and your ability to promote your music will increase.

YOUR PERFORMING TEAM

One of the hardest things about being in a band is . . . being in a band. Working with a group is stressful if you're not ALL consciously a team. Robby Baier says, "It is very important to me to have peace in the band. I try to keep the relationships clear between all of us before the show." If you're not clear about the role of each member in running your business, hard feelings can cause unnecessary static that's detrimental to your potential success. Evan R. Saffer of FIXER says, "Music is about working together—both within and without the band. It's about teamwork and reaching people. You have to collaborate." Lead singers with a star mentality should go solo.

Successful bands meet regularly to discuss band biz and who's responsible for what. Divide work according to everyone's strengths and weaknesses. Often one gung ho member takes the driver's seat and does everything. But as things escalate, it gets more exhausting and fun turns to resentment. When money starts to happen, the worker bee feels entitled to a bigger share. If the others disagree, resentment increases. Avoid this by dividing tasks fairly. Pat DiNizio says, "You have to be unified as a group in attitude, goals, and spirit. It's difficult to get three or four people in the same room and get them to agree on anything, much less music or career goals." Someone must book and promote gigs, contact radio and press, keep track of record and merch sales, handle paperwork and accounting, update your website, manage street teams, and do all sorts of other functions. One person shouldn't do it all! If you find you are doing it all, think about finding a new band. If each member isn't willing to do their share, it's an unequal partnership that won't work.

If you're not a solo act, have a band agreement. Put everything in writing, as businesspeople do. Tina Broad recommends, "Get things in writing with your other players so everyone knows what they're going to be earning; how their deal is structured; whether they'll be cut in on merch and, if so, by how much. Pay your players promptly." You're not taking your music seriously as a business if there's no agreement. Don't wait until you make money—that's when things get sticky. Stuff happens between band members. Of course you should trust one another, but this is business. Spell everything out at the beginning between everyone you work with or your business won't run smoothly. A written band agreement helps minimize issues between everyone in your act. Brian Caplan, Esq., says:

I have litigated a number of disputes among band members, which likely would have been avoided with the creation of band partnership agreements early on. Written band partnership agreements can save band members substantial headaches and legal fees down the road. Although newly formed bands often don't have significant resources to hire transactional attorneys, it is clearly in their interest to memorialize the respective ownership interests, rights, and obligations of each band member among themselves as early as possible. Litigation among band members is common when no partnership agreement exists. Issues that frequently arise are (1) who owns the name of a band when the band breaks up or a member leaves, (2) can a member get ejected from a band right before a large advance is due from a record label, and if so, should the ejected member have any right to share in such advance when he or she will not be part of the new record project, (3) what rights does a former band member have in continuing merchandising of the band's name and likeness, and (4) if there are unequal splits on record royalties and equal splits on other income streams split equally (touring, merchandising, etc.). A band's minimal investment in the drafting of a partnership agreement will be well rewarded down the road.

An agreement helps maintain stronger relationships. Are songwriting royalties split equally if one person writes most of them? Potential royalties are a lot to give away towards goodwill, so think carefully before agreeing to things like that. The band might break up and then others will own equal shares of a song you wrote.

Some singers pay people to play with them without actually being a band. Even so, Marly Hornik advises treating everyone well:

If you hire musicians, you have to pay them—it's your music, not theirs. They've spent years learning the craft that they're using to benefit you. Understand that even if you don't like the bass player on your tour, he's friends with tons of other bass players. If you treat him badly, others find out quickly. I take care of my musicians at every opportunity. I bend over backwards to make sure that they're comfortable but put them through the ringer too, because I can't afford to go first class. We all stay in one room.

Be careful about which musicians you team up with. Bobby Borg cautions that you really have to check the criteria of each member to make sure they have the same goals. He says you need more than just sharing a common interest in music. Ask the important questions: Do you see yourself doing this for years? Can you do this without making money for years? Can you invest money in the project? Are you in a serious relationship or married? Can you see yourself relocating? Would you change your image to what the band is going for? All these issues can create problems. Borg advises settling the answers before committing to work together.

Constant complaints between band members won't just go away. You need group decisions about what's acceptable and what's not. How late is late if you're paying for rehearsal space or studio time? What happens if someone isn't prepared for a gig? As the band improves, one member may not. Drugs and alcohol can also cause problems (see Chapter 8). Sometimes band members must be cut loose for the good of the group. It's important to have a comfortable relationship with those you work with. DiNizio says:

> If you're in a group, subordinate the individual ego to the collective ego of the group. It is a group. The audience can tell when it's a real group or just a bunch of players that don't relate to each other in any way. Be gentle with each other. The band has to be your family. There has never been a fight in the Smithereens. How else could we have stayed together for twenty-five years? It comes with respect and admiration for each other. You have to respect each other and give each other the space [you] need.

YOUR BUSINESS TEAM

Everyone wishes for a manager to handle business and an agent to book them. Life would be much easier that way. What does a manager do? Tina Broad explains:

> I run both the strategic and day-to-day aspects of our businesses: BROTHER Touring, the touring arm; BROTHER Productions, the retail arm; and Rhubarb Records, our own label. I liaise with promoters, venues, and agents

PROFILE

Hamish Richardson is one of the two lead singers of BROTHER, an Australian band. He and his brother Angus moved to L.A. and established their career in the U.S. Known for their unusual sound, their music combines pop/rock with the more traditional Celtic teachings of the bagpipe instruments and even the Aboriginal didgeridoo. Since 1994, the band has evolved into one that's out on the touring circuit in the U.S. every year, appearing at festivals, clubs, Borders in-store events, schools, and radio stations—they tour foreign countries, too. BROTHER's music has been licensed for film and TV. Their catalogue sales exceed 200,000 CDs.

on securing bookings; develop, secure, and manage sponsorships/endorsements; coordinate the marketing and promotion of all performances/appearances; manage the support team of engineers, road crew, merchandise sales people, and guest musicians; [and] handle all communications activities of the companies, including website promotions, database management, public relations, media liaison, and advertising.

Broad also coordinates the charitable and fundraising activities of BROTHER and stays closely involved in the creative side of the songs and performance. A well-connected and respected manager is beneficial. The music biz operates on relationships, so knowing industry players is a big part of the management game.

But these representatives work for a percentage of what you make, so it's hard to get anyone good until you make decent money. A manager will help orchestrate your career, so the wait for a good one is worth it. Robby Baier says, "Giving up a piece of the pie to a good manager is a great thing, especially if he/she gets you more work and opportunities. Being independent does not mean doing it alone." Baier, whose manager found him online and tracked him down because he liked the music, adds, "Keep a large presence online, be persistent, and the right people will find you." Musicians say the best time to consider a manager is when the business end takes too much time because you're accomplishing stuff. A manager who sees potential may come on board to bring it to fruition, so attract people to represent you by working hard to get your career going. The more you do on your own, the easier it will be to attract someone good. Matt Allison says:

You need to do every managerial task you can think of. I'm my own booking agent, manager, performer, CEO, publisher all rolled into one—I just switch hats when I need to. Ultimately, I'd like to pass on a lot of these responsibilities, but I need to find my team first. Research plays a big role in getting to managers and booking agents, and when you do, being ready and courteous helps. Many, if not most, don't respond to my emails/calls. But, it only takes one to get your foot in the door.

At first, use volunteers to pick up the slack. Fans or band members can help handle the responsibilities of a manager or booking agent. A big step for Rachael Sage came when she finally learned it was okay to delegate things to people who are better at doing them. She says, "I've always spread myself so thin—to the point where I'm about to break. At the very least, I'm learning more about building a team. That's easier with a smaller group, as opposed to a gargantuan company where you can't make your voice heard—when *you're* the product being put out."

When the time comes, carefully choose your representation. Preech says, "I've been making money since I was in school. I wasn't battling for twenty dollars. It was five hundred and up. When [my manager] came on board, it was like getting a different car. One car takes you from A to B, but a different car may get you there faster." A manager gets an average of 15 to 20 percent, so don't let desperation taint your judgment. I know the temptation when someone raves about what they can do for you and you're so tired of doing it yourself. There are many wannabe managers; some can be hard-working and effective. If someone has potential, try them out. Just don't turn everything over to someone without seeing a track record or observing them in action for you over several months. Don't sign a long-term agreement with anyone who you're not sure will do well long-term just because you're desperate for help.

Do you want an agent as soon as you start touring? Dream on! Eric Dimenstein, booking agent with Ground Control Touring, says, "It's good to experience booking shows/tours yourself, to get a good understanding/perspective on how things work, before handing it over to someone else." Agents look for artists with a following. Since they work for a percentage of your fee for live shows, they must believe you'll earn money. When is an artist ready to approach an agent? Dimenstein says, "Usually when legwork has been done and some aspects are already in place. It helps to have a bit of a touring history, a record label (independent or major) to ensure records are in stores in towns you will be traveling to, someone to help with press, etc."

Most agents say they're not interested until you've toured in a 300-mile radius around your hometown. They keep track of who's touring and getting press, and they want artists whose names they recognize. Once you've toured in several markets, begin contacting agents. Dimenstein advises, "We are very busy with phone calls and emails through the course of a day. It's best to be short and to the point. We try to get to everyone but sometimes take a bit of time getting back to people. You shouldn't take anything personal. Short emails are always better than phone."

Pollstar (see Chapter 9) has directories with managers and agents. When approaching agents and managers, send a cover letter with your highlights on a one-sheet (see Chapter 11). Don't send a huge press kit unless you know they want it. The letter should say that you'd be happy to send more if they're interested. If you're playing a lot, send a tour schedule too. Update your website (see Chapter 13) before you start, and invite them to visit it. If you keep developing your career, people will want to rep you.

● ● ● ● **CHAPTER 6** ● ● ● ●

Mental Independence

I f you want to succeed, prepare to develop patience, perseverance, and an ability to handle rejection. This chapter provides tools to maneuver potholes you may encounter on the road to success. I want to help you develop yourself as an indie who can go the distance.

USING YOUR POWER TOOL: FAITH

I used to be an atheist, which left me vulnerable. Then I read a book explaining that if I changed my thoughts, I would give myself power over my life. Slowly, I discovered that I always have support from a higher being. It's just up to me to use it. Now I believe I can get anything I need, and I'm rarely scared. No, I'm not at all religious. I just live a spiritual lifestyle; I know what goes around comes back to me. Indie artist Suzanne Teng (profile on page 116) advises, "Recognize that things are the way that they're meant to be. Don't stick to a set plan or formula. Understand there's a natural flow to things. Be open. If someone is openhearted, they can be spiritual."

Treating people kindly brings rewards. I expect people to be helpful, and most people that I meet are. The music biz is tough. I implore you to use faith to support your career. It will, if you expect it to. Believe in yourself and your ability to create and perform great music! When she first began,

Lorraine Ferro wanted to go to the Gospel Music Convention in Nashville but had no money. She prayed for a sign:

> I told God on Tuesday that He knew how thickheaded I was, and if I was supposed to go, He should send me money so I would know He wanted me to go. On Thursday, I got three checks from a jingle I had done the year before that I thought never got aired. On Friday, I got four more checks. On Saturday, two more came. By the next Tuesday, there were a total of twelve checks equaling over $2,000. I booked my flight!

That's how my world works! Positive thinkers make better independent musicians. Pessimists become their own worst enemies. If you expect negatives, you'll be "rewarded" with them.

Matt Allison says, "I thank God for his providence. My faith keeps me grounded. I know that my life is in God's hands—a far safer place than mine are. My art and faith go hand in hand. I often express my faith in songs. When faith is such a big part of your life, as it is in mine, it permeates whatever you do." Speech says, "We're a praying group and pray as a unit for all of our shows." Faith helps you stay strong. Ezina Moore shares:

> With crowds coming to see your shows and wanting autographs, it's easy to get caught up and start believing your own hype. It is so important to maintain your spiritual center because this business is cyclical. You have ups and downs. Maintaining your spiritual center keeps you grounded and comforts you when the unexpected happens. Nobody wants to hear that sales will slow or that crowds will thin out, but it happens at some point in every music career. During those times, we have to put aside the ego and be grateful for the blessing of being able to make music at all.

My strong spiritual faith allows me to accept life's glitches more easily. No matter what happens, I say *out loud* that everything happens for a reason and something good will come of it. I love finding those reasons later—they're always there!

When you go with the flow because you trust you'll get what you need, you get what you need. EXPECT good things to happen, and you'll get a lot more. Christine Kane says:

> I am one of those froofy people who believe that doors will open when and where they are meant to open. In my career, this has almost always been true. They just haven't always opened when and where I had thought they would. I recognize that my puny attempts to control my direction have never

worked, and it seems like something much, much bigger than my goals and my ego is at play here. And when I let that bigger thing drive the bus, everything works. And when I don't, nothing does.

Kane's successful career proves her point! To me, faith is the best antidote for stress and discouragement. Beth Wood adds, "I get caught up in worry a little too much. [Being an indie artist] is very uncertain financially, so you have to plan ahead for things and try to balance it out. The funny thing about worry is that every time I worry I won't make it through the next six months, I make it. I'm learning to have faith that if this is what I'm supposed to do, I won't starve!" I've learned to think the same way—hey, I'm independent, too! It isn't easy but faith makes it easier. I'd never have made it this far without having faith that I'm supported in my intentions. When I'm scared of taking a risk, I calm myself with affirmations such as, "I trust that everything will work out fine."

Canjoe says, "I am very spiritual and believe that what I do is a gift from God. . . . Each time I reach a point of giving up, my spirit is renewed by offers and situations that only He could make happen." I often look up, ask for guidance, and express my gratitude for each little blessing. I have NO doubt that I'm heard, so I follow my passions without worry. Barbara Tucker agrees: "I am a spiritual person first—one with God. We all are, but not all have come to that revelation. I am giving to the universe through my gift and my love. I know that's what I reap and get back. Givers always get, while takers will always be taken from." Tucker continues to achieve success in all she does. When we spoke, the joy with her faith radiated. Faith can do that for all of us. Choose your own spiritual path, but find one. Tucker advises, "Sit down and meditate. Go with it. See what it is that you want. God gave you the talent. Every day you thank God and let him open up those doors. Make sure you hang onto your integrity, your truth, and your honesty." Amen!

BUILDING CONFIDENCE

Often musicians work too hard to step back and just focus on the beauty of their craft. You're not ready to be an independent musician if you don't believe in your music with all your heart and soul. If you have doubts, work on improving your skills. Until you believe in yourself completely, it's hard to get others on board. Ezina Moore feeds herself confidence boosters. She says, "I am always reading a famous person's autobiography. I listen to motivational tapes and inspirational songs; I work out to them. I read *Biography* magazine." Corky McClerkin looks to Herbie Hancock for inspiration, saying, "Many musicians left for New York—unfortunately, some jazz critics and enthusiasts fail to credit the ChiTown influences. These musicians are a unique fusion of

Chicago Roots and New York inspiration. Herbie Hancock and I grew up in the same neighborhood, attended the same schools, and make music a primary force in our lives. His success continues to fuel my own sense of music's unlimited possibilities."

How can you build the confidence to go after what you want? One baby success at a time. Each review gets you closer. Let each new fan stoke the fire. If you believe in your music, let it wash over you like warm sunshine. When you're nervous about being taken seriously, think about your music. Know that it is worthy of the opportunities you seek. Confidence begins with belief in your abilities. Then you can fake confidence in other areas until it becomes real. Justin Lassen says he worked with a high profile DJ who was shocked to learn he was only 21 years old. Lassen had the confidence and posture of someone years older. He explains, "I've faked—acted like I knew what I was doing until people recognized my talents. I hear from people that I'd never imagine talking with, because they see my confidence. Then my work totally speaks for itself."

Confidence sells! And it doesn't cost anything. I often hear musicians speak about their music without conviction. That makes a difference! They have slumped shoulders and low energy, which won't impress anyone. But in this biz, we need to impress. Why would someone take you seriously if you're not confident about your music? Confidence is contagious. When people feel yours, your image is more positive. They're more likely to check out your music or make time for you. Henri Lessing of Media Records Benelux says, "An artist has to think he's number one to have enough drive to succeed. Then, if you fall, you get up. On the other hand, be diligent enough to want to discover yourself to improve and cope with your ego."

Confidence shows you take yourself seriously. Are you thinking, "I don't have a confident personality. What can I do?" I'll tell you: Nobody *starts* with confidence. It's developed and learned over time. I was terrified on my first few TV appearances. It took time to develop real confidence. I live by René Descartes: "I think, therefore I am." It's in all my books, and I live it. Before I felt real confidence, I'd shake inside but I'd exude that I was someone in control. If you do something over and over, it becomes a habit. The more you act confident, the more you'll feel it. Fake it until it's real—it becomes real if you keep it up. "I think, therefore I am." Here are some of my confidence boosters. If you practice developing them, you'll attract a lot more attention and success for you and your music.

- *Talk to yourself.* I do, and I'm not crazy (no arguments from friends, please!). I do it to encourage myself. In scary situations, I go to a mirror and say versions of, "I'm Daylle Deanna Schwartz and I know I can do it." Or, "I'm good enough to handle this situation."

Sometimes I repeat it like an affirmation until I feel the power of my words. You CAN do it.

- *Take deep breaths before speaking.* Trying to sound confident is stressful. Taking slow, deep breaths keeps your demeanor calm.
- *Keep a positive attitude.* If you sound positive, people will think you are. This is part of faking it until you make it. A positive tone of voice makes you sound confident. Develop some energy if you have none. The more energetic you sound, the more people will think you're confident.
- *Smile.* Nervous people don't smile. They may giggle inappropriately, but they don't have a confident smile. Smiling triggers confidence by stimulating positive body chemicals that make you feel good. Polish your teeth and show them!
- *Develop a confident stance.* Work on your posture. People judge you by how you carry yourself. Good posture can be faked easily. Stand straight and arch your shoulders back with your head held high. People will buy the image of confidence. It sets a tone for their immediate perception of you. Good posture makes YOU feel more powerful, too.
- *Develop a firm handshake.* A wet noodle grip doesn't cut it! In my seminars, I shake hands with as many people as possible. I tell about 50 percent to develop a firmer grip. This is something you all can do! A firm handshake communicates confidence whether you feel it or not.
- *Polish your balls!* In situations where someone is challenging your ability and you don't feel sure of yourself, challenge back. Ask questions to buy time to think. For example, if someone questions your

ability to perform, ask if there's something that elicits concern. Put the person on the spot to prove himself to you. Don't get defensive when someone tries to put you on the spot. Instead, make them own up to what they say. Being defensive doesn't impress. Asking questions back shows confidence.

EVERYBODY DOESN'T HAVE TO LOVE YOU!

Rejection stinks! But not being appreciated is part of the process of becoming a better musician. If you want to survive the music industry, you have to develop a tough skin. Learn to handle the downs so you can reach the ups. Mary Gauthier says, "My answer is just working. I treat it like a job and find ways to make it work. When it doesn't work in a city, I find one where it does work. If we took rejection personally, we'd all be in the fetal position. Even if it is personal, move on. It's hard to not feel it, but letting it go makes you stronger and keeps you moving."

Reviews that don't show you the love you hoped for are a learning experience. Howie Statland says, "I watch people that I look up to, like Lou Reed, who does what he wants. If critics slander him, it always backfires on them. Ten years down the road, the album they slandered turns out to be one of the best." If the criticism is constructive, get over your bruised ego and try something new. If it's nasty, maybe the critic is having a bad day, or not gettin' any. Some people need to criticize no matter what you do, and will always find something, fair or not. Don't let them undermine your confidence or slow your progress. Why waste energy lamenting someone's opinion? If a critic is being an A-hole, express your annoyance to friends and let it go. Why care what an A-hole thinks? Put your energy into improving your music and proving him or her wrong. Hamish Richardson says:

> I remind myself that the reviewer is obviously an arsehole with low self-esteem. It's never easy having something criticized that you've worked [on], sweated over, and bared you soul in, but not everyone is gonna get it. I try to have my ego-free filter on—process what's pertinent, disregard what's not, keep doing what we do honestly, and at the end of the day, not read everything that's written about us.

If a mean-spirited write-up bothers you, put your anger and hurt feelings on paper. Do this with your anger at the club owner who ignores your requests to play, the press writer who won't attend your gig, the band member who thinks he's above the rest, the friends who promise to support you but don't, the musician who never booked the gig she promised. Anger can be generated in the pursuit of a music career. Don't let it hurt you! Write down your feelings as if you were speaking to the person—it's cleansing. I read it out loud as if I were talking to the person. Then I burn it (safely, in the sink). My anger dissipates as the letter burns. Burn bad reviews, too. Burning negatives helps you feel better.

My company is called Revenge Productions because success really is the sweetest revenge. If someone does me wrong or puts down my work, I use the energy from my anger to improve. When my career began, I asked a well-known producer if I could include his name on my first record since he informally helped mix it. His name would have increased my credibility. I'd done him favors, but he said he didn't put his name on records made by "unknowns." Revenge Records succeeded without him. Two years later, this producer's career was stagnant when one of my acts got a major deal. He approached me all smiling and asked to produce some tracks. I pleasantly explained we were only working with current producers. Sweet revenge! What goes around really does come back to you! The producer had an attitude when his career soared, but it came back to haunt him later.

Use your anger or hurt feelings to do something that's good for you. Don't be afraid of being turned down by those you want acceptance from. Someone once suggested that I save rejection letters in a folder as motivation to succeed and prove them wrong; I use them to empower me. Rejections don't matter. I had 14 of them for my first book, which is still going strong. My book *All Men Are Jerks Until Proven Otherwise* got 16 rejections, but the seventeenth editor loved it and I got an excellent deal. Focus on your future success, not on past or potential rejection. Musician Anton Sanko (profile on page 180) advises you to decide whether you can put yourself out there on a daily basis and risk getting rejected, saying, "If you want to make a living as a musician, that's part of it." Barbara Tucker says, "If I'm turned down, I say that it wasn't meant for me. What God has for you, no one can take away from you. Don't get disappointed when something doesn't happen. Just work harder." Tucker has seen offers that she wanted but didn't get, then fall apart later. Knowing that not getting these offers saved her from bigger disappointment, she always says, "Thank you, God." It's impossible to please everyone, so don't worry if someone isn't pleased. When you believe in your music, just keep going until you find people who understand why. Then, give yourself the last laugh when you succeed.

HANGIN' IN THERE

Developing your music career can get discouraging at times. Prepare yourself. When you put your all into your career and it doesn't get you far, quitting may seem easier. Christine Kane says:

> *When you put yourself out there in any career, you'll be hit with hard blows, face your worst doubts, deal with unkind people, and have weeks, months,*

and years when you wish you'd gone to journalism school like everyone told you to instead of becoming an artist. I try to keep my focus on my intent and why I do this. Not all of my reasons are pure, but at the deepest level I know this is what I'm meant to do, and this is how I reach people. I remind myself of this regularly.

Have you noticed that things don't always go as planned? That happens way too often for most of us. Sometimes it's not even that bad, but we're just not in the mood for a curve ball. Matt Allison says, "It can be hard to keep focused to persevere, especially when you don't get the response you were hoping for. But I have learned to look back on where I started and where I am now, and it seems to put it all in perspective." Unexpected events or outcomes happen regularly. You can whine to friends and feel lousy, or you can view problems as opportunities to learn and see how strong your passion for music really is. Dean Seltzer agrees:

> *There's a million reasons to quit and one reason to stick to it—you love it. If you're in it for money, drugs, or anything like that, get out. It's hard work, you don't get much sleep, and you tend to be underappreciated. The only reason to do it is because you love it. You deal with so much bullshit— people stabbing you in the back. The only thing to keep you going is know- ing that there's nothing more rewarding and exciting than playing music in front of a crowd of people.*

Working way too hard for way too little hurts the spirit. Some musicians lose their desire to play live and write songs. Don't fight it at first. It's hard to write songs, or even practice, when you feel down. Sometimes you need to lick your wounds a little before continuing. Things improve if you ebb and flow gracefully. Alex Woodard explains:

> *Balance is a big factor. I try to keep my life supported with things not dependent on music: my dog, family, surfing, etc. That way, music and the business of music don't drain me like they do some people, and I stay pumped about continuing down that path. It's tough to always be inspired. I let the moments when I really am inspired hit me before I write songs. I don't force it. The main thing is, I can't imagine doing anything else.*

If you feel blocked creatively, play your instrument for pleasure or listen to your CD—a reminder of why you're pursuing a career in music and why you must persevere. Evan R. Saffer says, "In the end, it's the music we make that keeps my blood pumping. Every rehearsal, a new song, a compliment from a stranger, is pure energy." I still read my own books sometimes when I'm feeling down or considering a day job. It snaps me back fast to the reality of what truly makes me happy: writing and speaking. Christine Kane says that nothing helps keep her grounded more than writing a song. Listen to music you love in order to rekindle your general music passion. Gregory Abbott shares:

> To live the life of a creative person is a rare gift. That alone should be enough motivation to do whatever it takes to have it become a reality. Surround yourself with other creative people with whom you can share insights, strategies, resources, etc. You want folks around you who encourage and inspire, who themselves seek this higher goal. Persevere. At the end of the day, your most valuable asset is your belief in yourself.

Michelle Shocked says, "The nature of being an effective artist is that you have to focus on the big picture and not get bogged down by the flaws and imperfections that invariably come along." I always clean when I feel out of control. Organize your business materials so you feel more in control of what's going on. Accept that it's normal to feel discouraged. Your spirit will rebound if you don't let it sink you. Rachael Sage says:

> I feel vulnerable to the elements of this business most of the time. What keeps me going are occasional epiphanies that lasso me in and remind me of what it is all about. There are the moments of connecting with the audience. Someone tells you their story and how it relates to yours, or your music. It waves a big giant flag of awareness of how blessed we are to be able to do what we love, even if challenges are so great that we often question our purpose. In those moments, the purpose is clear. Many times it feels like those responses and signs are the road map. They come from people you would never otherwise have the opportunity to connect with—pure magic and

PROFILE

Speech is part of the hip-hop act Arrested Development. Signed to EMI until 1995, Speech still records and tours with the group. In 2004 they had a 32-city tour in Europe, and they tour Japan regularly, usually to sell-out shows. Speech has also developed a solo career with five albums, four of them independent. Speech and the group license their music to EMI in Japan because of their huge following there. In Japan alone, one of Speech's solo CDs has sold about 120,000 copies, and one of Arrested Development's has sold 200,000.

absolutely mystifying. In those moments, the grunt work fades, until it comes back in the morning. You just kind of go through this cycle.

When her music career discourages her, Marly Hornik says, "I try to think of other things I want to do but can't think of anything." Feed off your fans' enthusiasm for your music. I read fan letters when I question my direction, and then I know I must continue. Lisa O'Kane says:

The fan response has been overwhelming. I feel like I've been given a second chance to do something really great with my life and can't stop now. Sometimes there are hard days—juggling two children and a career and all that—but everyone has hard days, and the satisfaction I feel of being an artist makes it all worth it. Sometimes I think to myself, "What if I stopped?" Well, then I'd never know how far I could have gone, so I keep going.

When you're in a funk, take care of your health and your spirit. Be kind to you! Try not to dwell on negatives. Use affirmations to knock them out of your head. When things aren't so good, repeat your version of "My career will be successful in the long haul." You can't think two sets of thoughts at the same time. Bury your demons under positive statements, over and over, until they're gone. Danielle Egnew says:

If an artist's passion is truly their music, they will keep a strong focus in thrusting that music into the world, through some very tough times. I have certainly had my ups and downs in feeling enthused over the business end. The music is always amazing and fulfilling, but the rest is quite often laborious and unfulfilling, at least while doing it. But there is always a feeling of accomplishment after many press kits have been mailed, or a newspaper has accepted an invitation to a show. An artist will benefit from keeping their eye on the prize, which is showcasing their art.

Do something that's pleasurable to take your mind off what's not working. Get support from friends. Beth Wood says she's learning to pump herself up and give self-pep talks. She relies on the support of family, friends, and loved ones; just knowing they're cheering her on increases her energy. Wood adds, "I am very lucky to have them! Kind words and emails from fans help a lot, too. If I feel like what I do means something to someone, it helps me to continue on the path. There are lots of times when I want to give up. But then I have a little conversation with myself, and remember that this work is important to me."

Get a massage. Go for a jog. Do what you can to take care of your physical well being—it will affect you mentally. Hamish Richardson advises, "Stay healthy, fit, and sharp. You gotta have fun, but everything rides on you: load in, radio, in-stores, driving, show, signing, interviews." Nurturing yourself puts you back in touch with you. Get stronger on the inside and you'll persevere more easily. It takes self-discipline to become proactive. Jennie DeVoe explains:

Perseverance is the absolute necessity for an artist. There's not a lot of sitting around, waiting for your phone to ring. I never turn on my TV in the daytime. Self-discipline is a challenge. It's hard for artists I know to do what they should do every day, but we try. You do it 'cause you're driven. You can't wait for stuff to happen. Do whatever you can to move forward; promote yourself. Here and there, measurable successes take place. I go through down times and question why I continue. Everyone does.

Barbara Tucker says, "A disappointment is a setup for another appointment. A crisis is just something that pushes you to another level." When something doesn't come through, that means there's room for something else. Don't get down on yourself because you think you've screwed something up. Accept that it happened for a reason and it's okay. Lorraine Ferro explains, "Know you will make lots of mistakes! Welcome them with open arms if you can. There's no harm in making one, but understand the lesson in it. Sometimes a mistake hurts like hell, but it gets easier when you can rise to the occasion and learn from it." Patience is imperative for the long haul. If you quit, it's over. You may get turned down dozens of times for a gig or placement in a film; attendance at gigs may be small. But persevering changes all that. If your music is good, eventually it will be recognized. I've interviewed enough musicians to believe that. Stay positive to get more.

Zak Morgan says, "I'm just an ordinary person. If you believe in yourself and surround yourself with positive people, you'll do well. You can be an everyday person and do extraordinary things if you work hard. There are a lot of great musicians around me, but they have such a crappy attitude that they're not going anywhere." You may pitch dozens of music supervisors before a song gets placed in a film or TV show, or call a club 15 times before getting a gig. Musicians often whine about how many calls they've made. Do you want to succeed? Call more! If you don't quit, someone will eventually respond. Justin Lassen says, "If I get knocked down by anyone, I just get up and come back with ten times more charisma and hard work."

Each success makes it a tad easier to get the next one. As your press kit grows, so does your marketability. DJ Minx says, "I stay focused mainly because I'm optimistic. I know there's things I want in life for me and my family, and I need to work hard to achieve these goals. No pain, no gain!" If you hang in there, it does get better. Consider perseverance a success in itself and be proud instead of beating yourself up for what you haven't done. Baby steps forward bring rewards. Be patient! Christine Kane says, "When all of that fails, I call a friend and whine." But then she continues to march on.

CREATING A SUPPORT SYSTEM

I've heard people complain about what a lousy business this is and how people take advantage. This rarely happens to me. While people in this biz have a bad reputation, I expect people to be nice and they are. They may not give you what you want, but that doesn't make them bad. Ezina Moore has an OPP ("Only Positive People") approach. She explains, "I only hang out with positive people. We keep each other up during those times when life kicks you in the gut. When someone gets on a constant bitch fest that persists longer than a couple of days, I limit contact with her and stop answering her calls. Negativity is contagious."

As I continue to say, we get back what we put out. I support people, and people support me. That's my world and it can be yours, too. It's in your hands. Reach out to people with support and you'll create a supportive world. Having people who are there for you can make a big difference. Corky McClerkin says his desire to achieve excellence in memory of his encouraging mother and father and his music teacher, along with the consistent support from his wife, is what keeps him going. He says, "All gave me continuous encouragement and belief in my ability to succeed." As you network, keep in touch with like-minded musicians. Meet with them regularly to share information, critique music, and encourage one another. Do group shows. Expect to find supportive people and you will.

STOKING YOUR MUSICAL PASSION

No matter what your goals or perceived struggles, NEVER forget why you began doing music in the first place. If you're in this biz for fame and glory, going the independent route probably isn't for you. If you're in it because you love music, never forget that. Often musicians get so caught up in trying to achieve that they stop enjoying what they do. What's the point? Michael Johnathon says, "You have to start out with the right intentions and do this because you genuinely love what you're doing. You can't be there for the bucks. Be there for the people, the audience, because you want to share your music."

If you find yourself running in circles or ranting about what you have to do, stop. Take deep breaths. Play your music. Belt out your favorite song. List ten reasons why you began pursuing music. Then try to return to the passion at its core. Hamish Richardson says:

> *Make the most of every opportunity and enjoy the grind; we do what a lot of people would love to be doing. When you feel drained of new ideas, tap into*

music in general. Listen to it. Sing along. Remind yourself why you do music in the first place. Go hear live music with friends. It can help stir up the creative juices and incite the passion you've had.

Life is too short not to have fun with whatever you do. When you focus on your passion for music, it's easier to lighten up and enjoy. Robby Baier says, "I stay mentally in the music and not on the environment. All I need is the song and one person to focus on during the show, and I'm fine." Justin Lassen stays away from the industry as much as possible for clarity and productivity, explaining:

Sometimes you can get swept away in all of the bells and whistles of the industry and forget what you are doing, or get discouraged. I've been wined and dined, and I've been treated like shit, by both "big wigs" and "little wigs." It's very important to stay unjaded and positive. Always have hope. I heard in a war movie that "once you lose hope, you're dead anyway." It is most important to stay inspired and never relent.

I made a policy long ago not to ever do anything I don't love. I've been happy ever since. If you're not lovin' your music, figure out why not. Are you pushing too hard on promotion? If that's burning out your pleasure, do something else for a while. Your career can take a vacation if it needs one. Return to the music itself and put the biz aside for a bit. Without the passion and fun, there's little point in doing the business end.

CHAPTER 7

Recording Independence

New technology offers less expensive options for recording, but that doesn't mean you can just buy a bunch of tech toys and create music. I can't stress enough the importance of a top-quality recording if you want to be a successful indie artist. You're competing with a gazillion other artists. To rise to the top of the pack, you must create music that attracts and keeps fans who recognize how terrific your music is. If you want to make money, create the best product possible so you have the best product to market. Follow the tips in this chapter to get a great recording.

GOING INTO THE STUDIO

Be careful about who you choose to record your music. Price shouldn't be the only factor you consider. It's important to work with people who can make your project shine. If you use a small studio, make sure it's someone who knows how to engineer. People buy equipment and supplement their income by recording the music of others, but purchasing the gear doesn't mean they know how to use it properly. Get references from anyone you consider working with. How can you find a good engineer? Michael Gilboe of Copperheadz Productions suggests, "If you are in a large city, check the Yellow Pages. Get to networking sessions and ask around. When you talk to [potential engineers], ask to hear samples of their work."

Many artists say they don't need a producer. I usually disagree. A producer brings objectivity to your recording. Robby Baier advises, "Work with a good producer if you are not recording savvy." Many decisions will need to be made, and when you produce your own music, it's hard to accept that ideas you love don't work. Producer Billy Joe Walker, who's worked with many recording artists, including Travis Tritt, says, "The producer makes the final decision. He sometimes has to gently convince an artist to use one song over another. I try to be a receiver to help these people make their records and get to a better sonic level. Most songwriters think their last song is the best they've ever written, which of course is not the case. That's why it's good to have somebody objective."

What does a producer do? Walker begins by collecting songs. He advises which he thinks are best, then he finds the right keys and tempos for the artist. He also puts the musicians together and arranges the songs with them. Different mics sound better on different artists; Walker tries many to find the best one for each. He does most pre-production out of the studio, explaining, "We do pre-production on the songs before spending a lot of money. A song doesn't always work for the artist. I'm working with one now on a song we like, but it doesn't seem to be her style. We're trying different keys and tempos to bring it into her world." A producer can make a song work for you and can hear things you won't. Good production brings out the best in your music.

It can be hard to get good vocals in the studio. Walker strives to make an artist feel comfortable. Once a producer has cultivated that relationship, getting good vocals is easier. He adds, "Artists need to be shown how to stay right in front of the mic when they do the vocals." Network to find a good producer. Make sure someone is right for you before giving them the responsibility for your record. Lisa O'Kane agrees that the right one is worth it:

> My opinion has always been, you get what you pay for. Everyone wants something for free or work for really cheap. I did several gigs with Edward Tree before I asked him to produce am i too blue. I listened to albums he had produced and we had a few meetings before I decided. We have a great working relationship, and he brought out things in me as a singer that I didn't even know I was capable of. The experience of recording that album with him was invaluable to me as an artist. He taught me so much.

Until you work with a good producer, you may not understand the value. Please, carefully consider using one if you want the best recording results. And take the necessary time to create music you feel great about. Gilboe advises:

You can't force or rush it. Relax. If you are paying for studio time and your mind is on every second of the clock, you won't get a good performance. Likewise if you're recording in your own studio. Letting yourself get frustrated that you aren't learning fast enough or getting something done right won't help you. Music is, after all, about getting a vibe or feeling. You can't let all the technical elements get in the way of that.

Don't record prematurely either. Be ready to embark on *this* level of your career before taking that next step. Billy Joe Walker says, "You should feel confident about your performance before going into the studio. That helps you feel in control of who you are. I never tried to record an artist who didn't know who they are. At that point, you don't need to be recording. Find out who you are first." Decide what direction you want to follow before wasting money.

USING NEW TECHNOLOGY
As I mentioned at the start of this chapter, being independent is now more feasible than ever because new technology slashes recording costs. According to Rey Flemings, President of Memphis and Shelby County Music Commission, "Low-cost production tools have democratized recording and production of commercially consumable music; it's now the quality I can listen to. The do-it-yourself stuff years ago was bad. Nobody would buy it. The changing face of technology makes it available to everyone." Danielle Egnew says, "With so many terrific home studio options, I don't know many artists who still fork out lots of money to record." While you don't have to learn engineering, understand what's available to make economic choices that make sense for your music. Matt Allison says, "Magazines sites like Electronic Musician (www.emusician.com) and Sound on Sound (www.sospubs.co.uk) focus on recording and recording equipment. The articles give a good idea of what to expect in the studio and may help you understand the gear."

PROFILE

Robby Baier was signed to BMG Ariola in Germany with his band Pearls in 1996 and is now independent, as a solo artist and with his band Melodrome. He has opened for name acts, including Suzanne Vega and Los Lobos, and has placed many songs in film and TV both on his own and with Melodrome. His solo effort "Soultube" won the *Musician's Atlas* Best Pop Rock Song award in 2002, and Melodrome won *Musician's Atlas* Best Pop Rock Act award in 2003. Baier won second place in the 2003 International Songwriting Competition for Best Pop/Top 40 song. Melodrome's song "Sex Cash and Fuel" is licensed to Coors for its national advertising campaign.

The most acclaimed technology is Pro Tools, which put recording within the means of more musicians. Recording/mixing engineer Jose "Chilitos" Valenzuela wrote *The Complete Pro Tools Handbook*, an easy-to-use reference guide to mastering the art of digital audio production with Pro Tools. I asked Chilitos to explain Pro Tools:

Pro Tools is an entire recording studio in a computer. You can record in it and make masters of the entire production. It's more powerful than it's ever been. You can produce records and do post-production for a film in super-high quality. Musicians nowadays buy Pro Tools LE, which means "Limited Edition." A single MBox [music box] costs about four hundred dollars. You can do everything to your tracks that you need to and record thirty-two tracks at the same time with Pro Tools. Connect the box to your computer. If you're a songwriter, you can do all your sequencing with MIDI and edit. You can input a Quicktime movie into Pro Tools and make your own video; add music and make your own little film. The user interface is simple, unlike many other systems, so it's easy to use. The quality is amazing.

Chilitos emphasizes that you need a good computer to use Pro Tools effectively. He advises that if you're using the LE system, you need at least a G4 or G5 for Macintosh. There are other options, but a Macintosh processes the data faster. Once it's set up, it's like recording a cassette. He explains, "With Pro Tools, you just click a recording button right on the screen of your computer and you'll see the signal coming in for voice or guitar. That is enough to record. Just press like a cassette, play, and you start recording."

RECORDING AT HOME

Many musicians choose home recording over going into a studio. Be careful. Having tools doesn't make you an engineer—not even close. Think about what you want to devote your energy to. Engineers study and practice. Are you prepared to go to all that trouble? Michael Gilboe explains:

Many people think that if you get gear, suddenly you can record CDs. It is a whole other skill that needs to be developed and learned. Nobody buys a hammer and saw and expects to be a master carpenter in a week, but people do that with audio systems all the time. You need a lot of time and patience to develop this skill set. If you don't have it, you might be better off hiring a studio. This is a lot of work. If you want to be a performing artist, perhaps your time is best spent performing and developing your writing and singing than getting sidetracked with a studio. It is only in an act's interests to develop a studio if one of the members has shown a clear aptitude for it.

If you got an auto-repair tool kit, would you expect to fix your car with just an instruction manual? Your CD is a vehicle for your career. It needs to work properly, just like your brakes. I've taken an auto mechanics class, but I still won't change my own brakes! Real mechanics learn through experience, just like recording engineers.

That said, some people have an aptitude. If you plan to invest in home recording, Gilboe says that while each person's needs are different, there are some basics:

You need a hard disc recorder—a computer or other DAW (Digital Audio Workstation). It can be a computer with software, a stand-alone digital multitrack recorder, and various things that control it. If you record vocals, a good pre-amp and mic are essential. A good pre-amp also helps recording live guitars and basses. It is very easy now to record guitars at home because of all the amp modelers out there. You don't need to blast an amp while mic-ing it anymore. An electronic- or dance-oriented person might get away with nothing but a computer and software, and perhaps a keyboard for entering information. The needs for your general setup vary. Do a lot of research. Try to find an honest, knowledgeable salesman who is willing to listen to what you want to do and truly help. I recommend a budget of around $3,500 to set stuff up if you start from scratch, without a computer. Gear has gotten better, more compact, and cheaper than ever. It is possible to get a great sound that could beat out $250,000 studios from just over a decade ago.

If you're clueless about this equipment, doing your own recording might not be right for you. While I hate to sound discouraging, too many people buy toys but can't get a decent recording. And you don't just want "decent"—you want *awesome!* It can be done. Indie artist Adam Richman (profile on page 230) did his first CD at home. He found Pro Tools too expensive and says, "There are programs that are equally intuitive that are easy and affordable. My recording was bare bones. Artists like John Mayer were becoming established and their music proved you didn't need high fidelity for it to speak to an audience." Is it possible to get a good vocal recording at home? Gilboe thinks it is:

A good vocal recording is made up of many things. Try to get a room or area with very few parallel surfaces, differing materials all over, and different shaped things to break up reflections. The truth is, many cluttered homes are technically good, if not ideal for recording. But there are other issues. Is your home quiet? Can you silence your computer or refrigerator or anything that leaks into the mic? Can you coax a good performance out of the singer and relax him/her? A good mic and pre-amp make a huge difference. A singer shouldn't engineer himself. Find a friend and teach them the basics of stopping, starting, and recording, so you can focus on singing!

Often people who record at home take the tracks to a professional studio for the mix, which is critical for the success of a recording. Mixing sets the levels of each sound properly. Chilitos advises, "If you have the budget, [take your tracks to a studio] for the mixing. You should be able to grab your data, back it up on CD, and open it in the studio. Plug-ins are the effects. You have to purchase them and they are expensive." If you mix at home, Chilitos says you can rent plug-ins when needed. If he works in a studio that doesn't have a plug-in he needs, he uses it online for about $20 a day per plug-in. If you rarely use them, just rent them as needed. Get the best person possible to mix your music. You can hire someone to do it in your home. But don't let your ego convince you to do it yourself unless you have real experience and skills. Mixing is a skill you may not have.

Chilitos says the hardest thing for people who don't understand audio concepts is to figure out how to use the mixer: "You need to be aware of what a mixing board does. You should have an idea of what a signal level does. A signal level makes sure your recording is good, and not noisy. Everything is digital nowadays. It's good to know how the digital transfer format works so you can do everything digitally. If you use analogue, you lose the quality." Everything is spelled out in Chilito's book. Pay a good engineer to coach you at the beginning and show you the basics until you really have them down. Do the mix properly! Gilboe advises:

Have the best person possible mix your recording. Some people swear you can get a better mix in a "real studio," but often this is because of access to better gear/effects and the talent of the engineer who worked hard to develop his ear. It is doable to get a radio-ready recording with a modest setup. Many, many records that hit the top of the charts in Europe were done in home studios. The American music industry is still snobbish about it. But more and more, with the financial crunch in the industry, even American behemoths are realizing that some of these recordings are indeed releasable.

No matter which way you record, do your best to get the best possible results. Your recording reflects your music, so if you want a successful career, respect your music enough to do what's necessary to make it shine. It has to stand up strong in the marketplace.

CHAPTER 8

Healthy Independence

Are you so focused on your career that you ignore your health? If you don't consciously protect your body, you sell yourself way short. Staying healthy is a way of showing yourself love. An independent artist needs all the strength the body can give. Your body is the vehicle for the product you're marketing. All businesses strive to keep their equipment working properly. Don't take yours for granted! Being vigilant about good health is critical to your success, so I've devoted this whole chapter to helping you maintain your health.

GOOD HEALTH = PROSPERITY

The question "How do you stay healthy?" evokes a strong response from musicians who've learned that staying healthy enables them to make more money. Being on the road stresses your system. As an indie artist, you're responsible for yourself. Conscious planning makes it easier to stay healthy, especially when you're out on tour for long periods. Beth Wood advises, "Take care of yourself on the road. I sound like an old lady, but it's true. Try and get enough sleep, exercise when you can, and try to eat well. It involves more planning on your part, but it is worth it in the long run. Touring can wear a person down really fast if he/she is not careful." Be smart about not abusing your body. Jennie DeVoe agrees:

I am into being healthy. Leaving home makes you more vulnerable to getting sick. I drink lots of water, don't forget to sleep, and share driving with the band. I don't drink or smoke before or during a show. It can be fun not falling prey to obvious pitfalls. Decide why you do what you do. Are you in a band to live a rock-star life or are you an artist trying to make a living at using your talent?

Pay attention to the effects of touring! Wood recommends you take your own microphone to avoid sharing germs with bands that sang before you. George Baum warns, "Be careful about your back. Long hours in a van and heavy lifting can cause huge chiropractic bills!" Kyler England tries to get enough sleep and exercise, at least every other day when there's no time every day. Howie Statland learned the hard way: "I used to smoke cigarettes and drink a lot. I didn't take care of myself and was sick all the time on the road. I'd take a whole bottle of Robitussin™ just to go onstage. Now I don't smoke, and I sleep as much as I can." Robby Baier gave up late-night drives and gets a room if he can't be home by 2 A.M. so he's more productive the next day. He also won't play many sets in a smoky room or more than three shows in a row.

Exercise helps maintain a healthy lifestyle. There's always something you can do. Alex Woodard says he stays active at home and on the road by running. No matter how tired you are, exercise stimulates energy and keeps you fit. Wood says exercise makes her feel better after sitting in a car all day. Ask hotels about exercise rooms, parks, and jogging trails. She adds, "I belong to the YMCA at home, and many facilities in the country honor the membership. Before a trip, I go to the YMCA website and see where their nearest facilities are located."

Practice deep breathing. It helps you emote when you sing and it also relieves stress. Some people swear by meditation or yoga. Gregory Abbott meditates and does yoga every day to stay strong and light, both physically and mentally. Howie Statland says, "I do a lot of yoga and listen to a lot of music. Music keeps saving me." Most of these tips are just common sense! But when you're immersed in trying to maintain a hectic schedule, it's easy to neglect YOU. Don't! Maintain your health now and you'll be able to keep going. Wood advises:

If you can, stay loyal to your habits at home. Write in a journal every morning with your coffee. If you read at home, bring a book on the road. When you have a day off, go PLAY! See a movie, visit local attractions, break up the monotony. Don't forget that you're a person, not a music-making machine. If you don't take care of yourself, your performances will suffer.

Listen to that advice!

BEATING EXHAUSTION

Get enough sleep! Musicians say it's crucial. When you don't, it's harder to be productive and creativity can take a snooze. You need energy to keep going; sleep provides that. DJ Minx advises, "Get rest when time permits." So, permit time! Kyler England says, "If I had to pick one thing above all else as most important, I'd say sleep." Ezina Moore adds, "Being on the road is hard on your body. You have to get quality rest. I say quality because you don't always get eight hours of sleep. Sometimes you get none if it is your turn to drive after a late-night gig. I always try to have at least one hour of quiet time."

Jennifer Marks acknowledges that sleep isn't something you can always control, but she makes a point of getting up around the same time each day to keep a routine going. If you're young, be forewarned: Late hours and early mornings will take a toll on you. Hamish Richardson warns, "Don't party yourself into the ground—stop sometime before that, and catch up on sleep whenever you can." If you want a career, create good habits NOW. Lisa O'Kane says, "My biggest problem was jet lag. I've learned to fly two days before I perform. I try to nap when I can, even if I miss tourism stuff. I'd rather give the best performance I can, so I try to be rested." Danielle Egnew adds:

> Partying all night is fun, but when you don't sleep, you can't reset your physical system. Your most important tool on the road is yourself. You wouldn't go to a gig with a guitar that's missing strings. So don't go to a gig missing sleep and missing notes off of your singing range because you partied too hard the night before. That's bad business.

YOU ARE WHAT YOU EAT!

One consistent recommendation is to eat healthy on the road. Your body doesn't tolerate more junk and less nutrition just because that may seem like the music scene. Musicians who sustain a touring career say they must be even more conscious of what they eat, not less. Beth Wood says:

> I follow the same principles I do at home. As a rule, I don't eat fast food; if I'm in a bind, I'll eat Subway®. There are many options besides fast food—just dig a little deeper. Before I leave on a trip, I get healthy snacks—fruit, nuts, pretzels—so if I get desperate, I won't have to resort to fast food. I stop at grocery stores frequently; many have salad bars. Ask the hotel or local folks you meet where good, healthy restaurants are.

Hamish Richardson suggests bringing a supply of raw nuts and dried fruit to munch, finding fresh fruit when possible, and asking for raw and healthy stuff on your rider. He adds, "Eat less, not more than you would at home, 'cause you're doing a lot of sitting." Jennifer Marks says that eating well is her luxury on the road; well-rounded meals help her maintain energy to keep up with her schedule. Dean Seltzer brings supplements such as Ensure™ and Boost™, and takes one with a meal. Many musicians recommend making sure to have fresh veggies. Some say vitamins and other supplements help keep them going. Gregory Abbott says, "Become familiar with health food stores in whatever town you're in. . . . Focus on a balanced diet, fresh water, rejuvenating herbs, vitamins, and antioxidants."

Sometimes you can't avoid fast foods. But if you value your body, limit them! Visual says, "Eat salads, not just fries!" Fast-food restaurants have salads and other healthier choices—take advantage! George Baum says "We try to eat good food as often as possible, since pizza and McDonald's® find their way into your diet more than seems humanly possible." Matt Allison also advises trying to stay away from fast food, saying, "I love a burger, but junk food takes its toll on your body, especially on the road. Resist temptation to stop for it for every meal. Go to a local supermarket and buy fresh salad/fruit or make a sandwich. Don't ignore junk food, but be wise about what you eat." Another important suggestion: Always stay hydrated. It's easy to forget on the road. Water is the best medicine for your voice and your body. Remember it! Allison adds, "Drink lots of water, especially in smoky clubs, to keep your vocal cords lubricated."

CONTROLLING ALCOHOL AND DRUGS

I can't tell you not to indulge in alcohol and drugs. I'd like to, but it's your choice. However, I will implore you to use care if you choose to use them. Jennifer Marks warns: "I don't drink on the road. . . . It dries your chords out." Danielle Egnew explains:

> My biggest tip is such a bummer: DON'T DRINK! I love a great single malt Scotch, but alcohol is the WORST thing a touring artist can do night after night. It is a depressant, so it takes away energy. Alcohol is also a dehydrator, which for a vocalist causes a heap of problems—losing four to five notes off of your top range when those dry vocals chords won't stretch like they should.

If you drink on the road, don't drive afterwards. Make sure at least one band member is sober. Evan R. Saffer advises, "Keep the partying with drugs and alcohol to a minimum when you have a string of dates. You won't be much use for the fourth or fifth date if you party every night." I hate being a wet blanket by telling you not to party, but do it in moderation, and not right before a gig. Gregory Abbott says, "Although you should have fun pursuing your career as an artist, it is a business and not a party. Don't be the last to leave, the one to close the place down. You've got work to do and should always be physically at the ready and thinking clearly."

If you or someone in your band has a substance abuse problem, there are organizations that offer help. MusiCares (www.grammy.com/musicares) has resources for drug rehab and can help you in an intervention with a band member who has a serious problem. Drinking and drugging are no longer considered cool. An indie musician must rely on his or her wits to survive. Drugs and alcohol can kill your career. If you're serious about succeeding independently, get over the partying lifestyle. I've seen too many musicians lose their grip because they abused substances. DJ Minx advises, "What can I say about drugs? Just say *no!*"

PROTECTING YOUR HEARING

Listen carefully: If you want to maintain your ability to listen carefully, learn to protect your ears NOW. Many things can hurt your hearing, and musicians are exposed to some of the worst ones. Don't take your good hearing for granted. Loud music can deteriorate your ears over time. In 1988, Pete Townsend of the WHO shocked the music world with news of his hearing loss. He made a founding donation and gave his endorsement to H.E.A.R. (www.hearnet.com), a pioneering nonprofit organization. I asked cofounder Kathy Peck (a musician herself) for suggestions about preventing hearing loss. She says:

> Taking responsibility for protecting yourself today will help reduce the risk of hearing damage and loss later. A distance of at least ten feet between you and a speaker is extremely important. As your distance from the speaker decreases, risk of damage increases exponentially. . . . Check with your doctor about any prescription medications you take. Overall physical health affects your risk of hearing loss. Decreased blood flow to your muscles leaves you more at risk. Exercising regularly improves your resilience. Short-term hearing loss, like what you experience for a few hours after you get out of an event, is a risk factor for long-term hearing loss.

I can't stress this one enough: Wear earplugs! Peck says custom musician earplugs (ER 9, ER15, or ER 25; around $150) offer the best protection. Made from an impression of your ear canal, they're comfortable to wear. ER hi-fi earplugs (ready-fit; around $20) reduces decibel levels, too. Industrial foam earplugs (cheap) decrease sounds, but muffle speech and music. Sorry, but Peck advises that cotton and toilet paper won't help.

AVOIDING INJURY

Dr. Lillie Rosenthal, D.O. Physical Medicine and Rehabilitation at the

Kathryn and Gilbert Miller Health Care Institute for Performing Artists, encourages learning about your body to avoid injury. She says:

> Many musicians do not have body awareness and don't see themselves as athletes. Playing music, no matter what the instrument, is very athletic. Musicians are small-muscle athletes. The physical demand of playing music is extremely present. Training for music-playing is essential. That means good posture and being strong enough to not only play the instrument but also to carry it. Recognizing that this needs attention is critical. Most musicians just want to sound good and may not be aware of their posture. Crouching or things like that for six hours a day just isn't healthy. . . . Overuse or repetitive strain is really common. I see a lot of people with neck and back pain, which could be anything from muscle tension to permeated discs.

A common problem among musicians is repetitive injuries from using one finger or doing the same thing for too long. Dr. Rosenthal advises changing your posture regularly while performing, explaining, "Some musicians think I'm crazy when I say that there should be a break in music playing every twenty minutes. Unfortunately, people play for hours on end without changing their body posture. That is a very significant risk factor." While onstage, get up for a glass of water; take off your guitar strap. Do anything that moves you—literally. Do aerobics in downtime to strengthen your muscles.

If you already have an injury, it can be treated to prevent reoccurrence. Dr. Rosenthal says most problems are mechanical and don't need medication to heal. When you're young, you feel invincible. But those injuries will become a serious problem if you don't take precautions to heal them now. New injuries can be avoided by noticing your habits and consciously creating better ones. Dr. Rosenthal advises paying attention to general health rules, adding:

> Listening to your body is critical. You have pain and are not happy with the way the music comes out, so you play more aggressively and harder, with more tension. That is a downward spiral. Recognize general stress and tension. [Mental] tension is also something to pay attention to. It's a common theme that when [emotional problems] build up, stuff happens. It's a snowball effect. You have to pay attention to it.

Dr. Rosenthal says that relaxing the shoulders and being conscious of your breathing are very important. Keep your chin tucked. Reaching your head forward is bad because it strains the neck. Keeping your shoulders up to your ears also creates lots of tension in the neck and sets you up for bad posture and injury. She explains:

If you hunch forward with your shoulders up, by definition you need to put more tension on the lower hands and forearms when you play. You don't have the openness and freedom of movement in the upper body. It's a very common problem and relates to having an increased risk of injury. You really have to pay attention to it. Shoulder rolls are good. Stretch out the pecs. Put your hands [on a wall] and drop your body forward to stretch. Aerobic activity and other exercise really revitalize you.

Stretch your muscles as much as you can. Be careful when carrying an instrument. Dr. Rosenthal suggests carrying it knapsack-style rather than putting strain on the hands—or you can transport it on wheels. She also warns, "Pay attention to your mouse, keyboard, and overall computer setup. Most of these are sensible things that you just don't think about." Wrist rolls can help. Rubber band exercises are good, too, if done carefully. When you're on tour, Dr. Rosenthal advises that you watch your posture while driving and make sure you get rest. Don't grip the steering wheel too tight. If you take care now, your body will be healthier for the long haul of your career.

CARING FOR YOUR CHOPS

If you sing, read this carefully! You tune a piano or guitar to keep them sounding at their best; treat your voice with the same respect. It's the instrument that enables you to make a living. While your vocal cords are resilient, wear and tear can do long-term damage. Dr. Gerald Berke, an ear, nose, and throat specialist at the UCLA Voice Center for Medicine and the Arts—and mainly a voice doctor for the last 15 years—says that preventing damage to your vocal cords includes hydration, the right diet, getting plenty of rest, and not abusing your voice. He warns:

You can't go to baseball games and scream your lungs out. The voice is a very robust and strong instrument. It takes a lot to really injure it, but once you do, it takes a long time for it to recover. Most professionals watch the amount of alcohol they use and how much they're around smoke. . . . Musicians who have had longevity will tell you that they've taken good care of their voices.

PROFILE
....
Cari Cole is an independent artist and voice teacher. Her nationally distributed CD earned a spot on the 2004 Grammy nominations ballot for Best Female Pop Vocal Performance. Her Manhattan voice studio has helped thousands of other successful signed and unsigned artists to use their voices properly.

Dr. Berke says that a big potential problem is created by diet. Acid can burn your vocal cords if it backs up from your stomach into your throat, usually after eating very acidic or spicy foods late at night, and especially as you get older. If you're not prudent about food choices, over time this can cause hoarseness. Dr. Berke advises:

> *Make sure you have the proper diet, which includes not eating late at night, eating smaller meals, staying away from spicy and acidic foods, watching how much alcohol and coffee you intake, and making sure you drink enough water. . . . Taking antacids is important. You don't want acid coming up to the back of the throat when you're performing. It's very subtle but it can really hurt your performance.*

Many musicians suffer serious consequences when they allow their throats to get dry. Voice teacher Cari Cole says, "Drinking eight glasses of water a day is essential. Sip thirty-six ounces of water through a straw for best hydration and less trips to the bathroom." If you want a career that involves singing, make a conscious effort to stay hydrated. Dr. Berke says some performers go to an enclosed steam area to get a lot of humidity for their larynx. Others use something called the facial sauna, which is a little steam vaporizer that you can carry with you. He adds that drinking hot liquids right before performing can help "puff up" the vocal cords a bit. On the day of a show, some professionals don't talk at all when they're offstage. Many recommend running a hot shower in your hotel room and leaving the bathroom door open so there will be more moisture in the room. Do it when you arrive, at night, and in the morning.

Cole recommends, "A spoonful of honey moistens the vocal tract—it feels so good! Steam for ten minutes before performing. Even better, make a pot of Throat Coat® tea and steam with that." The manufacturer of Throat Coat (www.traditionalmedicinals.com) says it provides a protective coating on the lining of the throat. I've heard several musicians recommend it. Cole advises adding honey (no lemon) and bringing a thermos of it with you to gargle with at room temperature. She also suggests, "Sunbreeze® balm (www.sunrider.com) is the best balm for throat muscles on the planet! Use it before a performance." Thayers® (www.thayers.com) has a whole line of products for singers. Their dry mouth spray keeps your mouth lubricated, which also helps me as a speaker. And their Slippery Elm Lozenges coat and heal the membranes of the throat and mouth. Visual says, "My best advice came when we performed a music festival and some Native Americans gave me something with slippery elm for sore throats. It's beautiful, soothing."

Cole advises gargling with warm salt water for 30 seconds, three times, before every rehearsal, singing lesson, performance, and recording. She says the salt moisturizes your throat. Many musicians avoid smoke as much as possible. DJ Minx requests smokers don't hang close while she's playing. Kyler England says, "I do my best to avoid booking places I know will be smoky—my voice is really sensitive to smoke." Jennie DeVoe says, "My voice is my living. I don't want to put that at risk so don't do too many smoky bars anymore. I try to do more listening rooms, where you invent your own little 'VH1' storyteller situation. Make the situation what you want. A lot of artists declare their shows no smoking." Many listening rooms (see Chapter 17) respect no smoking.

Dr. Berke says professionals warm up for a long time before performing, adding, "They take a day or two and gradually warm up their voice. It's not an *on* or *off* process. It's like tuning any instrument." Handle your vocal instrument with care! Cole suggests you get professional voice lessons and learn correct techniques to avoid injury, especially before a tour. We go to the gym to work out our muscles; make time to work out your voice. Even famous singers work out with vocal coaches! Dorothy Potter credits her vocal coach for allowing her to tour Europe almost nonstop for three months.

Cole says there are exercises to relax the tense neck and throat muscles that accompany vocal fatigue and hoarseness. Get someone to rub your shoulders and neck muscles to diminish this tension. Cole shows simple self-massages on her website. She also suggests running in place or jumping up and down for five to ten minutes before performing: It strengthens your breathing. Exercise in general strengthens your heart and lungs, which increases your ability to sing.

How can you identify a potential problem? Dr. Berke explains:

If a performer finds his voice is not working properly, that's a good cue to rest it. A lot of performers take their voice for granted until they hurt it. . . . When vocal cords aren't working properly, artists will sing through it or think that it's a temporary thing. The bottom line is that if your voice feels like it's not functioning normally, it's a good time to say that you can't do a gig and take the time to rest your voice. Go on vacation or spend a few days at home and it will recover.

Dr. Berke reassures that with two weeks' rest, most voices recover greatly. Then, start using it slowly to stretch the muscles. He adds, "It's like an athlete using the muscles for their athletic performance." If you sprain your ankle, you'll probably stay off it for a while. Treat your vocal muscles the same for optimum performance!

INTERNET HEALTH RESOURCES

The Kathryn and Gilbert Miller Health Care Institute for Performing Artists is custom-designed for performing-arts medicine (www.millerinstitute.org).

Musicians and Injuries has resources for treating and preventing common injuries, a directory of physicians, and good articles (http://eeshop.unl.edu/music.html).

The Performing Arts Medicine Association lists physicians and others dedicated to improving health care for performing artists (www.artsmed.org).

The International Arts-Medicine Association is a nonprofit networking/education organization that gives doctor references (www.members.aol.com/iamaorg).

Canadian Network for Health in the Arts (CNHA) posts research and health services for performing artists (http://web.idirect.com/~cnha).

The British Performing Arts Medicine Trust is a specialist charity dealing with performing arts medicine (www.bpamt.co.uk).

Arts Medicine Aotearoa/NZ provides healthcare resources for New Zealanders involved in the arts (www.converge.org.nz/amanz).

Music Medicine of Germany (www.arts-medicine.org).

● ● ● ● **CHAPTER 9** ● ● ● ●

Indie
Resources

T here's a lot of support for independent music. Corporations can give you sponsorships. Many organizations are ready to help you and offer workshops that teach you how to hone your craft and enable you to meet industry pros. This chapter is a roundup of the many resources you can tap into. Searching the Internet and networking can lead to even more.

SPONSORSHIPS AND PROMOTIONS

There are many ways for musicians to affiliate with corporations. Some provide financial sponsorship; others give free or discounted equipment in exchange for promoting their name and product. Ezina Moore says, "People are more likely to give you product than financial sponsorship." Christine Kane is endorsed by Elixir® Strings and Takamine™ guitars and gets free products from them. Danielle Egnew explains:

> *The sponsorship backings we received came through our players—instrument and instrument accessory endorsements. A sponsorship is sort of a trade— they give you something like a guitar or bass, and in return you put their logos all over your promotional material—flyers, posters, websites, banners—so it is very easy to see. If a band tours, often they'll put up a banner with the company's logo when they play. It can be tough to get a sponsorship—so*

many players ask companies for free gear. But if you land one, it does look impressive on press kits and promotional material.

Bobby Borg says there are different levels of endorsements. Some companies promote your name and likeness, give you free products, and may pay you to endorse their product. Another sponsorship gets you something free, such as new guitar strings when they break. In other cases, they give you discounts on their products and that's it. The last two are more common.

Most musicians approach companies that make equipment they use, but some artists get approached. Rachael Sage says, "Kurzweil kept seeing me play these crazy hand-painted rhinestone keyboards that are Kurzweil, which I use at big festivals. Someone from Kurzweil got in touch and offered an endorsement deal. It was a no-brainer."

Sponsorship sort of found Jennie DeVoe, too. Corona™ beer found her on the Internet and licensed one of her songs for its radio campaign. She also did a print ad for Klipsch Audio along with some very high-profile artists. DeVoe adds, "The company owner and his wife really like my music and were aware of me because we live close by. I thought it would be a cool association and some free publicity." DeVoe also let some businesses use her picture and name because she saw a benefit to the free publicity. She advises, "Promotion is expensive, so if someone wants to affiliate with you, do it—as long as you have boundaries [and] time limits, and none of your own personal values are compromised." But don't sell yourself out! Ezina Moore says, "My first tour was sponsored by Budweiser. I had a real hard time looking at myself, because I do not drink. I felt like a hypocrite." Tina Broad warns:

> *There's always some kind of creative trade-off whenever you're partnering up with a corporate. Always. Sometimes it's worth it, sometimes it's not. Everyone has a different threshold about what's acceptable. My advice is, stay true to your values and have the confidence to walk away from a relationship that doesn't feel right. Remember why you're indie!*

Some companies find sponsorship a very successful way to promote their products. Jägermeister does no traditional advertising, only on-premise promotion with bands. Rick Zeiler, Director of Marketing & Brand Development, says they're dedicated and proud to be working with independent artists on a local, regional, and national level: "We as a company try to take care of some of the financial burdens that some artists generally have." They supply posters, lighters, shot glasses, T-shirts, etc., that can be given away or sold. Most of the bands, mainly but not limited to rock and metal, are unsigned. They look for bands that love to drink—those bands will do well promoting Jägermeister. Evan R. Saffer says:

> I called Jägermeister and said FIXER would be perfect for them. He was a tough dude and didn't want to hear it. I had to really give it to him. After hearing the music and seeing how much we tour, there was no question. We started as a trial band. Jägermeister received tons of photos of us slamming shots with fans on all our dates. Now we're an official Jäger band.

Jägermeister gives lots of support to bands that are enthusiastic about their product. You have to drink Jäger with fans and send weekly reports telling how many bottles sold each night. Bands that do well get the most products and attention. To apply for Jäger sponsorship, send a press kit to Adam Grayer, Sidney Frank Importing Company, 20 Cedar Street, Suite 203, New Rochelle, NY, 10801. If the company is interested, it'll send you a test trial—T-shirts, lanyards, hats, and other items—to promote at your next show. You supply photographs and feedback so they can see how well you do. Jäger also sends recognizable acts on national tours, with local and regional bands opening the shows. Zeiler says, "It gives all the Jägermeister bands the ability to play before a national audience, with national bands. Jägermeister puts a lot of money behind tours, and they're very successful. They play at fifteen hundred– to two thousand–capacity venues."

Mountain Dew™ and AMP Energy Drink™ have a program for emerging artists. I highly commend them for it! Jorge Rojas, Executive Vice President of FreedomZone, the company that created and implements the AMP Music Circuit, says it was first created to help emerging artists and new bands. Yellowcard was one of their first bands. Freedom Zone asked DJs at alternative-format radio stations in top markets to name their favorite rising bands and then signed some of them. They did a media buy on radio, creating a circuit of stations and venues that bands could tap into (before a band performs in a market, the

PROFILE

Evan R. Saffer is lead singer of FIXER, a rock band born in late 2000. The band has Jägermeister sponsorship and tours extensively up and down the East Coast. FIXER has released several EPs. After several DJs in Germany took a liking to and started spinning the band's latest release, they toured there. FIXER has won several Battle of the Bands contests, including the Sam Ash Future Rock Stars competition, and was asked by VH1 to headline a Save the Music benefit in NYC. The band's press and radio play continues to expand both here and abroad.

program buys radio spots for them). FreedomZone then turned to college radio and created 6Packs, which allow bands to create a six-minute segment with clips from three or four songs and talk about their music and philosophy—providing a good taste of the band and its music. Rojas says:

> We came out to CMJ in 2001 and displayed our concept. We were surprised when over one hundred and fifty colleges signed up for the program. We've been sending CDs out ever since. It's a really cool program. Many of these bands never see royalties. We told our client about this. Every time colleges report that it's played, the artist gets [a set fee]. Every time someone downloads it on the AMPenergy.com website, [royalties are paid]. The site is free to consumers. No one's getting rich, but we send checks that help people stay on the road and do other things.

Rojas says artists can submit music in any genre. If possible, send a full album and a press kit—they want to know about you. Rojas suggests you call afterwards to make sure they got it and ask if there's anything else you can offer them—that helps you stand out. Twelve artists are chosen to be on a special CD and put in the studio with expenses paid. The artists can decide what to include in their six minutes: songs, talking, etc. The AMP Music Circuit also initiated a video 6Pack that the artists direct themselves—a six-minute biographical piece that then goes to MTV2. Mountain Dew gets promotion by supporting emerging music, and artists are blessed by it! Rojas adds:

> We look for professionalism, passion, and people who are willing to work hard. A lot of our bands play up to two hundred shows a year. They're road warriors. We try to help set them up by getting them into college radio stations and giving them some tour support. We're not band managers; we're more about giving the tools to do it themselves. We try to offer them what a record label should offer them. We have many emails from bands and artists saying that we're more present than their record labels. We don't sign contracts with artists in which we take any percentage of what they make. We just help and see it as supporting the DIY mentality. The most exciting part for us: We get to see the bands we believe in succeed.

If you want endorsements, be proactive. Michael Johnathon says he was living in Kentucky and there was no club to play at. He had to create a means to find an audience. He called Pepsi Cola™ and said, "Your cans are all over the road. I'm sure that's not the advertising you want. I want to go to schools, libraries, and fairs and sing songs about the earth, traditions, your homeland, and things I believe." He played about 4,000 concerts in just over three years, including earth concerts in 14 states—all covered by Pepsi. Johnathon also sold 100,000 albums, which he didn't expect, and then got Pepsi to underwrite a music video. Matt Allison also took matters into his own hands when he emailed the owner of Mayes Guitars™ to share how much he enjoyed them. They became friends. Six months after meeting, Allison says:

> He told me to design the guitar of my dreams and he would build it, making me his first and currently only international endorsee! I got a beautiful hand-made guitar that I love and cherish. I perform with it live and get their name out among artists. We joke that while he has two Grammy-winning major artists in the U.S. who use his guitars, I, as an indie, have taken my guitar to more countries in the world than either of them. I thank all my sponsors in my album covers and have links to their sites from mine.

To get a corporate sponsor, specify the benefits of supporting you. What exposure will they get? Bobby Borg says, "It's not how good you are. It's how many people you will expose their product to. It doesn't have to be nationally. If you expose their product to many people, potentially they'll give you a deal." How many people come to your gigs? What's their demographic? This tells the company if your audience will potentially buy their products. How does your music fit with the company? Approach with an organized plan: A solid story gives you more potential to catch their interest. Explain how you'll display the company name on a banner and use the products the company gives you. They want to know how extensive your touring expectations are and how you'll accomplish those. State your promotion strategies—radio, flyers, emails, street teams. If you're going after cash, a potential sponsor will want to know exactly how you plan to use the money.

Be creative in choosing what company to approach. It doesn't have to be a music or alcohol company, though those are more common. Clothing companies also sponsor artists. Considering going after non-cash sponsorship that supports your tour in equally beneficial ways. Companies that supply what you need can cover costs—ask! Ezina Moore called and said she's a touring musician looking for tour support; then she sent proposals. The sponsorships department wanted to know how she'd spend the money. Moore says you need a good business head and a willingness to negotiate all the way, explaining:

> I walked around my house listing every name brand product I use. Then I listed every musical item: instruments, strings, vocal lozenges used before each gig. I called every company and submitted proposals. It is extremely time-consuming but very necessary. Marriott® covered our housing, National Car Rental® sponsored our vehicle, Diesel® jeans for clothing,

D'Addario® for strings, Yamaha® for instruments, and Shure® microphones. Kinko's™ makes a banner for the show. I was basically out-of-pocket for food and postage.

Moore warns that it's tons of work: "Prepare for three to six months of proposal hell. You need pictures of you using the stuff on tour." Most corporations have sponsorship departments. Get in touch with whoever handles their PR for directions on how to apply; it might be handled in-house or by another company. Justin Lassen says he was a fan of products made by the companies he approached for sponsorship—mostly musical and gear companies and some clothing. He says:

I made myself known to them. They liked me, and especially the way I used their products in cutting edge and "hip" ways. That is enough to get sponsored by most companies around the world. Capitalism is common sense. You want to sell your products, get someone hip to use them. Use a company's products in new ways that elevate the company to higher levels and they will love you for it.

Suzanne Teng says she got Yamaha sponsorship through the NAMM (International Music Products Association; www.namm.org) show. She gets her instruments much cheaper, adding, "I just met people and nurtured the relationships through time. I used to visit all the booths and talk to people." To be part of NAMM, network to find a company that attends and see if they can get you in to meet all the music-related companies. Bobby Borg also got endorsements through NAMM. He went up to everyone in different booths, said hi, and told them about his band. Afterwards, he sent them Christmas cards and postcards from his trips. When he was finally in a position to get decent exposure, he contacted them—and got deals on the spot. He adds, "It takes time to build relationships, but these people are in the business and they sponsor people who will promote their name." Rojas warns:

What you have to watch out for when you do a sponsorship deal is that nobody wants to get used. Be aware and demanding. Sponsors need to build a relationship with the artist. There are too many corporations out there that aren't approaching it the right way. They're not trying to build a genuine relationship. Artists are getting smarter, though; they realize now that you have to be careful. We feel like we offer a relationship, not a one-night stand.

Another opportunity to research is grants for artists. The National Endowment for the Arts (NEA; www.nea.org) offers grants for special projects, though as the government cuts funding, it gets more competitive. The American Society of Composers, Authors and Publishers (ASCAP; www.ascap.com) has song-writer grants listed on its website.

ORGANIZATIONS

Seek out organizations that support musicians. Many are great places to find the encouragement that nourishes the indie soul. Just Plain Folks (www.justplainfolks.org), is a community built around music, with more than 25,000 members. Founder Brian Austin Whitney says, "Anyone can record a nicely produced album and release it on their own label, but they need an organization that supports them. That's what we've become." They offer online forums where people from around the world share. Whitney does road trips across the country, arranging showcases in which all members can play a song and network all night. Whitney also has no-fee indie music awards, with an awards show in L.A.—all based on the music! They have about 100 chapters. It's FREE to join, so there's no excuse not to. The community feeling that you'll experience is a rare one in the music industry. Whitney adds:

> Joining appropriate organizations give you the chance to meet like-minded people to create a support system with. Support doesn't mean someone stepping in to do the work for you. Support is about having resources, sharing resources, and being a resource for others. Having friends who can offer you shortcuts to getting work done is invaluable. Connections to venues, places to stay while on tour, access to other artists' fan bases, trusted firsthand information on which companies to use for various career needs, and a sense of community to fall back on in a crisis, is what support is all about. And just as important is offering it up to everyone else that you can as well. You'll build far more support by helping others first, and letting them pay you the favor back, than the other way around.

Another organization that indies love is Folk Alliance. Phyllis Barney, President, says, "An organization like Folk Alliance helps you learn how to recruit and bring a system around you. It also serves as your networking organization. You have a chance to learn and interact with peers, find out what's going on in the field—and it's a home base for you as you develop your career." It provides network listings in business directories and the ability to be promoted as a member of the organization. Barney says most members have roots-based music that tells a story. The umbrella of folk is pretty broad; the organization serves people from lots of different backgrounds and musical genres—with an affinity towards folk and roots music—who want to work the folk festival and concert series circuit. It also has one national and several regional conferences each year. Barney explains:

The conference is a place to meet your peers, be seen, and have a chance to try out your material on audiences that are real familiar with acoustic-based roots music. You have to be a member to showcase. When you join the organization, you'll have access to the online searchable database, and the ability to be part of showcase performances. There's a level of showcasing that we sponsor with an application and jury process. In all regional conferences, we try to provide a platform where people can set up their own showcases. They can band together with other independent artists and put on a night of showcasing in a hotel meeting room or even a sleeping room. We have panels and workshops at the conference. We do a crash course the Wednesday before for artists just entering the field—on promotion, booking yourself, how to find an agent, [and more]. Throughout the weekend there are panels—how to get booked at a festival, etc.

Members get discounts for conference attendance and have access to the networking database of more than 3,000 listings in the folk community—media people, presenters, and other artists who can be searched by region. Barney says people view one another as colleagues instead of competition. Many work together. A newsletter keeps people in touch, and there's also Folk Alliance Canada. Finding support in the industry makes being independent easier. Barney encourages:

It behooves you to get into some sort of network, whether it's our organization or another. Or develop one informally. It's support and knowledge. A networking organization that you can tap into allows you not to reinvent the wheel. There are people with great ideas about promotion and other things, and lots of resources out there. Having the opportunity to meet others who do what you do can save a step or two and get you the skills you need ahead of time, without you having to do it the hard way.

AFM (American Federation of Musicians; www.afm.org) protects the rights of performers. Dick Gabriel, Assistant to the President, says the organization monitors to see if recordings are used for another medium, bill for that use on behalf of the performers, collect the money, and distribute it to them. If you play guitar on a track that's used in a film, as a performer you're entitled to something. AFM makes sure you get paid for each performance. Gabriel says:

If you have a chance to get your CD used in something and you're not sure, call our office on the West Coast and we'll check it. The record may get used for X amount of dollars, but along with that amount there may be more that no one knew to bill for. We'll do that if you're a member. Don't hesitate to make a call. That will get you a lot more money, without blowing the gig.

There are many sources of support online. Some come and go, but Indie-Music (www.indie-music.com) has sustained itself over many years. Its magazine reviews dozens of independent artists each month, plus it includes how-to-succeed articles for musicians—all for free. In addition, paid members have full access to an insiders' database of music industry contacts, including more than 7,000 venues. To learn of more sites, visit my website (www.daylle.com).

Other countries offer artists support, too. The Association of Independent Music (AIM; www.musicindie.org) offers its members services and information on marketing, promotion, and seminars in the U.K. Music Industry Network Canada (MINC; www.mincanada.com) provides services to Canadian artists and offers a list of music industry contacts and an industry calendar. Australian Record Industry Association (AIR; http://www.aria.com.au/) helps Australian indies with their own labels; they also put on seminars. IMMEDIA! (www.immedia.com.au) has industry directories with contacts needed to break into the Australian market. It also holds conferences and seminars and runs a website (www.themusic.com.au) with tons of info about the Australian music business. Next door, New Zealand has a supportive site, too (www.musicnz.co.nz); the NZ Music Services directory includes info about agents, songwriting, venues, and much more. Most countries have similar organizations that can be found online.

Songwriter Support

Many organizations support songwriters. In the U.S. there are three performance rights organizations (PROs): ASCAP (American Society of Composers, Authors and Publishers; www.ascap.com), BMI (Broadcast Music, Inc.; www.bmi.com), and SESAC (www.sesac.com). These organizations collect royalties for the performances of intellectual property on radio and TV stations and in other public areas where music is used, and distribute them to writers and publishers. Todd Brabec, Executive Vice President of Membership for ASCAP in L.A. and author of *Music, Money and Success*, explains:

> There is a specific copyright called a "performing right." The creator, mainly the writer, owns that initially. Many times it becomes assigned to a publisher who becomes the copyright owner. Any time music is being performed, within almost any context, whether it's a live music performance or it's on a jukebox, radio station, TV station, airline channels, [the bar owner, etc.] has to get a license from the copyright owner—the writer or publisher. They settle on a fee and pay that to the writer or publisher in order to use that work. Any time music is being performed, the company has to take out a license and get permission to use that composition, and then pay for it. Writers and publishers join us, and we negotiate the license

fees for whoever's using music. We also work internationally getting the music played all over the world. We send checks four times a year.

While each PRO varies slightly, they do the same type of job. Which one is right for you? I advise calling someone at each to see who you feel more comfortable with. Check each one's website, too. Then go with the one that seems most likely to help you market your songs. Paul Corbin, Vice President of Writer/Publisher Relations for BMI, Nashville, says:

If you're coming to the city for the first time, there are many things that BMI can and is willing to offer if you're affiliated with us. We have different kinds of workshops for our writers. We also have a round table where we talk about performing rights. We have a sponsored writers' series. Every Monday night we have a writers' showcase. We also have events that we do on an occasional basis. We have staff that will evaluate some of the music and talk to you about the current music scene in Nashville. If you're looking for a publisher, we try to connect you.

There are similar organizations in other countries. Here is a list of some of them:

Australia: APRA (The Australasian Performing Right Association Limited; www.apra.com.au).

Canada: SOCAN (The Society of Composers, Authors and Music Publishers of Canada; www.socan.ca).

France: SACEM (Société Des Auteurs Compositeurs Et Editeurs De Musique; www.sacem.fr), CISAC (Confédération Internationale des Sociétés d'Auteurs et Compositeurs; http://www.cisac.org).

PROFILE

Suzanne Teng is a flutist, percussionist, dancer, composer, teacher, and New Age music recording artist. She's an endorsed artist for Yamaha®, AKG®, and High Spirit Flutes®. Teng composes music for yoga and acupuncture videos, does session playing for record labels, and has extensive performance credits in film, television, and commercials. She performs in concerts, festivals, and dance and yoga events internationally; her band was featured at the Dalai Lama's World Festival of Sacred Music. Teng also performs flute meditations at events with spiritual leaders such as Marianne Williamson and Deepak Chopra, has performed for heads of state, and has appeared with top artists such as Sting and Jackson Browne.

Germany: GEMA (The German Society for Musical Performing Rights and Mechanical Reproduction Rights; www.gema.de).

Italy: SIAE (Societa Italiana Degli Autori ed Editori; http://www.siae.it).

Japan: JASRAC (Japanese Society for Rights of Authors, Composers and Publishers; www.jasrac.or.jp/ejhp).

Spain: SGAE (Sociedad General de Autores y Editores; www.sgae.es).

Sweden: STIM (Svenska Tonsattares Internationella Musikbyra; http://www.stim.se).

U.K.: PRS (The Performing Right Society; www.prs.co.uk), PAMRA (Performing Arts Media Rights Association; www.pamra.org.uk).

The NSAI (Nashville Songwriter's Association International; www.nashville songwriters.com) is one of the best support systems for songwriters. The heart of its mission is to protect American songwriters' copyrights. Executive Director Bart Herbison says it's the largest and most productive organization for assisting aspiring songwriters. Its ProShop program has produced Grammy-winning songwriters. Herbison adds:

> Many of our members want to become professional songwriters, but a number of them just want to grow in their craft while experiencing the songwriting community and bonding with their peers. We have an entire series of programs and our song evaluation service, where we have professional writers listen to your tape, put an oral critique on it, and mail it back to you to help you grow as a songwriter. The song evaluation service is part of the basic membership. We're proud of our affiliation with country music, but we have done songs in every genre and language. Primarily, the focus is on the song. We have professional songwriters in every genre of music.

Feedback given on songwriting applies to any genre, not just country. NSAI has many chapters across the country; check their site for one near you. Get involved! The SGA (Songwriters Guild of America; www.song writersguild.com) has offices in several cities and offers inexpensive and free workshops. The Film Music Network (www.filmmusic.net) provides a forum for music biz professionals to meet, network, and share info. Membership is reasonable and gives you access to their *Film & TV Music Agents and Managers Directory*, Film/TV Music Jobs Database, Film & TV Music Salary & Rate Survey, 24-hour streaming audio of Film Music Network events from all cities, and a premium listing in *The Film Music Directory*.

There are many more great songwriter resources online. Jodi Krangle, the proprietress of The Muse's Muse (www.musesmuse.com), says, "It's your place for songwriting tips, tools, interactivities, and connecting with other songwriters around the world. Drop by for musician classifieds, busy message boards, links, songwriting association listings, music reviews, artist spotlights, copyright and publishing info, contest listings and market information, articles, interviews, a monthly newsletter and lots more." Krangle is a songwriter who started The Muse's Muse to learn more about her trade. It's a fantastic resource! Unisong (www.unisong.com) lists songwriters associations and other organizations and has many other resources. Christian Songwriting Organization (www.christiansong writing.org) is an online organization of Christian songwriters, with many songwriting resources. The Songwriting Education Resource (www.craftof songwriting.com) has loads of information for songwriters. It has a song-writers' chatroom, resources, and links, and also offers songwriting courses. The British Academy of Composers (www.britishacademy.com) is a trade association for songwriters in the U.K. It helps protect copyrights and offers benefits and services to all British songwriters. The Australian Songwriters Association (ASA; www.asai.org.au) is a national, nonprofit member organization that supports Australian songwriters.

Local Support

If you have no access to organizations where you live, create your own coali-tion of musicians. Some cities offer more support than others. New York and L.A. are tough places to break into music but have many events with industry people. The Los Angeles Music Network (LAMN; www.lamn.com) promotes career advancement and goodwill among music industry profession-als. LAMN offers professional development opportunities, educational programs and seminars, opportunities to meet and interact with peers, a job bank, a mentor network, and a newsletter. Austin, Texas, has a music office through its convention center that gives support to musicians there. The mayor's office of the city of New Orleans has a department for music business development, and the Tipitina's Music Office Co-Op offers a do-it-yourself business incubator designed especially for musicians and other digitial media professionals (www.tipitinasfoundation.org). The Co-Op provides tools, train-ing, and other support for those who need it. Seattle's Department of Economic Development has a music and film office, too (www.seattle.gov/music).

I went to Nashville to check out the scene there. While it's a very tough town to crack, it's a smaller music community that offers a lot. People know one another well. If you have THE GOODS, there are people who can help you advance. There are many workshops for songwriters. The NSAI is based here and offers a huge support system. I found the people to be friendlier and much more open and accessible than in other cities, and I loved being there. I think everyone should visit Nashville to experience the small-town atmosphere of this powerful city.

The Memphis and Shelby County Music Commission in Memphis (www.memphismusic.org) offers support for its indie musicians. According to Rey Flemings, President, what the commission does there has been launched out of the independent music community since there are no major label companies in Memphis. It's now setting up the Sam Phillips Center for Independent Music as a recording company, with all the services of a record label but on a nonprofit basis. Flemings explains, "We'll walk five to ten artists through the entire process for twelve months. Then we'll induct a new class. The purpose is to jumpstart the careers of artists based on [a screening process]. The artist won't have to put up any money." The commision plans to give lots of support to the independent music community. Yeah!

Legal Support

There are other organizations that offer legal support to people in the arts. Alexei Auld, Esq., Director of Education and Senior Staff Attorney for VLA (Volunteer Lawyers for the Arts; www.vlany.org) in New York, says there are similar VLA chapters throughout the country. Each has different services; some offer pro bono programs and can refer you to attorneys in your area. Many are linked on the VLA website, and most are listed in my book *The Real Deal*. Auld encourages you to use its services, saying, "We have an art law–line that's open to everybody. If you're outside the New York area it's a long distance call, but we'll still field questions: (212) 319-2787 ext. 1. If you call, regardless of your economic level you'll get your question answered." VLA has a clinic every other Wednesday for members, where you can talk to an attorney for a half-hour private session about any type of artistic legal concern you have. Membership is $100 for individuals and covers unlimited clinic access for a year.

There are other great legal resources that you can take advantage of. NOLO (http://www.nolo.com) is an online legal resource with many of the legal basics in plain English. Music Law Advice (www.musiclawadvice.co.uk) is an independent music law site for musicians in the U.K. providing legal info on the music business, including articles on subjects such as copyrights and contracts. The Arts Law Centre of Australia (www.artslaw.com.au) is a legal resource for that country's music industry.

PUBLICATIONS

There are many directories and books that are helpful for breaking into the indie music biz. Most are available in bookstores, and I've included the websites when applicable. You can never acquire enough knowledge about the music industry! I mention many of these resources throughout the book, but here's a roundup of them.

Every indie should own *The Indie Bible* (www.indiebible.com). It lists thousands of music-related websites; e-zines, and print magazines; online and real radio stations; and thousands more sites that can help you market your music, for all genres. It's reasonably priced and updated regularly. *The Musician's Atlas* (www.musiciansatlas.com) is another must-have for any artist who wants to tour or get exposure. It lists clubs, radio stations, press, record stores, colleges, conferences, festivals, organizations, record labels, publishers, and much more, all organized by city.

SRS Publishing (www.musicregistry.com) has several directories that can be ordered by calling (800) 377-7411. Their *Music Publisher Registry* lists most music publishers with direct dial numbers. The *Film & Television Music Guide* is a directory of music supervisors and much more for film and television—it's a great reference! The *Producer & Engineer Directory* lists the complete contact information for more than 1,000 record producers and recording engineers.

Billboard (www.billboard.com) has some good directories. The *Billboard International Talent & Touring Directory* lists U.S. and international talent, booking agencies, facilities, services, and products. It includes many cultural arts and civic centers that book music. The *Billboard Musician's Guide to Touring & Promotion* is a city-by-city guide to touring resources. Besides its regular touring publication, Pollstar (www.pollstar.com) also puts out a wonderful series of comprehensive contact directories: Artist Management, Agency Roster, Talent Buyers & Clubs, Concert Venues. The Management and Agency Rosters are cross-referenced so you can look up artists who are similar to you to find a manager or booking agent who might be appropriate.

In addition to these resource directories, there are many good books that emphasize the importance of learning the biz. I'll discuss a few that I think are especially good. I'm a bit biased, but I highly advise reading both of my other books: *Start & Run Your Own Record Label*, 2nd ed. (Billboard Books), which has a lot more info on the specifics of creating and marketing a CD, and *The Real Deal: How to Get Signed to a Record Label*, 2nd ed. (Billboard Books), which has a lot more details on the basics of artist development. Jeri Goldstein's *How to Be Your Own Booking Agent*, 2nd ed. (www.performingbiz.com) is a comprehensive guide to creating a lucrative touring business and has great resources for venues that aren't clubs, such as corporations. Bobby Borg's *The Musician's Handbook* (Billboard Books) is jam-packed with information to provide a solid foundation on the music biz itself.

When it comes to the business of songwriting, there are three masters— Jason Blume, Jeffrey Brabec, and Todd Brabec—who have written books that you should study if you're a songwriter. Blume's *6 Steps to Songwriting Success: The Comprehensive Guide to Writing and Marketing Hit Songs*, 2nd ed. (Billboard

Books) is an easy-to-understand guide to writing great songs and then marketing them. The appendix lists songwriter contests, organizations, song camps, and much more info that isn't readily available elsewhere. If you want to make money from your songs, this book is a must-read. His other book, *Inside Songwriting: Getting to the Heart of Creativity* (Billboard Books), is a personal look into the world of songwriting that will entertain and inspire you. The Brabecs' book, *Music, Money and Success: The Insider's Guide to Making Money in the Music Industry,* 4th ed. (Schirmer Trade Books) is another must-read for songwriters. It's regularly updated with the latest industry standards and expanded information for the songwriting biz. All sources of songwriting revenues are detailed with up-to-date rates and current laws, including Internet issues. This book is an essential reference for taking your song biz seriously. The more you learn, the more prepared you are to succeed.

CHAPTER 10

Independent Street Marketing

The operative phrase for indies is "grassroots promotion." While money may be tight, you can be rich in people resources. A BIG difference between major labels and independents is the value of fans. Majors are mainly concerned with selling records, but indies know that loyal fans can support a long career. Grassroots promotion is an inexpensive resource that uses fan power. If you treat your fans right, they'll reward you with promotion that major labels can't buy.

SHOWING YOUR FANS LOVE

If you show your fans love, they'll give it back to you multiplied. How important is it to interact with your fans? Daniel Lee Martin says:

> For me it's number one—right up there with the quality of the music. From the beginning, I decided if I had a chance to sign an autograph, not only would I make eye contact with the person, but I would make physical contact—a hug or handshake—and ask their name and where they're from. They stand in line and support you, and if they don't deserve a hug, I don't know what would. It's been said that country music is different in the interaction between artists and fans. Pop artists should do the same thing. It's really important.

Fans greatly appreciate having personal contact with you. Do what feels comfortable, but interact whenever you can. Mary Gauthier explains:

> *After a show, I go to the table and sign CDs for people—all night if I have to. I shake hands, introduce myself, and give people access to me. That really works if you want to sell CDs and build a fan base. The star routine is not the way to be an independent artist. People need access to you. It's part of the building process. That's hard—I am honestly quite shy. Take away the microphone and lights and I don't know what to say to people. I've learned to let them talk, sell CDs, learn their names, and when I come back to town, remember their names. It allows me the opportunity to do this for a living.*

Being accessible fuels grassroots promotion. As fans feel closer to you, they'll support you more, too. Visual says Little Egypt is known for interacting a lot with fans, talking to them for hours after shows. He explains, "They want to rhyme with us and ask questions. We love to meet new people. I don't think it's too much to give a few hours after a show. We build relationships. If you just take the time, you may have a fan for life." Speech suggests:

> *Set yourself up to meet people after the show. People want autographs. We respect fans and don't sign for a brief moment. We'll sign until the last one comes up. It's sometimes a long line but we'll stand there until it's done. The fans greatly appreciate it. We don't just sign and have them move along like cattle. We talk to them and ask what they thought about the show. Find out what they want from you. It's about connecting.*

Connect and keep connecting. A personal approach allows fans to bond with you. Go the distance and fans will take you further. Jennifer Marks says an eighth-grade fan missed a show because she and her mom got lost. They emailed her that night, very upset, and Marks did a private performance in her hotel room for the girl and several friends. Marks enjoyed making her happy. That's how fans develop!

Keep in touch with fans on the Internet, too. Gregory Abbott says, "Loyal fans who consistently support my music not only help sustain me, but motivate me to create more. For this reason I have open communication on my site to get feedback from them. They tell me what they like, what they'd like to hear more of. I appreciate them immensely." What goes around, comes around. When you show fans love, the love is returned. Marly Hornik didn't have the money to record a full-length record. Fans said she had to do it, so she asked for $20 from whoever could help, saying she'd put each name in her liner notes and send them a signed copy. At this point she had nothing, not even a producer—just the idea to make a record. She says, "Six-and-a-half weeks later, I had ten thousand dollars in cash. I think about that constantly because it's an affirmation of what I'm doing."

A great live performance keeps fans coming back. Beth Wood also advises connecting with your audience:

> Look them in the eye at least sometimes while you perform. Don't look at your shoes all the time. If interaction is hard for you, encourage someone in your band who is really good at audience interaction to engage them. Give him a mic so he can say hello, plug CDs, etc. When your show is over, do not break this audience connection. Walk straight into the audience to the CD table and talk with people. People want to support indie musicians. Make it easy for them by being approachable and kind. Being an indie musician is all about grassroots promotion, so be willing to shake some hands.

Danielle Egnew adds, "Some artists act like they are doing everyone a favor by sitting at the table and selling their product. Remember that it isn't a chore to sell anyone a CD, it's an honor that people buy them from you." George Baum says:

> We make it a point to be completely accessible before and after concerts. Lost And Found is spread by word of mouth. The only way folks hear about us is through an enthusiastic friend or by seeing us play somewhere. One reason this works is because we have a very unique sound and approach to our performances. We keep the house lights on and chat with the audience. It gives our concerts a markedly different atmosphere than most bands' shows we've seen. We personally answer every email we get.

Showing fans love returns it multiplied! Keep them in the personal loop with newsletters, journals, or other written stuff about you. Fans love details. It makes them feel closer to you, which strengthens their loyalty.

FREE MUSIC SAMPLES

The best way to hook new fans is to let them hear your music. While you should value your music enough to not give it away in all cases, it's good to let people have samples. Major labels are scared of people getting music for free because all they care about is record sales. Don't worry about that. Create fans first. Loyal fans will buy your CDs and come to shows, even (or especially!) if you give them music for free. Beth Wood suggests:

Be willing to give some things away. Technology makes it easy for us to burn our own CDs. Try giving away two- or three-song samplers of your new material. Your audience will feel like they are in on something, and hopefully will be intrigued and want to buy your new material when it comes out.

If you can afford it, give out CD samplers in areas near an upcoming gig. Marly Hornik says she get them for 55¢ each at Media Services CD and DVD Manufacturing (www.mediaomaha.com). These are bulk CDs that come without a jacket; you can get plain paper sleeves for about 5¢ each. She considered getting a CD burner, but it was more expensive. Samplers are great grassroots promotional tools. Hornik explains, "I bring mini-CDs into a bunch of nontraditional outlets. If we're in town three hours early, I'll go around town to women's clothing stores or other outlets, give CDs to people, and let them know that we're playing that night. I definitely get good feedback." CD samplers speak in ways that flyers can't. Many record stores will give them out because they like giving their customers added value.

Tape every gig, and give away the good ones. Encourage fans to make copies and pass them out. That attracts people to shows and creates a buzz with only a small investment. People who get excited about your music love to burn CDs to share. Musicians say they mention fans' names when performing and offer free CDs of those shows. Fans will want to play it for everyone to hear their names mentioned and then, of course, the music is heard, too. Take pictures or videotape gigs, and get email addresses for those who want to know when the pictures are posted on your website. Encourage them to pass your website address on to friends. This is a fantastic way to create a community around your music. If you don't want to give out too many CDs, have a web page that can only be accessed with a coded URL. Tracks can be downloaded off that page. Giving potential fans this link makes them feel special. When releasing a new CD, offer free downloads of unreleased tracks with preorders. Ask stores to post this offer; they like preorders, too.

If you give music away now, sales will happen, too—IF you have good music. Added value appeals to music lovers. Beth Wood suggests, "Throw

PROFILE

Preech-Man is a hip-hop artist who started rhyming seriously at age sixteen. He began by making mix tapes and battling for real money—$500 and up—while he was still in school. Preech was featured in the Ruff Ryders *The Documentary, Volume 1.* He consistently does a lot of shows at clubs, festivals, events, and battles, and has opened for many other well-known artists, including Trina and Luke, DMX, Doug E. Fresh, and Ice T.

in free stickers (great for advertising your name) for people who buy CDs. Stickers are fairly inexpensive and will help you get name recognition." If you have a like-minded circle of artists with music that appeals to the same audience, create a compilation sampler. Each artist can contribute songs, chip in equally to manufacture it, and distribute it to places where potential fans shop or hang out. Consider doing a group show and using the sampler to promote it. Working together gets your music to a broader circle of people.

STREET TEAM POWER

A career isn't built alone. Once you get others excited about your music and develop a fan base, begin building a street team to support your career. Preech says, "Street teams are important because you can't be everywhere." This way other mouths spread your word, too. Beth Wood agrees:

People volunteer to give my music to someone they know [at a radio station, etc.], put up posters, call venues or newspapers, and spread the word about shows. That is how this music grows—it is very much word-of-mouth. I equate being an indie musician to owning a mom-and-pop restaurant. Sometimes it will be the best food on the block, even without corporate dollars. People find out about it, tell friends, their friends tell friends, and so on. The key is to give something in return—if someone agrees to hang posters for you on their day off, put them on the guest list or invite them backstage. It's a give-and-take.

Street promotion is the mainstay of indie artists. Until you have a street team in place, do it yourself. Evan R. Saffer says, "We're junkies for flyering and postering. You'll find FIXER outside of rock shows frequently meeting new fans, passing out flyers and stickers, and hitting the streets." Grassroots efforts reach potential fans. If you catch their interest with your music or a flyer, the word spreads. This type of promotion must continue no matter how many fans you get. Danielle Egnew agrees:

We flyer a lot, still to this day. Sure, the flyers are printed, not xeroxed, but we still hand them out. Where it's allowed, we leave postcards and flyers with our website address so people can see our latest album. It's about getting your name out. Leave business cards everywhere. There are clubs that allow you to slap a band sticker up on the wall, and we will. It doesn't matter if it's a rest stop in Hoboken. I'll do it, if it's allowed. You never know who is going to see your name and web address.

Organize fans to work for you. Fans love being part of your career. Marly Hornik says, "Without them, I wouldn't be where I am." Put a link on your site to sign up for your street team. Announce it at gigs. Fans will respond. Hornik says her fans put posters up. They call venues, saying they want to see her, to convince the promoters to book her when she's having a hard time getting in. She adds, "That's pretty convincing because the promoter just wants to know that they're going to make money." Be patient. Saffer says, "It takes a while. Even the most dedicated fans have to be organized and want to work a little to be part of our street team. We have a fan club and street team, each with different functions and perks. The info is on our website."

When you tour, ask street teams to spread the word. Ask anyone going to a concert or going anywhere with people who might like your music to wear your T-shirt (with your website on it) and to give out flyers or samplers. Hearing about you from enthusiastic fans is the best promotion. Give them perks for helping: free passes to your gig, CDs, T-shirts, and verbal appreciation. Alex Woodard says:

Establishing a street team has been a big help. I have been blessed to have people willing to help me because they love to do it, and want to help me. The street team is an extension of that. I have street team members in many markets. They hand out my music samplers at shows they attend, promote my shows in their area, and just spread the word-of-mouth thing around.

Kyler England sends her street team e-cards to forward to their friends about when she will be coming to their towns. Danielle Egnew appreciates a fan in Kansas City who started Pope Jane's online Yahoo!® fan club, which enabled the band to stay in touch with many fans. Ask for help from those who love your music and you'll get it. Don't feel funny asking; fans are happy to support you. Jennifer Marks says, "At first I had a really hard time asking for help. But I realized it is silly not to use resources. I have friends who bring CDs to work with them to sell and people in cities who put posters up and hand out flyers. Others have posted things online and just spread the word as much as possible." Ezina Moore never had an official street team because she thought she'd be bothering them. After getting wiser at my seminar, she sent out a newsletter telling fans what she'd been up to and asked them casually to join her street team. She was thrilled with the response:

I got email after email saying "Yes, I want to be on your street team." I asked them to go to chat rooms, tell their friends, go to concerts of other musicians and pass out flyers, and have their friends sign my guest book. I said for every twenty people they got to sign up on my site, they would get a free T-shirt.

Something amazing happened. I sent the email to the 3,900 people on my mailing list; I now have 6,000 names and it grows every day. They became like warriors and single-handedly sold 5,000 more CDs for me and secured me bookings in Texas, Illinois, Canada, and Tennessee. I scrambled to reorder CDs, I ran out so quickly.

Figure out what you need and let your street team know. A forum area on your website is particularly helpful, because allowing an online community to communicate with one another can mobilize them into an organized street team. Make them feel important. Have special perks that are exclusive to them: special T-shirts or caps, special downloads or hearing new songs in advance. DJ Minx gives them mixed CDs or vinyl, T-shirts, stickers, or whatever they might appreciate from the label for passing out promotional flyers at clubs. Stay in touch with a street team newsletter. If you mention members who do good things, it can inspire others to do more, to get their name in the newsletter.

CREATING OPPORTUNITIES

Indie artists are known for creating their own opportunities. Suzanne Teng does concerts for her hometown of Topanga, California. They gave her a chance and the people of her town support her career. She gets paying gigs now, but she still does peace concerts and other fundraisers, especially since most of her work has been found through word of mouth. Barbara Tucker promotes the Underground Network for dance music, which she started, and says it's helped her career a lot: "Being a promoter/activist in my town helped me because I was wearing the promoter's hat, not the artist's. When you are the promoter, you meet a lot of people and are able to network. People would come and want to book me. It helped a lot." Get creative about live appearances. When Preech goes to a town he's never been to, he tries to find someone from there who's popular and invites him onstage to do a little of his own music. This helps to initiate Preech into that market.

PROFILE
David Ippolito is known as That Guitar Man from Central Park. He began playing in the park in 1992. As crowds continued to return week after week, he recorded CDs and sold them; people put money in his case as a thank-you. Ippolito has won the Abe Oldman Award for songwriting. He puts together his own concerts in winter months, and he also did a one-man show at the Soho Playhouse about being That Guitar Man from Central Park. He's been written about in both the *New York Times* and the *New York Post* many times, and PBS did a documentary on him.

Go ahead and ask! Ezina Moore proves that if you ask, you will receive. When she worked as a manager for MAC Cosmetics®, she played her music in the cosmetic department at Marshall Field's® on Saturdays to attract customers. She explains:

> I asked them to play my record, and they were excited to. The store manager found out and announced it at the morning staff meeting. From there, other staff members inquired about purchasing the CD, and I sold them to the staff. Some also told their customers that it was the MAC manager singing, and customers began to purchase the CDs from me as well. I asked the regional manager for MAC if we could play it in all the stores in the region. She agreed. From there I called the store operations department and asked if the record could be played in all stores nationwide. They said yes.

Many artists play acoustic sets and do signings at retail outlets. You just have to know where your music sells. Daniel Lee Martin says Walmart® accounts for 90 percent of his sales. He explained this to his distributor, which liked his music so much that it contacted Walmart and set up a tour. Martin and his label paid the expenses, but it was worth the promotion he got. When his album came out, he did two appearances a day. He says, "It's grueling but necessary. In the first three weeks we were floored by our CD sales. After being in many stores in the Tampa–St. Pete area we were the No. 6 top-selling country artist in that area." While Martin didn't get paid, the tour created a huge awareness with people who might never have heard him. Creating awareness is valuable, too. Martin does a half-hour set for Walmart patrons, but he's learned to also do a private show for the staff:

> A manager asked me to play for the associates on their fifteen-minute break. I was absolutely beside myself at how many of them bought my CD and brought it back for me to sign. It seems like almost half of our sales right now are through the employees. We make sure to do a meet and greet every time with the associates in the back. Then we go out and do our show. It averages about an hour and fifteen minutes with the signings.

Michael Johnathon created a platform for himself on a great grassroots level. When he put out his first WoodSongs album, he packaged the album with a book he wrote, went on a 186-city book/concert tour that he booked in Borders and Barnes & Noble® stores, and moved about 20,000 copies. He says the major label world would look down at that, but in the folk world that's a huge number, especially when you own it. This led to his live radio show. He explains:

We had the idea of celebrating grassroots, independent, acoustic music that WoodSongs is about and thought it might work as a radio show. I had one little college radio station and a friend that owned a recording studio that seated eighteen people. The show is taped before a theater audience. There are two artists per show. I started the "WoodSongs" radio show and [more five years] later, we've moved from the eighteen-seat studio to a four hundred–seat theater that is full every Monday. It's aired on 416 stations in thirty-two countries. It's bluegrass, country, Celtic, singer/songwriters, struggling artists selling CDs out of their trunks. The only thing we want an artist to do is to be great. We don't care who you know, who your manager is, who you opened for. We don't look at press kits. We found a worldwide radio audience that wants to hear these grassroots artists. Every Monday night at dinnertime in Lexington, Kentucky, hundreds line up to try and get tickets to see artists they don't know sing songs they've never heard before.

Johnathon syndicates the show. He charges $5 admission to cover the cost of sending CDs to the affiliates. He and the crew work for free; artists aren't paid either—this is a passion-driven enterprise. Johnathon is starting a National Association of WoodSongs Coffeehouses in the U.S. and Canada, a string of local hometown coffeehouses with the synergy of the "WoodSongs" radio hour—it could be in someone's living room or a church—for people who love the music on the show. Past "WoodSongs" shows can be heard for free online (www.woodsongs.com); the website sells a majority of Johnathon's CDs. But his prime purpose is being true to music he loves, and sharing it. He says:

Music became a commodity only fifty years ago. For thousands of years it was a family, person-to-person, town-to-town, community-shared art form. The fundamental idea of what music is hasn't changed. More than ever in America, people are comforted by going back to how things used to be. That's what grassroots independent is: a world where there are no stars. The audience comes first. It's a community of people willing to help each other.

● ● ● ● **CHAPTER 11** ● ● ● ●

Creating an Indie Buzz

Working the media creates a foundation for your career. It's hard to get people to buy your music or come to shows if they don't know about you. To be a successful indie, make an effort to use everything you can. It's possible to work the media and create a huge buzz, even if money is tight. Are you ready to put in some hard work to build your biz? If so, the information in this chapter will help you get busy!

BUZZIN'

Artists ask, "Why would someone write about an unknown artist or play their music?" Lose that mentality if you want to create a buzz around you and your music! If you've got THE GOODS, the potential is there. Once you believe your music is worthy of media exposure, you can work to inform others. Kyler England says:

> There are many great indie-friendly magazines, radio stations, and record stores that can help make your music visible and accessible to potential new fans. There are more resources than you could ever make use of, so it's important to decide what is the best use of your time and energy. At the end of the day, that's one of the biggest limiting factors.

Build your story one press clip and one radio show at a time. Take baby steps up the ladder from teeny publications and local radio stations to larger ones. As your story builds, so will opportunities to expand it even more! According to Dalis Allen, the producer of the Kerrville Folk Festival:

> It trickles down. Having your record reviewed in Austin magazines and things like that may not propel your career to the degree that you want it to end up, but every one of those things adds up. If I see a review of someone's record in Performing Songwriter and then hear their name somewhere else and then see their package, I've seen their name over and over again. It doesn't matter if it's not the most important thing that you're going to do. It's one more step in what you're going to do.

Let people know about you and your music through the media. Robby Baier says he pressed 1,000 CDs, sent them to newspapers and magazines, and started playing regional clubs. His exposure mushroomed from there. It may feel useless, especially in the beginning when hard work doesn't seem to pay off. Don't lose hope! Every CD that goes out is another chance for progress. Jennie DeVoe says, "I give CDs to radio and anyone else who should have it. It's like planting seeds. Give your music to the right people—they do a lot of the work for you by testifying to your talent and turning people onto your music." Plant your own seeds once you have something to pass out. It takes time, but if your music moves people, your career can sprout by means of reviews, radio play, and other exposure that builds your foundation. If you plant enough, you may have a lovely garden blooming in a year or three. Canjoe says:

> The business of music requires public awareness and major marketing in order to sell. Major labels have major money to market with. Independents must get publicity in order to survive. I send well-written press releases out on a regular basis. I look for every opportunity to get in the news, TV, radio, newspapers, magazines. If I'm in a new town, I call newsrooms to try and get a story. I've been very successful at this and consider getting major free press as much an art as performing major stages.

As you get your name and music out, the chances increase that people will find you. For example, Evan R. Saffer says, "VH1 heard of us and asked FIXER to headline their Save the Music benefit in NYC. FIXER has also done radio and TV interviews and live appearances at colleges and public access stations in the Northeast." Exposure builds your press kit! Some artists make videos. They're always useful, but don't spend a fortune on one unless you have a plan for it.

Nowadays videos can be made inexpensively, but making copies and mailing them is pricey. A performance video is helpful on your site—promoters, fans, and the press can check you out there. It's not easy to get videos aired on TV, but if you can, it's good exposure. Marly Hornik says, "I got onto television by making a music video. I don't know how helpful it's been. Then again, I'll play a show for fifty people but my video plays and five thousand people see it. There are a bunch of independent music video shows throughout the country."

Start by creating what's known as a one-sheet: a summary of your story on one sheet of paper. Design your one-sheet so it looks organized and includes whatever ammunition you have, including radio play, press, and venues you've played—any selling points about your act. College promoter Rev. MOOSE of The Syndicate says, "You can fit a lot of information, including comments as to who produced it, who guest stars, a short bio of the band, a track listing, a tour routing, some quick press quotes." The one-sheet can be sent along with CDs to press for reviews, to radio for airplay, or to potential agents, managers, distributors, and almost anyone else you want to support your music or give you media attention.

Choose your priorities based on your budget, both financial and time-wise. David Ross, Publisher of *Music Row* magazine, says if you have millions of dollars to spend, you can go up against major labels and try to chart on radio. Otherwise, he advises:

> *The independent of today has to be a whole lot smarter. That means looking at the game and figuring out how you fit in to create a career for yourself that's profitable, fun, self-satisfying, and still doing what you want to do. You're going to lose at the chart game, so don't play it. Instead, go carefully and watch your expenses. Get airplay where you can. Start touring, find online opportunities to get the word out, and create your own plan. You can find a way to make a living. A lot of independent artists now are doing it.*

WORKING THE PRESS

I believe that getting into magazines and newspapers is the best way to begin building the foundation of your career. While it's not easy, if you have THE GOODS and work hard, press will open doors. Danielle Egnew says: "We go after press as much as possible. It looks terrific in a press kit sent to clubs and labels, as well as for getting your name out." Press is written proof that your music is appreciated by more than friends and family. Jim Merlis, President of Big Hassle Media, says, "Publicity increases the odds that you'll have a successful career and you're actually considered an artist."

If you can afford it, hire a publicist to maximize your opportunities. Jennifer Marks says, "I am a believer in hiring the right person to get the outcome you hope for." Publicist Martha Moore, head of So Much Moore, says: "The most important reason to get PR is to build your press kit. If people don't hear or read about you, or see your picture, they have no idea who you are." Hiring a publicist can help. Lorraine Ferro says:

> *If you can swing it, get a publicist. There are many companies that cater to indie artists. I got a chunk of money from commercial residuals and put it into a publicity campaign. [My publicist, Ida Langsam of ISL Public Relations,] and I worked as a team to further my career. I entered contests and got showcase slots. She put out press releases all over the media. I'd book and she got reviewers to come. We tag-teamed at [a music conference] by phone. I spoke to panelists and asked if my publicist could send a press kit. When they said yes, I'd call her, and she sent it immediately—a more professional approach. Ida got me many radio and magazine interviews.*

Corky McClerkin says, "Having someone speak for you elevates your status." The press takes you more seriously. Moore says, "It's professional to have someone else tell your story and present you. Having representation shows you're professional and serious about your career and puts you on a different level." A publicist knows who to call and has relationships with them. Daniel Lee Martin has a publicist and says, "We've had press releases in every country. Out of the top forty country singles in Finland, we were No. 20, 21, 22, and 23. They found me through my publicist! She does press releases to every major publication. A publicist takes networking one step further."

Music SUBMIT (www.musicsubmit.com), an Internet PR and music promotion service, offers affordable Internet publicity. Publicist Ariel Hyatt (www.arielpublicity.com) says her PR firm has an infrastructure in place for every genre, and for a reasonable fee they'll submit your music to hundreds of music-related web sites, Internet radio stations, music writers, and online music magazines. The more places with your music, the more chances to make money. Look for these types of opportunities.

DIY PUBLICITY

If you can't afford a publicist, you CAN do it yourself. Use an alias to make it look as if someone's doing it for you. I have a publicist's name on my press material—but it's me! Do what you have to do. Whining about not having money to hire someone isn't the indie spirit! Israel Vasquetelle, Publisher of *Insomniac Magazine*, says you can do the job of a publicist if you're dedicated and do your research. Find magazines you want to be in and make the calls: "If you're serious about making it happen, there's nobody better than you to represent yourself."

Target publications that write about your genre. Look at daily and weekly papers, alternative publications, and trade magazines. Be creative about where you can fit into publications that target a specific audience. If you have a good story or technique relating to your guitar-playing, pitch a guitar magazine. If you've made savvy business moves, pitch a business magazine or the business section of a local paper. Find something special about you or your music and look for music and general publications that might write about it. Everyone wants to get into *Billboard*, which isn't a consumer magazine. With so many indie artists, it's hard to get in. Ken Schlager, Executive Editor, advises:

> *Billboard's primary readership is people within the music business. Our main goal is to inform. It's a very narrow, very specific audience. It's not a mass consumer audience. Look at the magazine and get a sense of what we cover. Figure out how to present a story that fits into what we're covering. You have to understand who at the magazine would be most likely to cover it. If it's an artist who's also a songwriter and they have an interesting story about their songwriting, we have a person who covers songwriting. If it's a dance artist, go to the person who covers dance and electronica.*

If you want to get into *Billboard*, the masthead is very clear about which editor handles each section.

Spend some time reading at stores with big magazine sections. Matthew Fritch, Senior Editor of *MAGNET* magazine, a bimonthly national magazine that covers mostly alternative and independent rock music, advises, "Pay attention to what magazines/papers write about, where your reading audience might be. You wouldn't show up at a honky-tonk joint to play punk music, would you?" Study publications carefully so you know which are appropriate for you. For example, David Ross says there are opportunities to get into *Music Row* if you understand that the publication deals in fact and in the business. He explains:

PROFILE

Michelle Shocked signed a deal in 1987 with Mercury Records (Polygram). Because she negotiated a good deal, after her third record the company put her album aside because she refused to renegotiate to give up all rights to her masters, which she'd licensed to them. Eventually, Shocked got out of her deal and the masters were returned to her. Touring has always been her mainstay, and her loyal fans continue to support her. Shocked released an album on her own label, Mighty Sound, in 2002.

We routinely print stories and information on a wide range of different artists. You do not have to be on a major to get mentioned in our publication. The Country Breakout chart is based on secondary radio, so they have a broader playlist. Music Row deals in facts. If you have hard news about your tour, a change in management, a new album being released, anything that's a factual sort of deal, send it to news@musicrow.com. I don't like press kits anymore. We do everything online. Send it by email and it goes to everybody in our building. They all read the news every morning as it comes in. Attach pictures with it. Give me some jpegs. I like to see pictures in the email, even if they're low resolution.

Gather the names of editors and writers, check who reviews or writes about your genre, and send material to that specific person. Martha Moore says:

I do a lot of cold calling. Find out whether to send your material to the writer or editor; their deadline; do they want it by fax, email, or must you mail a press package. Every editor is different. If you can get everything in a cold call, you've done the publicist's job. If you never get them by phone, search out the info—go online or to a sourcebook. Ask for the [specific editor for your genre]. You have to dig for the info.

Ask for assistance from your street team. Who's better to talk you up than a savvy fan with good phone skills? Create a press kit first. Moore recommends using a professional writer for your bio. She says, "It should be only one page." Jim Merlis adds: "A bio explains why they should care about you. Words like 'great' mean nothing. Every band thinks they're excellent. Figure out what makes you great and who you are as a band. Be more original than saying you sound like Radiohead. Use something more obscure that may raise eyebrows."

PROFILE

Jonathan Williams is a member of Hoodz Underground, a hip-hop group in the U.K. The group began in 1994 at the local youth center. Williams started and runs their label, Trackshicker Records. They've had five-star reviews and full-page-spread interviews in 12 national magazines—including *Hip-Hop Connection, Undercover, DJ Magazine,* and *Blues & Soul*—for each of their three releases. They get coverage on MTV Europe, where they've performed live. Their music video airs regularly on MTV's Channel U and they get regular airplay on several shows on BBC Radio One. Hoodz Underground tours the U.K. constantly.

Include clips of press you've gotten—Merlis says it makes an impression—but don't send piles of sheets. Put your contact info on everything you send. Moore adds:

> If you can't get articles written about you at first, at least get quotes. Start on a local basis—ask local DJs who play your music to give you a one-liner. Build up your quote sheet. Put them on your website. Every time you can regurgitate what a credible press person has said about you, there's a domino effect—other media will think that you're credible.

You also need quality photos: Merlis says color photos are key. Your photo should reflect you and your music. Dress how you do for performing. Before your photo shoot, think carefully about the image you want to introduce to the world. It's good to have some fun or interesting photos available on your website, too.

Some editors want full press kits. Some just want the CD with a one-sheet and a URL for your site. It's best to email them and ask before sending anything. Fritch says he just wants a CD and a press/bio sheet: "99.5 percent of the time, a promo photo goes straight into the trash." He prefers you don't call before sending the package. Christopher Porter, Editor of *Jazztimes*, also doesn't have time to receive phone calls. He advises sending a printed one-sheet with some quote highlights and biographical details, "Something clear and snappy that stands out from everything else we see all month. Then direct us to a well-produced website, especially with photos. It's a better idea to direct someone to a website with color photos than to send an 8x10 black-and-white."

Jim Tremayne, Editor of *DJ Times*, a magazine devoted to music that people dance to, wants the music. He says it's more difficult if you have almost no track record. If it's your first dance track, he advises getting your music played by other DJs, adding, "For dance music, the buzz needs to happen inside the clubs. Sometimes I'll get a package and it says that the CD is being played by this DJ or that DJ. If I'm into one of those DJs, I might give it a spin. Don't send five pages of stuff. A short bio or one-sheet is good." Tremayne says they read the different DJ charts to find out what's hot. Get your music played in clubs before approaching him!

Why is one artist chosen over another? Israel Vasquetelle says it's how your package looks:

> We get a lot of stuff that doesn't look like it could be good. Poor packaging or a CD in a blank case with the title scribbled on it doesn't help. If it looks good, it enhances the chance that someone will want to look at it. Be professional, but also be unique—make someone want to listen. It could be an

interesting picture or a stand-out name. The majors have made rap music a very cloned genre. When you get something unique, it can feel special.

I emphasized earlier that packaging is important. Impress people with yours so they want to know more. JJ Koczan, Editor of *East Coast Rocker/Aquarian* in New Jersey, a weekly that focuses on indie and major label rock, says he wants a professional-looking package: "The more there is to look at, the more there is to see." Merlis suggests sending out CDs that are in packaging with a spine: "It makes them easier to pick up. Make sure there's writing on the spine and the track-listing is not only on the CD but also on the artwork." Porter says what makes him choose one artist over another is presentation:

> *What works best is a good-looking, well-put-together package that doesn't look like your sibling did the artwork. If it has a bar code, it means that it can be distributed. Have an overall look that people in the industry will notice because it's real—not just burned. I would say most magazines are in the same boat; we get about two hundred CDs a month. There are only a couple of us here who can listen and make decisions about the records, and not enough time to look through them all. Therefore, presentation is a huge part of it.*

Have an electronic press kit on your website, too, with a good assortment of photos (see Chapter 13). Some editors prefer to take what they need without talking to you. Moore says the media no longer likes press kits in a folder, so she advises investing in a two-sided color sheet (if you can afford it) or having color on the side with your album to grab their attention. She explains, "I call it a two-sided press sheet. On one side, have album information, musicians, and quotes. Have info—anything critically important—on the other side. That plus a CD is all you need. Your presentation should be creative. A lot is the art on your CD." This is a variation of your one-sheet and works well for the media. I recommend getting a plastic folder that your sheet can slide into. Put a photo in, too. Some even have a pocket for a CD.

Send your CD, with a cover letter, to every reviewer you find. Koczan says, "A spotlight or live review is the best way for us to introduce somebody." They will come see you live if you catch their interest. Contact e-magazines and ask if you can send an electronic file of your music. If possible, send a CD directly to people who do reviews. Tremayne says, "I try to review the records I think will work best for the dance floor. I also have record reviewers and leave it to them to decide what moves them." Moore advises, "Start with your local newspaper, then move on to the next level—regional, then national. It's necessary exposure, not easy to get but not as difficult as some people think."

While you may not get press immediately, keep press people in your loop. Send announcements and press releases to get on their radar screen. If they keep hearing about you, their interest may be piqued. Press begets more press. Include new clips with your next press release. Use your best clip as the top sheet when you send out material; it makes a bigger impression than what you write about yourself. Put a handwritten note right on the clip, inviting the writer to come to your gig or asking for a review. Jonathan Williams networked before releasing his CD. He used the names of known and respected people whom he met within the scene to get to others, explaining, "I could say that a certain person said I should contact them. Many DJs I met also did reviews for the hip-hop section in national magazines. When we got into a mainstream magazine like *Hip-Hop Connection*, I sent other writers promo flyers of our shows and magazines we've been in."

Williams got tons of press by *working it*. Create a reason for press to write about you. Your music isn't enough—something else must be going on. Merlis advises building a story, saying, "A hard, earnest rock 'n' roll band is not a story. 'We play good music' is not a story." He recommends figuring out something interesting about you or anything different that might make a more attention-grabbing story to write about. Tremayne says *DJ Times* tries to find what they think their readers—every DJ from the rave to the bar mitzvah—are most interested in. Think about what would interest the readers of any publication you approach. If you give the press a ready-made story, there's a better chance they'll write about you! Matt Allison advises:

It is all about finding the angle. Mine was having the most downloaded song in Africa on MP3.com. I tried for ages to get national coverage from a paper. I looked for a noteworthy item to get me in. When I hyped my headline—"Local Music Hits the Big Time in Cyberspace"—I had them begging for an interview. I told them how we had had a song doing well online and just hit being the top download in Africa. That got them thinking maybe I was worthy of some press. Once they published the article, it led to a spin-off: Local stations that wouldn't give me the time of day before started playing the song. Even the number one talk-show station couldn't help giving me a play in a face-off against a well-known international artist, which was great!

Hype sells! Embellish what you have into something that sounds exciting. Spin a story around your music. Writers need something to write about. Evan R. Saffer says, "FIXER has buzz now. We've got fans, artwork, tours, sponsorship, and celebrities showing up at our gigs. These are the types of things the press love to bark about."

After laying the groundwork, continue to get your name out with press releases, which are announcements of something specific, such as an upcoming gig or a new CD. Don't make things up, but try to find things to announce so the media can get familiar with your name. Moore sends all press releases by email—no attachments! She says the media doesn't like graphics and won't open attachments, so only send a jpeg if someone requests it; she puts a link in the release that the person can click on to get one. You can also send a release out through Entertainment Wire (www.entertainmentwire.com).

Give your package time to arrive and for someone look at it. Then call or email to make sure they got it and give them a reason to check you out. Vasquetelle says communication is another factor that gets you into a magazine. He explains:

> We're flooded with submissions. The reality is, a lot of stuff isn't listened to. Call to check up. Even if you get ten answering machines, continue to call, follow up, and get the names of people who need to hear your music. It's good to call beforehand—it drops your name into someone's head. When you follow up after sending a package, eventually they'll remember you, like after seeing a commercial fifty times—it's your name brand. You must follow up!

Merlis suggests having a friend do it so it sounds as if you have a publicist. Or, try to enlist a street team member as I suggested earlier. Koczan advises, "Keep following up. Many times people will try to brush something off, but if someone is making the effort to keep in touch, we do take notice as opposed to someone just sending a package and there being no follow-up." Porter says, "Email is best. I respond relatively quickly and can look in my files and tell you if I got it."

If you call someone, be prepared beforehand. Moore says, "I give good phone. That means knowing what you will say, and saying it in short doses." If you get someone, don't hold them hostage on the phone! Have a script if necessary, but stick to important facts and then get off. Don't express impatience if people don't get back to you promptly. Sometimes you must send several packages before they notice it. Make a good impression with manners. Do it without bitching—it's part of the process. There's lots of competition for press, so save your energy for getting noticed, not getting angry. Those who persevere with a positive attitude will get more. Keep following up, even if there's no response. Danielle Egnew says:

> The key to pursuing press is following up on contacts you've made. Keep a detailed listing with dates and who you last spoke to. An artist never wants to hound anyone, but checking in once a week on an editor who expressed

interest in covering the artist is good. These people are very busy balancing many projects and can sometimes use a respectful and gentle reminder.

Persistence helps, so follow up—but don't be a pest! Tremayne says, "You don't have to be overly persistent. Just say you've sent it and check to see if we've received it." Fritch adds, "Even if editors don't respond to follow-ups right away, be patient. Please don't follow up more than twice by email. That email is probably sitting in an inbox and will at least get noticed." Bugging editors and writers won't get you press! Koczan says, "There's a delicate balance. It's one thing to follow up and another thing to stalk somebody. Also, be polite. It's crucial." Show respect for their time. If you call, ask if it's a good time to talk. If you get into a publication, send a short note to thank the person. Porter advises being patient because the market is saturated: "Don't rely on one publication to make or break your career. We had to pass on one hundred thirty CDs this month." Koczan agrees, "Keep trying. Even if I don't take somebody, someone else might. It's easy to get discouraged, but there's so much out there. The people who really stand out are those who put the extra effort in."

GETTING RADIO PLAY

Jennifer Marks says, "TV and radio have a wider audience. You can reach a lot more people quickly." Radio play is the best promotion for many indie artists, but it's also the hardest to get. Mary Gauthier says:

> *It's not going to sell a million records, but it helps create a buzz for your name. You have to do it. People start to know who you are—your name is out there, you become a contender. It's an opportunity to reach people, like talent buyers who may give you a chance to be on their stage. You need to build your name, which is your brand. The value of building it won't pay off immediately. But you have to build your brand before you count on this to be your income. It doesn't take that long. I did it in about three years, but I'm a really focused person. A lot of musicians don't want to do this hard work. They want to write songs, play them, and have someone discover them. I'm not one to be at the mercy of any company.*

While college and public stations are more indie friendly, you don't get the same results as commercial radio. But any exposure is good. This is explained a lot more in my book *Start & Run Your Own Record Label*. Beth Wood encourages, "The current system keeps indie artists off of mainstream radio. But there is hope for us. There are still lots of indie radio stations and DJs who support indie music. Just seek them out."

There are two key players at stations: the Program Director (PD) and the Music Director (MD). Jim McGuinn, Program Director for WPLY 100.3 FM (Y100) alternative rock station in Philadelphia, says:

> The program director is in charge of almost everything. The music director is in charge specifically of the music and reports to the program director. The program director often makes final decisions and is usually involved in marketing, managing the DJs, and many other duties, including overseeing the music. But the music director is the one who mainly digs into the music.

Ezina Moore got radio airplay by doing the networking she spoke of earlier. She asked everyone she knew if they knew someone that worked at a station. Her sister-in-law went to college with a station program director, so she called and asked him to play her CD. He listened and played one track on the air. Moore took it a step further: She asked if he knew other program directors who might help her, and got a list of his friends. Don't be afraid to ask, as long as you have THE GOODS, as Moore did. Rachael Sage broke into radio by doing research. She says:

> There are directories and websites that list every type of radio show and station. It's been a long process. I started out just doing college radio in limited quantities. The next year I sent out to more college radio, then national and Internet stations. It mushroomed. Now we have radio stations actually soliciting us for catalogues. You plant the seeds and start to build a database of people who are on your side.

As an experiment, Sage sent out her first CD to radio stations that report to CMJ (www.cmj.com), an organization that targets college radio. CMJ publishes a trade magazine, and college radio power stations report their playlists to it, as do key Internet, community, noncommercial, and a few commercial radio stations. Sage says she circled every station in the CMJ magazine that seemed to play artists like her. She sent out 150 CDs, each with a pitch letter, pretending it was from a manager. She adds, "I just put it out there. Amazingly, I charted in the top thirty on a variety of stations. I printed it out and put it in my press kit. It's one more dimension that shows a venue that I'm getting myself out there."

Rev. MOOSE says there's a big difference between college radio and college music. College students play a variety of music. Usually, the radio listenership doesn't draw from the college as much as they do from the college community. But noncommercial station listeners are usually bigger fans of *music* than a commercial station's audience. Noncommercial stations are more likely to interview you and let you play live on air—offer to do this. Matt Allison does many live shows for radio, mostly college and community stations that invited him after seeing him live or getting an introduction from another artist. He says, "The DJs are great. They love music and often have an emotional response to it, unlike those at a commercial station whose bottom line is money and who often don't bother with indie artists and approach it from an analytical angle."

It's said that college radio play doesn't necessarily sell CDs. But Israel Vasquetelle says, "If nothing else, this builds awareness that eventually *leads* to sales." That exposure is a foundation for future sales. MOOSE says the most important aspect of college radio is the relationships you build. He explains:

> *Most college radio stations are like a club, with a staff of between twenty and one hundred and twenty people. If someone on staff hears something they like, they'll tell all their friends about it. Most people at college radio stations wear different hats. They may also be editor of the local fanzine, book shows at the local garage, work in a coffeehouse that books local talent, are friends with a band that is just starting to get a career nationally, intern at a publicity firm. A large chunk of college students want to do this for their career. An artist that goes to college radio may not get support from the actual station, but they may build their fan base.*

Developing relationships at the ground level helps you down the road. MOOSE warns about only coveting larger college radio stations. Everyone goes after them. He advises targeting smaller stations with just as strong a staff that can make something happen in their community. Try both. Send your CD with a description and a good one-sheet. College radio doesn't need a huge press kit. When a college gig approaches, promote it with flyers, posts on the community board, and notices to radio stations. MOOSE adds:

> *It helps if the college radio DJ sees that you put up posters in the local record store and somebody put flyers in the cafeteria. Have a well-timed PR campaign that lands at the same time you're doing college radio airplay. It's all about making impressions at the same time. What affects airplay more than anything is being able to take advantage of all the resources at once. The tricky part of doing it yourself is balancing all that.*

Some public radio stations have enough clout to break new music. Nic Harcourt is music director for KCRW in Santa Monica and also DJ of its very popular show "Morning Becomes Eclectic." Many well-known artists have gotten their break on his show. While commercial stations have mandates about what they play, Harcourt says his show is free-form and very different. Since he's not restricted by playlists, he can try out material and play music that he likes: "Because we're able to do that, we put a lot of different stuff on the air and constantly discover new things." Harcourt describes his audience as intellectual and responsive, adding, "A lot of decision makers, people who put music into television shows and things like that, listen to the show. If something in particular that we play is new and fresh, those people gravitate towards it like I did."

Harcourt says if he really likes an artist, "[Playing their CD] 'a lot' may be three, four times a week as opposed to commercial stations that beat you to death with it." Commercial radio is different. McGuinn receives several thousand records a year from major and established independent labels and about 500 regional/local CDs a year. WPLY adds two to three songs a week to its rotation. Commercial stations put records in what's called regular rotation. McGuinn says those songs are played more than ten times a week: "They're the songs we think could become hits. Every station is different. Most songs are played about seven times a day. Some stations play a song as much as one hundred times a week."

But McGuinn says that in addition to WPLY's regular rotation slots, there are many nooks and crannies of airplay. There's a new and local music show on Sunday nights, and every night at 11:00 p.m. the station plays a local or regional artist. McGuinn adds that it's harder for indie artists from out of his region because they don't have built-in places for that kind of music. To get airplay, he says your music really has to stand out. But while it is harder, don't assume breaking into commercial stations is impossible. So many musicians only go to noncommercial stations for exposure. Sage didn't listen when she was warned that noncommercial was the only way for indie artists. She says:

We focus on noncommercial, but my last release was the first that we serviced to commercial Triple A stations that play artists [similar to me]. We did pretty

PROFILE

Ezina Moore is a rock/R&B artist who has used serious networking to advance. She released her first album in 1995 and got permission to play it in the MAC store she managed; other stores started playing it, too. In 1998, Moore left a $50,000 salary to do music full-time and has now sold more than 15,000 CDs. She tours colleges, festivals, and clubs, and has also performed in Europe and Japan several times. Networking helped Moore get gigs in corporations and at trade shows, and she now gets more commercial radio airplay than a majority of indies do.

well—added to a number of stations in big cities and smaller regions. When I toured near a commercial station that played me, we made it a point to visit, thank them, and give them T-shirts to give away. We made sure they knew that we appreciated their support.

What catches commercial radio's attention? The packaging, as I keep emphasizing! Steve Richards, Operations Manager for the mainly hip-hop Hot 107 in Memphis, advises, "Send it in a creative package, a nice, neat portfolio that has some effort put into it. That catches my attention. A package with something scribbled on it won't. If there's creativity in the package, I'm a lot more likely to look at it." The key is sending material that makes you look professional enough to be taken seriously. McGuinn explains:

It has to be presented professionally. When we open the package, we have to feel confident that you know what you're doing. I should be able to say, "Wow, look what's going on with this person." It also has to stand up sonically to be compatible with records that we're getting from major labels. Actually, the music has to be better. We have to feel that we should play your band over something that's on MTV or in Spin magazine. That's not easy.

For Harcourt, it's about the music. He says, "The less material the better—a CD with a one-sheet—one piece of paper that tells us who you are and if you're getting any attention, with some quotes." Richards prefers you send a package first. Hot 107 listens to everything at a weekly music meeting, so he doesn't like being called and emailed daily. McGuinn likes a one-page bio and a fact sheet with bulleted facts: how many gigs you've had, what bands you've opened for, what compilations you've contributed to. He advises, "I like something that in thirty seconds gives me an accurate view of what the band has achieved. Bios say that they're the most unique band ever, but don't say why. It rings hollow. I also like a quote sheet where you take one key sentence from each review you've gotten and string them together on one page." He warns:

Don't send an album without instructions. If you do, someone's going to listen to the first twenty seconds of the first track and if they don't like it, they're done with it. If you can't send a CD single or a promotional sample, at least indicate the two or three tracks that you think will work. If track eight is the great song on the record but you started the album with a four-minute song with insects buzzing, I'm not going to make it to track eight. That's the reality of the time constraints.

McGuinn says music and program directors won't go to a website and listen to an MP3: "We would have to download and burn it, and we don't have time for that. If anybody tells us that, we email back and ask them to please send us a CD and press kit. Oftentimes *then* I will go to the website if I like the music on the CD." Once you send radio stations your music, follow up. McGuinn says, "I'm quicker with email." Richards says, "You can check in with me with a phone call once a week. That's what a record rep would do." Most commercial stations have specific hours each week to touch base with them. Harcourt says he can't follow up on emails because there are hundreds, but they have hours for people to call and follow up. He adds, "If they send something in, they can call on Wednesday from 12:00 p.m. to 3:00 p.m. and check to see if we've received it and listened to it—and whether it was added or not."

Sending packages to stations and flyering an area can get expensive. Some people at radio stations say that the most bang for your buck is buying advertising time on radio. If you have a gig coming up, check out rates for an ad during the night, when it's cheaper. It's also cheaper in smaller markets. Have your catchiest song playing behind the verbal info, and include your website. Leave time for just the music to play at the end. If it's really good, it will speak to music lovers. Nothing speaks louder than the music itself!

Build relationships, one person at a time, and you can make it on radio. Many indies get commercial play. Preech got a drop (a 16-bar verse talking about the station) on Hot 97 in NYC. His manager called, got friendly with the guy who answered the phone, and kept in touch by email. It helped Preech's CD get airplay. He got on other radio shows by going to their events, like open mics at Promo Radio (an underground station) shows. Alex Woodard emailed the 91X afternoon drivetime DJ in San Diego, asking if he could send her a CD. She liked it and played a song on her new music show, where the listener reaction got him ranked No. 2. You can develop relationships, too! Jonathan Williams says many DJs he met while networking in clubs also DJ'd on pirate stations. When he had a master copy of tracks, he sent promo CDs all over the country to these DJs, four weeks before the release. Those relationships helped get airplay.

Daniel Lee Martin got far by building relationships. A childhood friend knew people at the largest country radio station in the Southeast. In the spring of 1996, he set up a meeting that Martin thought was for a quick radio interview. It turned into a lot more! Martin says he learned how important networking is when this station, the official Tampa Bay Buccaneers broadcasting network, got him involved with the Bucs. He explains, "I played opening day at Raymond James Stadium in front of 75,000 people—all through the radio station! They got me into many events at Tampa Stadium and other things they were involved with. They believed in me and gave me every opportunity."

Martin also did a three-month radio tour. He targeted stations to visit, got to many of them, and played his music and talked. Many didn't want to give a new artist the time of the day. Martin says they drove hundreds of miles to hear, "Thanks for the media kit. See you later." But many other stations were receptive. Martin personally called and sent media kits to stations he couldn't get to. He wanted to create as close a relationship with them as possible without being face-to-face. His persistence paid off—he charted. Martin adds, "We debuted on No. 72 and made it to No. 52. That was a major milestone. It's networking—stations said they remembered me on the chart. I want to be taken seriously. I want independents to be taken seriously and to be competitive with the majors."

Many stations support artists they like. Richards says, "Seeing something live can really affect how you feel about it. If I get a package and think they seem interesting, I may go out and see them live." He also does live interviews with artists the station is supporting. Harcourt says his station does live performances with interviews if it's an artist they like or one they're playing. (If you'll be touring in his region, he'd like to receive your material at least three or four weeks in advance.) McGuinn says WPLY is very active in the regional music community.

> We book shows with local bands a lot and help people get gigs and get on the radio. We try to set up relationships with acts. If someone sends us a CD and we like it, we'll try to create a dialogue and help them. Maybe we'll know a new punk rock band, and someone we know is coming in and needs that type of an opening band. It really becomes a relationship. An email from you every week to tell me you're playing a gig may not be necessary, but every once in a while can help.

Radio can be worth pursuing if you research to find stations that play indie music. *The Musicians' Atlas* is a great place to find many of them. Danielle Egnew says Pope Jane has been on heavy college radio rotation, with some commercial FM play. She says, "That certainly helped us! Radio promotion always gets out the music. That assists when you go to an area to play."

Some people hire radio promoters. A college radio promoter helped Woodard send CDs to stations, and his album debuted as the eighteenth most added CD in the nation on college radio. MOOSE says, "Independent promoters are familiar with the people you need to get in touch with and what they're looking for. If you as the artist call and know nothing about the radio station, the person probably won't give you the time of day." A promoter knows exactly where different genres would fit into a station's format. When a person knows they'll hear from a promoter again, they're more likely to call back.

When should you consider an independent promoter? MOOSE says, "When you can't do it yourself anymore, or have a national tour or national exposure coming up, it makes sense to hire someone." Beth Wood adds:

> When I released my third CD, I hired an independent radio promoter. This was costly, but I built the expense into my recording budget. He promoted to Triple A and NPR stations. This helped tremendously to get my music out there, and it did translate to record sales in other parts of the country. With my last two CDs, I didn't have the budget, so I contacted as many stations as I could myself and sent CDs. If you have extra cash, it is definitely worth it to hire a radio promoter. This is a side of the business that is an insider's game, and people rarely fully understand it.

Promoting your music to radio can open more doors than you might expect. If someone from a station becomes a fan, it can make a big difference for your career. McGuinn says:

> We discovered Good Charlotte. I saw them live one night. The next day the music director said he had a demo by this band called Good Charlotte. We both loved the same song and decided to give them a spin on a feature we have called the "Cage Match." It's a battle. They won fifteen nights in a row. Their bidding war price inched up a quarter of a million dollars. It's rare, but that was pretty much an unknown band from Baltimore, and we gave them what we thought would be one spin. It helped lead them to where they are today.

No matter how you plan to promote your music, be true to yourself—not to what you think commercial radio wants. Nic Harcourt advises, "Make music because you love making music, not because you want to be a pop star. Think of the reasons why you're doing it. The happiest musicians are those who are doing it because they love to make music."

PROMOTING YOUR TOUR

The difference between a successful tour and one that bombs can be good tour support: working the media in each city and using street teams to promote gigs. An indie artist who learns how to do this has the best chance of making money. Martha Moore, explains, "Tour press means exposure in each market. It's all a building process. You have to knock 'em down one at a time. If you don't get it this time you tour there, next time you know who the person is." Editors assure me that while they might not cover you the first time you come to their town, or the third, if you keep coming back they will eventually give you press. Keep in touch with the editors you want support from. Tell them about your progress. Marly Hornik says, "Tour support does make a difference—it shows that you're serious about what you're doing. Even if it doesn't make that much difference in a first show, it can have a long-term effect."

Jim Merlis says that touring absolutely helps to attract press. Club owners know the dailies and weeklies, so get the club you're playing to support you. Merlis adds, "Every club has a media list. Get the list and send out CDs and press kits. Try to do a personal letter. If you're opening for someone, make sure you put that. Go from the daily papers all the way down to college and high school papers." Don't hesitate to ask! Jennie DeVoe says radio and press are key, so she tries to do radio shows and press releases before each of her shows. DeVoe arranges an in-store acoustic performance in a local music store on the day of her show. She advises getting your name seen and heard as much as possible to raise curiosity about your performance and pull people in, adding, "It's great not to have to arrange all of this yourself, but sometimes we have to."

Some artists splurge on a publicist for tour support. Jennifer Marks says, "I figure it is worth the money to play to a room full of potential fans who could buy CDs and merchandise instead of not spending any money and not making any either." If you've never been to the markets you're touring in, a publicist can open doors. Then you can try it yourself the next time, as you'll already have names. Beth Wood adds, "If I am on tour to promote a specific project, I will hire someone to do press for me. It can be a little costly, but some publicists give you a better deal the more shows you do with them. A publicist has a better chance of getting through to major outlets—he or she has the contacts and know-how."

If you can't afford a publicist, do it yourself if you want a successful tour. Martha Moore suggests sending a press release about the tour with a list of dates. Tweak the headline to localize it to each market. She says since it's hard for a developing artist to get press, get it where you can. Try for something in

PROFILE

Daniel Lee Martin is a country music singer whose records are released on Chin Music, a label founded by Major League baseball players who believe in Martin and invested in his music. In 1997, Martin left the advertising agency he had founded and moved to Nashville to pursue his music independently. He gets commercial radio play and does extensive Walmart tours. He's opened for top artists, including Tanya Tucker, John Michael Montgomery, and Lonestar. *Country Music Today* magazine picked his first album as one of the best albums of 2003, along with mostly major label artists.

the smallest markets. If you get a little nugget in a local paper, Moore says it can lead to more press. JJ Koczan says if you're going to tour in his region, send material three to four weeks in advance. Doing tour support is YOUR job. Michael Johnathon says, "I make myself completely available to the promoter to work. I'm not there to sit in my hotel room and doodle on my guitar. Put me to work during the day. Promoters need to hear that; they assume that you can't be bothered. I'm not there to watch TV during the afternoon."

Marly Hornik says she and her publicist send press kits to press within the region she's playing. Then they call and try to get features, or even just a mention in the paper. It's crucial to follow up. If you're not famous, they probably won't do much—unless you stay in touch to remind them. Many musicians think it's okay to just mail out packages and hope for the best, but editors take you more seriously if you call. Try to establish at least a minimal relationship. Publicists advise sending material four to six weeks in advance of your tour. That allows plenty of time to consider writing about you. Beth Wood tries to get into the local concert listings:

> This gets info about the show out there without taking too much space. You can't expect to get a full-page article every time you come through town. Unless you have something newsworthy, I recommend keeping it on the level of concert listings. Send a photo with your info to make it stand out—lots of newspapers have photos on their concert calendar page. One thing to keep in mind is that newspapers usually like lots of lead time—at least two weeks. Most papers like to have the info two Fridays before your show.

A great photo can get onto the concert listings page. Editors prefer photos with energy and may opt to use an indie artist's eye-catching one over a boring photo of a well-known signed act. Have an assortment of photos they can choose from on your site.

Try everything. Go after local radio to get exposure for your music. Support from radio is possible, especially in smaller markets. Rachael Sage says they try to book radio appearances, interviews, and on-air performances in every market: "If I'm flying in somewhere and playing that night, I can make two radio appearances before the show that afternoon. Even if they haven't added [you] in the past, oftentimes they're very open to having you come visit and perform a few songs on the air." Dean Seltzer says he's developed relationships with radio stations, so he can call if he's in their town and bring down T-shirts and CDs. But it's not always rosy. Seltzer explains, "Some are too big and important to pay attention to an artist like me. I've had some radio success at many smaller community stations. They come and put banners up at my shows. I'll play a couple of songs for the station and do an interview on the air." Marly Hornik adds, "I either email or call local radio stations and tell them I'm coming. People are fairly receptive." Danielle Egnew calls newspapers, tells them where her band is playing, and asks if they'd come down and do a live review. Don't forget to contact local TV shows, too. Tina Broad says:

Regional TV—network-affiliated morning shows, for example—are an important part of our publicity push when we go into an area. It helps that we're Australian and can talk up the exotic instruments. Likewise with radio. Anything that is profile-building, that we don't have to pay for, is a big plus in my book! Liaise with the event promoter and marketing people and make sure they know you're available for pre-show interviews and media appearances. Make sure you get a tape of the appearance.

Be creative when promoting your tour. Forge says Little Egypt takes out an ad in the school paper when the group plays colleges. Marly Hornik sends mini-sampler CDs to coffee shops, record stores, guitar stores, bookstores, music stores, and other places that fans of original music might congregate. Hearing your music can lure folks to your gig. Send flyers that announce your gig with the samplers. Hornik says in small towns, you'd probably send them to the venue. For a city, go to Citysearch (www.[name of city].citysearch.com) and search for "best music store in this area" to get a list of ten, ranked in order. She recommends, "Call and ask if you can send samplers. They give them away for free, probably in a box on a table. Often I'll pop in the store while we're there to say thanks. Sometimes they'll ask for more because they've gone so well."

Artists have different takes on using flyers to promote. Kyler England says, "I focus more on having street team members pass out postcards to their friends. Word of mouth is a powerful tool." Preech, on the other hand, likes flyers and says, "If there's another party, we go and get DJs to announce it." Dean Seltzer says if he can't arrive early, he asks the club to put flyers up. He makes it easy, explaining, "On my website, I have a flyer that is blank on the bottom so that they can write in the time and [other info]." Having PR materials on your site that can be downloaded saves the cost of printing and mailing them. Design stuff that clubs, your street teams, etc., can download and distribute. Find whatever way works best and work it! Robby Baier says, "We send emails to our list and print posters to send to the venue two weeks in advance. We call or email special fans that we call 'agents' in the area of the gig and ask them to get the word out. They get on the guest list." Find your own best way to create the indie buzz, and work it with your heart and soul!

CHAPTER 12

The Indie Store

Your business has products to sell: CDs, merchandise, and your performances. Your store is portable and in many places. If you don't handle it as any other store would, you lose out. Create your own version of an indie store to market you and your products. Corky McClerkin says, "CDs give your audience an opportunity to bond with you and your music. They give you feedback on what you have done and need to do, help target the right audience for your music, provide a chance to demonstrate your talent to those who have never seen you in person, and earn steady income." Find outlets to sell yours!

CDS AND MERCHANDISE PAY BILLS!

If you want to be a successful indie artist, make a top-quality CD. The packaging should be competitive with major labels. Your products reflect you—make it a shiny reflection! Evan R. Saffer says, "That's your product—what defines you most. The first priority is product—get an amazing recording, then sell it." Musicians agree that having a CD is a must. Matt Allison says that without them, he wouldn't have a living. He earns about 80 percent of his income from album sales, especially at shows. Jennifer Marks adds, "Selling CDs at shows and on the Internet makes a difference in my income. I also sell merchandise. If people like what they hear, they often support you in any way that they can. I have made quite a bit of money that way."

CDs also spread your music. Alex Woodard says, "They serve as vehicles for word of mouth more than anything. People like to support independent music they love. They help the music pay for itself." People take you more seriously when you have a CD. Lorraine Ferro says, "*Product* in this industry is your main calling card. You can't get a CD review if you don't have a CD!" Jennie DeVoe views CDs as a promotional tool. While she's sold more than 25,000 CDs, she puts a lot back into touring, making professional press packages and shipping them, and taking a band on tour with her. Dean Seltzer adds, "At my level, the profit for CDs is not huge but it's mandatory and necessary. No one takes you serious without one. Clubs that haven't heard me ask for a demo. When I say that I have a CD out, they think I'm a for-real musician." Jonathan Williams got major national promotion and distribution in the U.K. for his hip-hop act, Hoodz Underground, after setting up Trackshicker Records in 2001. The Hoodz got reviews and features in 12 national magazines and were on many top radio shows. Their CD was the vehicle. Williams says, "I realized that waiting to do that magic gig, on that magic stage, where that magic A&R person offers that magic contract, wasn't going to happen. Setting up a record label was the best thing I did."

Musicians say that selling merchandise is a staple for survival, too. Create a variety of merch to sell at shows and on your website. T-shirts, sweatshirts, and caps are the most popular. Jennie DeVoe says, "Merchandise is invaluable. Selling T-shirts, CDs, and posters keeps your name afloat and works for you even after you're gone." Add products as sales increase. Fans eventually buy everything. Manager Tina Broad (BROTHER) says:

> We make three times more across the merch desk than what we take in tour guarantees. Touring is the best retail promotion we can do. Web sales significantly increase when we're on the road. Downloading, piracy, and the gradual erosion of the consumer's perceived value of the CD as a "must-have" item have forced a rethink about where we're going as an indie. We're tending to look more at our CDs as a kind of sonic calling card rather than the endgame product. We're working hard to diversify our merchandise.

Selling merch can pay many bills. Touring artists say they wouldn't survive without it, especially at first when gigs don't pay much. Sales fund gas, food, motels, and side musicians. Lisa O'Kane says, "I sell a lot of CDs when I tour Europe. That helps me pay the musicians I hire when I'm there." When fans love you, they want to take something home. Make product available. Visual says, "We have two lines of T-shirts. We sell a lot of them, especially at festivals." Danielle Egnew (Pope Jane) adds, "Selling merchandise helps. T-shirts and hats sell quite well on tour and in the less music-centered areas of the country. Merchandise is a smart way to leave a little piece of you behind, to remind everyone what a great time they had. Plus, it makes great giveaways for your website promotions."

Evan R. Saffer says, "Merchandise helps finance FIXER as well as promote. We have a very identifiable logo and artwork the people love." Howie Statland says he likes to give away stickers, adding, "I have a cool T-shirt. If your merchandise looks good, people will buy it." T-shirts are a walking advertisement for your music. Fans can explain who you are to people who ask questions. Their enthusiasm makes others want to check out your music. Beth Wood says:

> The most important thing about merch is it gets your name out. My T-shirts and hats have my website prominently displayed. I can't really measure how effective this is, but if one guy walking down the street checks out my music because he saw my website on the back of a T-shirt, that's awesome! It's also a subliminal thing. When I was in a band in college, we had stickers with our band name. We stuck them on every telephone pole, wall, inch of every corner that was not covered with something else. The result: When you mentioned our band name to someone new, they had a reaction like, "I think I've heard of you guys but I can't remember where." Pretty sneaky.

T-shirts and caps can be given out for promotion to key industry people: club promoters, retailers, etc. Anyone who wears it serves as your walking poster, so include your website. Don't cut corners on merch. Fans appreciate good quality. Put time into designing your products. Make people want them!

MARKETING YOUR CD

It's your call how to price your merchandise and CDs. Many indies sell CDs and T-shirts for $12 to $15 each. Alex Woodard has a different philosophy:

PROFILE

....

Danielle Egnew is a solo artist who is also the front woman for the band Pope Jane. She produces and writes for other musical artists and does underscoring for film and TV. Egnew has played music professionally since 1992 and has sold over 75,000 CDs. She's played with many national acts, including Joan Jett and Ann and Nancy Wilson. Egnew is also a columnist for many music periodicals and e-zines. She's won numerous awards for production and artistic contributions.

I usually sell women's tanks and most of my records for ten bucks. People are more willing to spend ten. The people I play for pay to get in and buy drinks. To me, ten bucks for a record is totally reasonable. I fight with people all the time, especially people I open for or who open for me. They price their stuff higher and tell me I need to price mine higher—they feel bad about charging so much more. I won't. I want to make a living but it's just as important to get it out there. People can buy all my records for thirty bucks. In the stores, they're twelve dollars because the stores take a cut. It's hard to straddle that line between commerce and art. I do what I feel is right.

Danielle Egnew, whose band has sold more than 75,000 CDs, agrees that price affects sales: "We sell ours for ten dollars. If we have a new one, it sells for twelve or fourteen, but then drops down to ten. Artists freak out about price. But you will sell two CDs for ten dollars each before you sell one for fifteen."

Should you run to a major city with a new CD? Egnew says geographical location makes a big difference in sales, but not how you might think. She says Pope Jane moved lots of product right away because they were in a more rural area and there weren't many bands producing original albums that sounded like they did. She explains:

Artists who live out in the Midwest, Northwest, South—anywhere not a major metropolitan area—will sell more product than artists in L.A. In less congested parts of our country, there is a totally different culture—one that really enjoys being part of a band they see play. In the larger, more artistic centers, many artists are more on a quest to get noticed, so fans are less apt to buy a CD than the rancher who sees us play in Wyoming and buys seven CDs for his kids. Artists who tour anywhere outside of L.A., New York, Chicago, Houston, or other big musical centers sell TONS of product to those who CDs are meant for—the general public!

You'll have a much better chance to make money and get promotion in what are known as the "softer markets"—smaller cities and towns that have less people and aren't known for being strong music markets. Major labels invest less time in them. Radio stations are easier to connect with. There's less competition. All these situations favor the indie artist. While everyone else flocks to the major music cities, try to tap into markets that you might not expect to help you. Book a tour in a smaller market and work it hard. You may get a boost to move to bigger ones.

Indie artists don't count on retail stores as much as the majors do. Woodard says, "I don't have a *national* distribution deal but do have it in select markets. I think as an independent artist, it's a waste of time until you get to a certain level." He says that tracking sales is a lot of work and you're better off focusing on your online presence and selling that way: "Record stores need to sell at least three or four CDs a month to keep them on the shelf. When you're a bigger indie, like Fountains of Wayne and the White Stripes used to be, it's worth it. Until then, it's better to sell records at shows and online." At first, place records in stores on an individual basis yourself. Beth Wood says:

> Many indie artists think they need national distribution, when they may not be touring nationwide. It does not make sense to have ten CDs in Akron, Ohio, if you have never play there and don't get radio play. Concentrate on your area first. Get in touch with local DJs. See if they will spin your CD on their show. Take a handful of CDs to a record store and make a consignment deal—even some major chains sell indie CDs on consignment. Check in with the stores occasionally and collect money if they sold any. With national distribution, you may get thirty percent of what they owe, six months later.

Jonathan Williams says that before the first release by the Hoodz was in stores he spent 18 months networking. He created a promotional tape with some of the group's freestyles and live performances on radio shows, and then he traveled to every city in the U.K. with a hip-hop scene. Williams went to hip-hop nights and introduced himself, his new label, and the group to promoters, DJs, and acts from that city. He gave each a tape and handed out more to the crowd, letting them know the release would be out in the next six months. He says he also visited record stores in each city:

> I introduced myself to the manager and vinyl buyer who deals with hip-hop and left fifty tapes. I figured if you give out fifty tapes to people, that can reach one hundred—each person will let someone else know. I also left tapes in other stores where potential hip-hop music buyers would visit, like clothing stores and skateboard stores. It made people feel like they couldn't get away from us. Each tape had a bright yellow cover with my contact details. Our first release was on 12-inch vinyl with quality artwork in black and yellow—the same color as the artwork on the tapes, to remind people.

Williams' efforts paid off when the record was released.

Target stores in markets where people might buy them. It does you little good to have CDs in markets with no buzz about your music. Retail stores aren't like those on the Internet. With the exception of some indie-friendly stores that allow customers to listen to your CD, people don't go in looking to discover new music. They come in because they've heard your music and they want it. Go the consignment route first—you leave some CDs and get paid when they've sold. Rachael Sage says:

> I marched down to the person who handled consignment at Tower Records and asked if he would take on a few copies of my CD. I told people at my gigs that they were available. Somehow, the fellow there was nice enough to put my record on the listening booth. He said my CD was the biggest selling consignment CD ever. I asked if I could quote him and added it to my press kit. It was very helpful. You have to make something out of nothing sometimes. It can help you get a better gig.

As your buzz gets louder, try more stores and distributors in regions where the CD sells. Suzanne Teng says she learned who distributors were through her alternative market, adding, "I also asked friends and looked at magazines. It was a lot of groundwork with people I knew who were doing the same thing." You don't need national distribution until you're a national act. Distributors carry product that sells. Create a demand first. Work with regional distributors until you expand further. Tina Broad says BROTHER hasn't had a good retail distribution partnership since INDI (a distributor) went bust owing them $30,000. She explains, "It's made us a bit gun-shy. At this stage, we're working with some regional, smaller distributors, all nonexclusive, and also servicing retail arrangements with individual stores on a consignment basis."

As your career escalates, getting distribution is absolutely crucial. Sage tours nationally and says, "There's no way we could reach all of those people who are sort of a by-product of word of mouth, print promotions, and stuff like that. We can only physically get CDs into so many venues before we would need the help of a distributor." Sage says her distributor, Big Daddy, approached her after seeing her chart in *CMJ* magazine. She'd already done a bulk mailing to distributors, but she chose to use Big Daddy because:

> He left a personal message on my answering machine, very excited. He said he could do a lot with my stuff and wanted to put it out there. He knew I

PROFILE

Jennie DeVoe is a full-time singer/songwriter who's run her own Rubin the Cat Records since 1998. She's sold nearly 20,000 CDs. DeVoe has done shows with many big-name acts, including Joe Cocker, John Hiatt, and Susan Tedeschi, and has played on the Lilith Fair tour. She's earned three John Lennon Songwriting Contest Honorable Mentions. DeVoe continues to license her songs to major television shows and to Corona Beer.

was about to go on tour with Ani DiFranco and was excited to help me get my music into regions where I would tour. We met, and I really liked what he had to say. He got what we were trying to do. We worked out an arrangement and I've been with him ever since.

When your buzz gets loud, getting distribution usually isn't hard. Distributors make money by selling CDs. If you show a big enough demand, they'll want to carry your products. Gregory Abbott says:

We work on a project-by-project basis. I have good relationships with three or four distributors who specialize in one genre or another. A new CD will inevitably be most appropriate for a particular niche, e.g., Urban, Smooth Jazz, Dance, or Caribbean. The distribution method will be dictated by the style of music. I also offer my CDs on my website on a song-by-song basis as well as each CD in its entirety. If I distribute the album independently, I use many of the same promotion people, subdistributors, and publicists the majors use. It's quite a bit of work, but very rewarding. We've done quite well.

When Matt Allison looked for distribution in South Africa, he spoke to other artists and producers to get input on various distributors. Another artist introduced him to the president of Sarepta Music. Allison says:

When he heard my music, he signed me for distribution, which has since evolved into a pressing, distribution, and marketing deal—my debut release was a good seller. In the U.S., I was introduced to the CEO of Grassroots Music in Houston, Texas, who offered me a marketing and distribution deal. The A&R guy at Sarepta Music relocated to New Zealand. A fan of my music, he played it to the staff at Parachute Music, who signed me there.

So much depends on the relationships you develop and whether you have THE GOODS. Williams says when his release was ready, he had relationships in all the main stores and asked them who distributed to them. If you don't know what distributor to try, ask the stores who they buy from. But wait until a demand is created. Williams says, "Six months after the release, when we'd received press and were touring constantly, I contacted the distributors whose names came up all the time, using contact names they knew from my local record stores, and things went from there."

If stores like your music, ask for quotes. People who work in stores can be your best allies. Develop relationships with them. Many have contacts and know the biz well; they'll guide you if you ask. They can also promote your CD—play it, put it in an unpaid-for spot in a listening booth, or display it. The more exposure, the more doors that open. Christine Kane says the founder of Putumayo Records was in a Borders Books & Music when they played her CD. He then invited her to be on his *Women's Work* CD. Ask to do an in-store promotion, especially in markets where you have gigs. If you're friendly to record store employees and they like your music, they might help. When you treat people right, it comes back to you.

There are many more details about marketing a CD in my book *Start & Run Your Own Record Label*—it can guide you in the many decisions you must make. And the future of independent music will mean a whole new way of selling your CDs. Clint Black's Equity Music Group now signs other artists—to *fair* deals. He didn't want to get a great deal for himself and give other artists unfair terms. Black explains:

> We wanted to create something that would be positive all around and also show the industry that a company geared in the artist's interests really can be successful. We've had good success so far with sales, airplay, and the media. Equity is staffed like a major label, walking, talking, and acting like the pre-existing system, with the exception being that the artists own their masters— they get paid from the first SoundScan, full statutory rate. Once they've sold a half-million records they become part owner of the company. It's acting like the same old animal in all the best ways but a new one in all the best ways. As Equity proves itself, there will be others who do it, and artists won't have to go to labels with fuzzy accounting. It's a tough battle because artists want so desperately to get signed to a record deal. To the uneducated person, it all seems so unattainable. It's got to change. It's looking like this little machine didn't need the big machine to get it done.

ALTERNATIVE MARKETING

Be creative about alternative ways to market your CD. Alex Woodard says, "The alternative retail channels are little hidden gems. I have more sales in those stores and it won't be as much work as having to track down consignments [in stores all over the country]." Woodard says finding these markets has been word-of-mouth, like when someone saw him perform and introduced himself:

> He asked if I wanted to sell my CD in his furniture store. It was very successful. He plays it in the store and when people get to the register, the CD's there. For ten bucks or twelve bucks, it's easy to buy. Stores are very open to it. I have one of my other records in a furniture store in Chicago and it sells well. That will be a big part of what I do. It's better than going the traditional route because there's no competition. I'm working now on getting my new record into clothing and other retail stores.

Offer CDs to stores that play music, and ask to leave some on consignment. Decorate a small box that holds five or six CDs with the CD artwork, to be used as a POP (point of purchase) display near the cash register. Beth Wood leaves CDs in coffee shops where she's played and gift shops owned by people who like her music. She warns, "It can be tricky keeping track of these—it takes good organization to keep it up to date." Danielle Egnew says Pope Jane is the queen of nontraditional marketing: "Since we started in a rural place, we had to be very creative. We placed CDs in truck stops, clothing boutiques, metaphysical bookstores, and tourist stops in Montana. They all sold!" Ezina Moore leaves no market untapped. She says, "I sell CDs at my doctor's office, dentist, at airports, in clothing boutiques, nail and beauty salons." Ask anyone who likes your music to sell CDs where he or she works or make other suggestions. Gregory Abbott says:

> On a grassroots level, cross-fertilization can be effective. There are many opportunities such as fashion outlets, sporting events, coffeehouses, malls, restaurants, ringtones, clubs and airplanes, etc. Getting your music played in these venues can generate artist awareness and sales. My people work very hard at this. It's important to establish a distinctive, recognizable sound and persona so that you can go after a defined niche. Then proceed in your efforts in getting your music played in places which cater to people likely to want to hear your music. From here you build and expand.

Get some invoices for consignment sales. Leave the store a receipt and keep one for yourself to help you keep track. Jennie DeVoe advises selling wherever you can, including bookstores, wineries, and coffee shops. She finds people receptive.

PROFILE

....

DJ Minx founded Women On Wax—a collective of lady DJs from the Detroit area to support up-and-coming female talent—in 1996, focusing on their recordings. In 1999, she became a resident of world-renowned Club Motor, playing with Basement Jaxx, Afrika Bambaataa, and many more. German booking agencies got Minx playing in Paris, Berlin, Cancun, Switzerland, and Spain. She tours overseas at least twice a year and regularly plays clubs around the U.S. and Canada. She was a key component of the legendary "Deep Space Radio" program on Detroit's WGPR 107.5 FM and can now be heard on "Rhythm Gallery," an afternoon mix show she co-hosts on Canada's CJAM-FM 91.5 FM.

You have to ask them to carry you. If your reputation precedes you, there's a good chance they'll say yes. Most places will take five to ten CDs on consignment. As they sell, keep restocking. You come to an agreement on what the store sells the CDs for and what you want. They tell you when they settle up. In some cases, stores buy them outright from me because they have proven to sell well. Sometimes you can use that as a negotiating point: Tell them you'll give them a price break if they buy right now.

KEEPING TRACK OF SALES

Keep track of your CD and merch sales if you want to run your business properly. Find whatever system works for you, but find one. Record all new products when they arrive. How much did it cost you? Separate each item. If you have more than one CD, record individual figures for tracking inventory and sales of each. Note how many you give away. How much of each item is in stock? Write it all down. Make sure your sales and expenses match what you have in the bank for your business-related stuff. Keep your biz account separate from your personal one to make it much easier to keep track. Beth Wood says, "I have a separate bank account for CD sales, and I pay for smaller expenses like gas, postage, and supplies out of this account. When I do have a slow month, I don't have a problem covering these expenses." Write everything down regularly— don't get too backlogged. It's easier to create a routine for recording sales and expenses as they happen. I make notes on my bank deposit slips of what the money is from and write on each check exactly what it's for.

When your sales start to build, you can track product through SoundScan. Danielle Egnew says, "Once you begin selling CDs, register with SoundScan so your sales are reported. SoundScan reads the bar code on your product when it's scanned at the cash register." If you plan to sell in retail and you'll benefit from showing sales, you should consider getting a bar code from the Uniform Code Council® (www.uc-council.org). Tina Broad adds:

> *The whole SoundScan thing is a bit overstated for indie bands. If you want to build your business by getting some kind of buy-in from a label or distributor, it's important as one sales verification tool that the labels take notice of. But most indie bands are precluded from SoundScan membership in the first place if they're a one-act setup. They say you have to be a multi-act label to be a member. We pleaded our case with SoundScan on the basis that our own label had multiple releases, a very strong sales record even though the sales were all BROTHER, and we'd been in business continuously for more than five years, so they made an exception. But they're not set up yet to accept reports on our web sales. Whatever SoundScan publishes as BROTHER's sales figures*

is an incomplete picture of our sales. We've let go of the emotional attachment to SoundScan reporting. We'll still report on big festival sales, but I'm not sure it's got a whole lot of value to us at this stage.

SoundScan has a system for reporting on-site sales at gigs, but as Broad said, they don't allow labels with only one artist to use it. Sometimes you can go through your distributor, or if you co-op with other labels, you can apply under the umbrella name you create. If you may license your music to other labels, consider getting an ISRC (International Recording Standard Code). DJ Minx discovered its importance:

> *When I signed a license deal with a record label in NYC and they asked for my ISRC code, I didn't know what it was or why I would need one. When I found out that this code is very important in receiving royalties and was used as a "fingerprint" for each track, I filled out an application for it on the RIAA website (Recording Industry Association of America; www.riaa.com). It's free, and well worth it! If you don't have an ISRC code already, I strongly suggest you log onto the website to get one today!*

CHAPTER 13

Buzzing Online

The Internet is a fantastic promotional tool—the biggest factor in why the playing field is leveling between majors and indies. It gives you unlimited access to millions of people around the world. You can do a lot online for free. Yes, it costs time. But if you're talent rich and pocket poor, this is where you can make moves. Kyler England says:

> *Because of the digital revolution (digital recording technology, the Internet, email, MP3s), artists can produce high-quality recordings on an independent budget, start touring and building a fan base, and stay connected with fans through a website and email mailing list. While I get frustrated with technology sometimes, I have no idea how independent artists made a go of it before the Internet and cell phones. I'd be lost without MapQuest®!*

ORGANIZING YOUR WEBSITE

If you want to be independently successful with your music, you MUST have a website. It's no longer optional. Alex Woodard says, "It's my portal to the world and one of the most, if not the most, important tools for me. Anybody, anywhere, anytime can listen to my music and buy my stuff. That is everything!" A website allows people from all over the world to find your music and support you. Zak Morgan says:

A website is like your online business card—direct someone there if it's an impressive-looking website with all your information. I book gigs with people who found my website. It's linked from other sites. You don't have to send anything—no postage. If someone goes there, they hear bits of your music and see a little video clip—boom! It's like a mini-showcase—a great tool.

I admit, when I consider an artist for an interview, I lose respect for them if I can't find them online. Your website is a showcase for your bio, photos, tour schedule, samples of your music, news, and much more. Beth Wood agrees:

I cannot emphasize enough the importance of having a good, informative website. You can keep people apprised of what you're doing without having to spend money on stamps. You make your music accessible to the world—they just have to find it! Keep good quality photos, bio, and touring info for promoters to use—save the time and money of having to send out promo packages. Post tour updates, info about your CDs, poems, recipes, whatever you want! This is a wonderful forum to let a little of your personality show. Many artists do a notes-from-the-road journal. Having a good website gives you a bit of legitimacy as an artist—it is worth the expense.

Canjoe says his website is critical for success—everything he does is promoted from it. He explains, "Instead of expensive promo packages, most promoters just go to my website for all details. Media use my website for news stories, photos, etc. You can't survive this business without a professional website."

Are you convinced yet? Most artists tout a website's value. Jennifer Marks agrees, "Mine is a great marketing tool. People get to see and hear you and then decide if they want to take it a step further and buy a CD." Robby Baier says it's not so much about CD sales. You want presence on the web. More and more people locally and internationally are looking to discover new music or book up-and-coming acts. They turn to the Internet to find you. When you're not around, your website is. Ezina Moore says:

My website is my personal salesperson who never needs a day off, a coffee or bathroom break. I stream my entire album so fans can hear it. It increases sales because they can hear the entire thing. I book three times as many gigs with my website. When I call a club in a new city, I send them to it. They hear my music, see my music video, or watch a clip from a live show. It is worth every penny. You gotta have a website with your name. It is the most important step in branding. Be creative so you can get the .com or .net. If it is not available, change the name or add another word.

But be careful: A less common name causes confusion. Moore implores you to get one that's direct. Corky McClerkin recommends, "Hostbaby is efficient and cost-effective for my website. I highly recommend them to anyone who doesn't know where to begin. As the consumer listens, he or she is provided with photos and information about the man behind the music." Hostbaby.com, created by Derek Sivers, the founder of CDBaby.com, is geared to a musician's needs. Some people park their site on someone else's, resulting in a long name with slashes. If you can't afford your own site, have your domain name forwarded to a cheaper site. It's a worthwhile investment. Gregory Abbott says, "My website is the backbone of my communication with fans. Making it work requires a real commitment. It must be advertised aggressively and kept interesting. That said, it can become a bulletin board, listening room, viewing room, store, and meeting place for fans to keep abreast of all your activities."

Make sure your website is organized and easy to navigate. I get frustrated quickly on a site that's so cutesy I can't figure out how to find things. Be clear. Update your site often, especially tour dates. Make contact info clear. I'm amazed at how many sites I go to with no way to get in touch. That's counterproductive! Zak Morgan advises:

> It's got to be easy to buy your product. People sometimes make their websites so artistic that you can't find your way around. Remember, this is not to show people how artsy you are but to get people to book you and buy your product. People shouldn't have to click on nine hundred different things just to find a phone number. I am always dumbfounded when people make it hard to get a hold of them. Ease—that's the most important thing. Make it easy to reach you and to understand what you do. Make it easy to navigate the site so that even an idiot can do it. Have samples of your music and video clips. Let people get a taste of you in an easy, quick way.

An electronic press kit on your site is essential! It's a link you can send to media, club promoters, A&R people, music supervisors, and others who want info on you. It allows them to read your bio, check your tour schedule, and download photos—all without speaking to you. If they're interested, they'll get in touch. Jim Merlis, President of Big Hassle Media, says having an electronic press kit makes it easier: "A music journalist gets hundreds of records a week. If you send a press kit, chances are they'll lose it." Holding onto your website address is easier. Photos should be 300 dpi, a downloadable quality. Have a large assortment, in black-and-white and in color. A great fringe benefit: no money for postage. Matt Allison adds, "It is like having a press kit available 24/7, especially living in South Africa, which is hours ahead of the U.S. My bio and tunes are available for people to peruse and listen to, mostly while I'm asleep on another continent."

Design your site with care. The more bells and whistles, the slower the download time. You don't want potential fans to leave because they have an old computer. There are sites I can't get onto without getting a new system, and I'm not ready for that. If you go to a higher-tech format, have another one in simple form. I love having a choice when the computer screen says, "Enter the latest macromedia or html." I prefer simple; others do, too. Make your site user-friendly. Add some personal touches. People should be able to get a sense of who you are from your site. Post lots of photos and add more regularly. Fans like to see you in different scenarios. It motivates them to return often. Have a place for people to sign up for your street team. Update it often, so people want to return. If you can't do it yourself, tell fans that you need help with your site.

Have music samples on your site, too. Many indies stream the whole album so people can hear it. When you stream music, people can't download it so it's the same as them hearing it on the radio. If they like it, they'll buy it. People are sick of spending CD prices to buy an album and only liking one song. If you believe in your music, let potential fans hear a lot, or even the whole album. Let your music be heard! Have sound files ready to send out if you get a request for one. Some magazines and radio stations accept them. DJ Minx says, "I send MP3 files to record labels that may be interested in licensing my product. I send mixes to various Internet radio stations. They set a time and date for it to air. It can be heard online around the world."

Create "private" pages with full songs that you can direct specific people to. Create a URL you can send only to people who need to hear your music. If you're nervous about protecting these pages, change the URL regularly. Instead of emailing large sound files, send an assortment of people—venue promoters, music supervisors, producers, record labels, and even special street team members—to a private page. They can request hard copies of what they might need.

SELLING CDS AND MERCHANDISE ONLINE

Musicians agree that the Internet offers a source of income from CD and merch sales. Corky McClerkin says: "Internet CD sales give me the opportunity to communicate with fans and artists like myself, introduce my music to people around the world, and learn how music helps in defining cultures." Make your music and merch available on the Internet. It gives you a presence, even if it doesn't sell millions. Danielle Egnew says:

Selling CDs on the Internet has been tremendous for us. More and more people shop on the Internet for everything, and music is part of that. I highly recommend you have some sort of Internet storefront, for both CDs and products. It can never hurt when someone is surfing and shopping late at night and they have their Visa card burning a hole in their pocket!

Jennifer Marks says, "Some months are great and some are slow, like any retail store." While most artists don't rely solely on the Internet for sales, they all agree it supplements the other ways they sell CDs. Not everyone buys at gigs. If fans have your URL, they can order from home. George Baum says Lost And Found's Internet sales have really picked up. He adds:

> *Those sales augment our current sales, rather than provide anything approaching a healthy income. We think of our Internet sales as a means to catch the folks who would otherwise fall through the cracks. Our hope is that in the future, our Internet sales will continue to increase. We do everything through our website. The company we use to process the orders is called Verisign. We're very happy with how it all works, and our website sales amounted to about six percent of our total gross last year.*

Some artists prefer to take credit card orders directly. Lorraine Ferro advises setting up a PayPal.com account or similar system, such as CCNow.com, that accepts credit cards. Ferro says, "If you sell CDs or do any work in which people would rather pay you with their credit card, you'll need an account like this, or miss the opportunity to get paid." But most artists prefer to sell through links to online music stores. Jennie DeVoe has PayPal on her website and sells on CDBaby.com and Amazon.com. It's good to cover all bases. DeVoe thinks it's great, explaining:

> *I've seen sales from Italy to Japan to the Netherlands. The Internet is so valuable in this way. I'm actually still on a learning curve to take much more advantage of what it has to offer. My website is beneficial in many ways. I usually have table cards at all of my shows with my website on it. If people can't buy a CD at your show, they may track you down later on the website and order online or just check your tour dates so they can see you again.*

PROFILE

George Baum is half of Lost And Found, a Christian duo who started playing together when they were 14 years old and developed what has become their unique sound, called "speedwood" (it's like speed metal but with no metal, just wood). They released their first album in 1980 and have worked their music full-time from 1990 on. They have released more than 20 independent albums and tour the country playing churches and youth groups.

Even if you take credit cards on your site, get your music into online stores, too, for more exposure. No such thing as selling in too many places! Artists have mixed feelings about working with Amazon. Try it and see if it works for you. The one that I consider essential is CD Baby. I can't include all the positive statements from artists about this site and its founder, Derek Sivers. Sivers is a former indie musician and caters to the needs of artists who want to get their music out online. Beth Wood says that working with CD Baby has been a very positive experience. She explains how it works:

> There is a thirty-five-dollar setup fee for each CD. They sell them for whatever price you decide. CD Baby keeps four dollars, and you keep the rest. This is a significant resource for many reasons. It takes the work of filling orders out of your hands. It is also an online community, with the folks at CD Baby and other musicians sharing tips with each other. And it gets your music in front of folks that might not otherwise hear it. Many people tell me they were just browsing the site, found my music, and bought it. This gives me hope—it means there really are people who are seeking out good music. I KNEW IT!

The Internet can make you an international artist. Rachael Sage says, "A lot of people from overseas order my CDs through CD Baby." People in foreign countries (see Chapter 19) are bigger indie music lovers than Americans. They know they can get great CDs and great service by cruising CD Baby. Ezina Moore adds, "CD Baby has become the industry standard. I make many contacts worldwide through this website." Music supervisors also cruise it, looking for music for their projects (see Chapter 16). Robby Baier says, "I placed a song in a major commercial for thousands of dollars, just because someone found me on CD Baby." Having your music on the site brings many opportunities for artists who have THE GOODS. Lorraine Ferro adds, "Through CD Baby I have been played on XM satellite radio, placed on iTunes and other websites that pay to download songs, entered into contests, and gone on tour. So far, among music-related websites, only CDBaby.com has done all those things successfully."

Adam Richman has his CD exclusively on Awarestore.com, an online store run by Aware Records. Music is screened for quality before it's sold. Richman says, "A lot of artists sell their CDs exclusively on there. It has a great built-in college-age audience. All my mailing list members buy it there. They have a Top 10 Sellers list. I got on it right away and haven't left it. I'm advertised as a Top 10 Seller and everyone that comes to the site sees that." Another online music model, iTunes, has blown up fast while other models stumble. According to Alex Luke, Director of Music Programming and Label Relations for iTunes:

From my perspective it's the result of having a full-service music service with the collection management and the music store embedded in the sort of jukebox collection management. For a consumer, you can burn CDs, move music to your IPOD, build playlists, and buy music. A lot of the other services have really complex models and don't have a clear portable device. From day one, iTunes was built to address all of these issues.

Luke says iTunes frequently works with unsigned musicians and promotes them on the site. He says the best way to get your music sold there is through what they call a "digital aggregator," such as CD Baby. You get paid through CD Baby, not iTunes. Luke explains, "They provide the minimal services of a record label to get artists familiar with the digital world. It's a means to connect the dots for us. If you're an artist starting out looking to make a dent in the digital music space, that's a great way in." Digital aggregators inform iTunes weekly about artists who are touring, gigging, or getting radio airplay so iTunes can take note of them. Sometimes iTunes works with an unsigned artist. Luke explains, "Someone on my programming staff will find a band, bring them in, we'll feature them on the service. Frequently we will route them to one of these companies, a digital aggregator. It's the fastest way in." iTunes features artists on the site. You can send iTunes press material to attract promotion; it has an editorial staff that goes through that. Luke says to keep things convenient, you can send an email with your bio information. If you have a West Coast gig, they may even check you out.

Explore every option. Downloading music will continue to escalate as a format of choice. That benefits indies. It's much cheaper to sell that way. Find your own path to Internet success as more opportunities open up. Luke sees electronic sales continuing to grow, explaining:

In the past eighteen months it's gone from almost zero to nearly two percent of the U.S. music business. I think the opportunity is tremendous. It's definitely shifting to where it's going to be a bigger percentage of the business. When we started, the concept of music programming wasn't even there. We tried to put a lot of platforms in place to promote developing artists. I think within the next year you'll start to see bands getting their big break online. That hasn't happened to date, but we're getting to a place where it will happen.

Share information with other indies. The indie community will be big in the future, so get your music out wherever you can. This is the time to establish your presence and develop relationships. You'll be ahead of many others when the indie biz explodes.

ONLINE PROMOTIONAL OPPORTUNITIES

There are endless promotional opportunities online. Robby Baier advises, "Have a strong presence on the Internet. Make it easy for people to find you." Some artists say they spent many hours exploring at the beginning. Do the same and you'll learn the best ones for promoting your music. Danielle Egnew says:

> I place our Pope Jane website and my Danielle Egnew site on a host of web rings and music-related message boards found on many record labels. When Pope Jane started, I spent about six hours a day, five days a week, listing us with indie music directories and websites. The key to doing anything on the Internet is investing time in it. Mostly, Internet promotion has to do with forging relationships through the written word. When I lived in Montana, I'd be amazed at how many people I'd meet in L.A. not only knew who I was, but I knew them—we'd been friends online for months! There is plenty you can do for free—simply spend time to ticky-tick on your keyboard and chat about your project or your band, wherever it is appropriate.

Once your website is ready, visit sites that might be helpful to you. Visual says the Internet is Little Egypt's biggest research tool in finding information for shows, getting contracts, and marketing: "We have a spreadsheet with three hundred sites. I put our music up on as many as possible for people to download and listen to. You never know. We can't send CDs to everyone in the world. So we put the music out there and if someone listens to it, that's a bonus." You'd be foolish not to own *The Indie Bible*, a huge book listing most sites related to music—the ultimate web resource. It contains thousands of e-zines that review music, radio stations, websites for non-Internet radio stations, magazines, etc., and much more for all genres. If you want to cover every avenue for marketing your music on the Internet, this book will take you there. It's reasonably priced and updated regularly. Israel Vasquetelle (*Insomniac*) says:

> There are many radio shows and websites that broadcast shows on the Internet. The better ones are the real stations that have an Internet community, like college stations. They have a real world presence, with fans that tune in. We track more than two hundred radio shows in the U.S. every week and publish a national chart for independent hip-hop on college, Internet, and community radio with a few mix shows. We list our reporters and the stations on the website. A search on Google would get that information.

Search for the best online stations for your music. Look for e-magazines to review your CD, and link the reviews to your site. List URLs for your reviews or articles in print magazines. Jennifer Marks says she tries to get interviews, reviews, features, and anything she can get, on any site she can get on, adding, "It is a matter of spreading the word. People who are interested in independent music seek it out. You never know where someone will find you." Most artists agree that the more websites with something about you and your music, the better. Ezina Moore says she swaps links with musicians and buys ads on sites geared towards women.

An email newsletter is another great tool. George Baum says, "The trick is to drive traffic to our website, so people remember to check when we're coming to their area and buy any new items. That's where the bimonthly newsletter comes in. We announce every two months through an email to our entire mailing list." Newsletters should be personal. They provide a connection between you and your fans. Write in a warm, friendly tone that makes fans feel like friends. Include added-value items—useful info, artists you like, etc.—to make people want to read it. I put out *Daylle's News & Resources* every two months (subscribe by sending an email with your name, city, and state to daylle@daylle.com). I write articles and include interviews with artists and industry pros, and I also throw in some self-promotion. When you have a good newsletter, people want to subscribe. You can promote what's going on to a ready-made audience. A mailing list is gold to an indie artist. Keep in touch with people on your mailing list in whatever way works for you. Matt Allison says, "My mailing list is a huge help. Keeping folks up to date on my movements with the click of a button is invaluable."

A good database program organizes your biz. Using one for your mailing list enables you to sort your fans into different fields, such as location. The Indie Band Manager (www.indiebandmanager.com) is an inexpensive database program created specifically for musicians. It helps you book your tours and has other useful functions specific to the music industry. You also have the option of buying a huge mailing list of student activities people who book music at colleges, as well as a huge list of PR people. Stay organized or you'll get lost in all

PROFILE

Matt Allison is an independent folk/pop artist from Cape Town, South Africa. He began in 1995 and has had three songs chart in the Top 10 on many stations including a No. 1 song on the largest regional station in Cape Town. Allison quit his nine-to-five job in 2003 and did a national tour of South Africa, followed by a tour of New Zealand to promote his latest record, licensed there and in the U.S. He's the only international artist with an endorsement deal with Mayes Guitars. Allison has toured the U.S. and U.K. several times by networking on the Internet.

the Internet stuff that comes in. Organize your email folders to separate the variety of emails: fan letters, biz stuff, personal, etc. All emails about your music should be answered promptly—and I mean PROMPTLY. Do your business right! If you wait to respond to someone from the press or a club, you may lose a good opportunity. Fans want to hear from you, too. George Baum has a program to notify folks about concerts:

> By signing up on our mailing list, people receive email announcements telling them about concerts in their area. We invested significant resources on this aspect of our website, and it seems to have paid off. The fellows hired to design our site developed a program that merges the ZIP codes in our mailing list with the ZIP codes of upcoming concerts; it sends out an email every two weeks to folks within a one-hundred-mile radius of each concert.

CREATING AN ONLINE COMMUNITY

It's extremely valuable to have message boards, chat rooms, and other vehicles for fans to communicate. If at all possible, have one on your site. Matt Allison says, "Since I added a message board, I feel more hands-on with my fans. I regularly post replies and even get topics started by asking questions." When your fans interact with one another, passion about your music is fueled. As you join in discussions, they love you more. Fans meet on your site and work together to push your music. They meet at gigs, encourage one another to promote you, and keep returning to your site to chat. That's a biggie! The more they visit, the better chance they'll eventually buy merch. They'll tell friends, too. Mary Gauthier says there's a discussion group on her website where they post her set lists and discuss other details: "Talking on the discussion groups allows them to meet each other, so there's a *community* of people who like this music."

An online community can be your biggest source of grassroots promotion. Search for news and email groups that might attract potential fans, and then join them. Visit websites for popular artists in your genre, or one of the thousands-plus groups that exist, such as those at Yahoo.com. These sites offer opportunities to network and get answers to questions related to marketing your music. Once you establish a presence, talk about your music and include your website. Every group is different—spend time and gauge how soon you can bring your music up. Some are friendlier than others. Allison has toured the world from South Africa by developing relationships in these groups. He explains:

> I shared who I am, where I am from, and that my music is similar to the artist whose board I posted on. I often used topic titles that got attention, like "What's up with all this folk music anyway?" on a singer/songwriter board

read by those that love folk music. That title prompted them to read my post. Many folks just listened out of sheer curiosity, and somehow it worked. The music kept them. I got emails from indie music magazines that wanted to review my album. One of them asked if I had thought of playing in New York, their base. I hadn't, but for the first time I thought about touring the U.S. They helped book the first few shows and it snowballed from there.

Allison continued networking in groups and made good friends who helped in other cities. Of course, you must have THE GOODS or it won't work. If you do, you can find folks all over the country and the world to swap gigs. Preech says, "If I'm going to California, I'll go into a California chat room and say I'm coming to town." The possibilities are endless. Ask for recommendations. Explore the Internet for music forums with lots of people and something related to your genre. It's time-consuming, but participating can reap many new fans. Danielle Egnew adds, "Since the Internet is a free tool, I encourage you to find Internet communities that you like to chat in, whether it is a music-related site or a rock-climbing site—whatever community fits you. Share your passion with others in the group. You never know who is interested in what you do as an artist."

Check out the MySpace network (www.myspace.com), a web portal that creates communities around shared interests. It allows artists to connect with fans and develop a social network around common interests. It's used for many interests, but music is very prominent. You get your own space to upload your music, promote shows, and be accessible for new fans to find your music. The best part? It's free! Visit and bring your fans with you.

● ● ● ● **CHAPTER 14** ● ● ● ●

Marketing Your Talents for Cash

Y a gotta pay your bills! You can't eat passion. It takes time to earn a good living. Smart indies find ways to supplement their income with their musical talents. Even if a gig isn't your preferred direction, making money from an aspect of music is better than a day job that's not at all related to it. Why sell insurance when you can teach guitar lessons? Weddings may not be your favorite venue, but you can earn good money at them. Jennifer Marks says, "I did demos, played at parties, sang on jingles, and anything else to help pay bills and meet people. I did not get too wrapped up in [doing these things]—I didn't want to lose focus. But if it pays the bills, you do what you have to."

BRANCHING OUT

Music is everywhere. There are tons of opportunities if you look for them. Indies get creative about using their talents to generate income. Corky McClerkin says that while playing jazz is his preference, about 30 percent of his time goes to supplementing his income by performing for weddings and parties, as a session player, and at various other gigs. Danielle Egnew agrees:

I have made lots of cash off of various things—singing at funerals, weddings, session work, writing for others, working as a producer for other artists. I owned a jingle company and composed and sold jingles to many people. I've even played for tips on a sidewalk. There are a lot of ways to make money while using your gifts.

Alternative income sources are opportunities to expand your talent. Clare Cooper says, "I do music copying (using Finale software on the computer) for theater auditions and work as musical director for cabaret shows. I've done lots of unusual gigs and am always amazed at and appreciative of opportunities that come my way." Lorraine Ferro sings on songwriting demos for other people. She's also sung jingles and done voice-overs. Ferro makes a good living using her talents in a variety of scenarios while pursuing her artist career. She adds:

> *I've sung in all kinds of cover bands, doing weddings, corporate parties, clubs, and even was lead singer in a band on the Spirit of New York cruise line. I've written songs for others. . . . I have a trio that plays Caesars in Atlantic City. I'm producing many indie artists and have a voice-over manager. I sing backup regularly for a number of artists, including touring overseas with Ritchie Blackmore and his band Blackmore's Night, and doing spot gigs for celebs like Wayne Brady. I do session work on CDs and sing for songwriters who want someone to sing their songs in a live show. I have been the voice singing "as Celine Dion" for karaoke CDs! I do a lot of artist consulting. I prepare bands for big shows and contests and travel with them to the performance to coach them right into taking first place!*

Whew! Ferro illustrates that there are many ways to make money. Barbara Tucker has worked with and written songs for several signed acts; one album went double platinum. She's also hosted parties, and with her husband produced the first gospel/house music album featuring church singers. Tucker is busy since leaving her label deal. She does production, she still gigs, and she does the voice of C&C Music Factory on their tours. Justin Lassen's original direction to become an artist led to him becoming a remixer for acts such as Nine Inch Nails, David Bowie, Madonna, Linkin Park, and many more: "It's funny how life can do that to you. You want to get from Point A to Point B, but end up going to Points C, D, and E, then maybe eventually back to Point B. The experiences, résumé, and friendships I create by giving my heart to a project or venture are invaluable." Seek and ye shall find!

GETTING THE JOBS

How do you get music-related work? You ask! Keep your eyes open. Let people know you're open to alternative musical work. *Network like crazy.* Justin Lassen says, "I worked in a music store and met really cool people, some with connections. I also sent demo CDs to strategic places that my music would fit well with." Lorraine Ferro says networking helped get most work, explaining, "I can't name one job I got that hasn't in some way come because someone recommended or vouched for me. I strongly believe in the power of a good team—we cannot be successful alone." The more networking you do, the more people know you. The more you get your name out, the more people think of you. Drummer Bobby Borg, author of *The Musician's Handbook* (Billboard Books), says he never waited for someone to do it for him. He got his name out as a professional drummer and played often with other people's bands. Borg says:

> I did a mass campaign to let people know about my drumming. I put together a very small brochure about myself and what I did, and put it under the door of every college dormitory room in Boston. I mailed the brochure to all the teachers, too. Finally, someone needed a drummer for a wedding. The person who had hired me recommended me for another wedding. Once I got the first gig, people referred me. It grew fast. I made myself available to perform on demos in the area, for free. I went to clubs and told acts if they ever needed a band, I would put it together for them, rehearse them, and play on their demo for free. I got lots of recording experience from this, which led to a great demo. It all snowballed. You can't wait for someone to hold a magic wand over your head and say "Voilà! We're going to take you from Point A to Point B." You have to create some momentum.

Market your talents if you want work. Create a brochure and leave it in studios, at music organizations, at music seminars, and anywhere else you think of. There are agencies that book gigs you might not have access to.

Kevin Kinyon runs Gigmasters (www.gigmasters.com), an online entertainment service that connects performers with people wanting to hire entertainment. He explains:

> Different types of people look for entertainment: festival planners, club owners, brides, corporate owners who want music for office parties. If you're

PROFILE

Clare Cooper is a singer/songwriter who works on an assortment of musical projects, independently earning a living from her music since 1997. She produces for other artists, writes award-winning songs, and has regular club gigs. Cooper was a musical director substitute for "Tony n' Tina's Wedding," Musical Director for cabaret shows at clubs including Don't Tell Mama and Rose's Turn, and Assistant Musical Director for "I Love You, You're Perfect, Now Change" in Memphis.

flexible about the types of events you'd perform at, we can bring you customers who allow you the opportunity to get paid to play. We open a lot of avenues you haven't considered or known about. Customers do a search on our site and get accurate results for exactly what they look for. They can listen to audio samples and watch a video, if that's been provided. They can read about pay rates. Through our site, bands can do online what they did offline, sending out press kits and overnighting a CD. We generate lots of leads for the majority of our entertainers, which turn into bookings, which hopefully turn into longer careers than they might have otherwise.

Gigmasters connects acts with people who might book them. If you're interested and agree on a fee, the customer can click on a link that books you, pay any deposit agreed to and forward it to you—or it can be booked by phone. You set your fee, and Gigmasters charges a five percent finder's fee to customers who hire their bands—the only fee for a booking. There's a yearly membership fee to join, and all memberships have a 30-day money back guarantee. Great cover bands and soloists do best, but Kinyon says almost everyone gets bookings. How much can you make playing alternative gigs? He says:

I've seen as low as seventy-five to one hundred bucks. Some corporate planners are just handed a blank check to find great entertainment. A solo guitarist, who might only make one hundred to one hundred and fifty bucks for an hour or two, can do really well. Musicians put a pay range on their web page. Corporations can go for up to four thousand dollars for a good cover band. We book about five hundred-plus gigs a month in the U.S. and Canada.

Kinyon says almost 55 percent of the bookings are from corporations and weddings.

If you have THE GOODS, let people know about you, and are open to new options, you have the best chance of earning a side income in music. There are many agencies that book these kinds of gigs in a variety of ways. A few side gigs a month can pay your basic expenses. Then you can devote the rest of your time to your passion!

TEACHING

Many people want to learn how to play an instrument or improve their vocals. If you have skills and feel you can guide others in improving theirs, consider giving instruction in your area of expertise. Bobby Borg says, "A lot of artists or independent bands teach private lessons. I gave drum lessons for forty dollars an hour—all cash! I was a twenty-three-year-old kid, so that was an amazing situation." Once you teach a few students, word gets out. Teaching is part of how Suzanne Teng earns a living. She says, "I teach private lessons and do workshops for percussion. We also do workshops at schools." Lorraine Ferro has coached artists for many years and loves teaching. She explains:

> I love the environment and watching students "get" who they really are, beyond the stuff they thought was the limit to them. I teach privately, for the Songwriters Hall of Fame, and give seminars on creating for artists. One thing begets another. Performances garner me students; those students garner me more students. Some tell peers that I am a good singer, and I get calls to do demos for them.

Clare Cooper says that singers she played for approached her for vocal lessons. She saw it as a good chance to branch out into another way of making money that she can keep doing throughout her life. She explains:

> I see a lot of singers making mistakes that are very easy to correct, and I enjoy helping them with their performance skills and choosing material. I get my vocal coaching clients through personal referrals and people who approach me at gigs. A lot don't follow through, but the relationships that develop with the ones that do are really rewarding.

Cari Cole adds:

> A singer/songwriter/performer needs to support their own career with other work that brings in money. One hundred and twenty days on the road along with recording and promotional expenses can end up taking money out of one's pocket! Teaching voice at my Manhattan studio has been a way for me to support my music career and to give back through teaching, creating a community and network of musicians helping musicians. Besides, how cool is it to teach someone and watch them become a star!

SESSION WORK AND JINGLES

People hire good musicians and vocalists to do backup vocals or play an instrument in the studio and on tour. Jennie DeVoe says she knew she wanted to sing and make a living at it, so she does session work in singing and voice-over, lead and backup. DeVoe enjoys having this income source:

> I worked in a studio after college. They did music and post-scoring for commercials for radio and television. I poured coffee and tried to be in the right place at the right time so I could make money doing something I was good at

and loved. I offered myself every time there was something I could do. Little by little I made a pretty good living at singing and talking for commercials. I quit my day job, and commercials are still the best supplemental income to writing and singing my own music that I have. Commercial work is a horrible thought for some artists—all the more work for me! My living is made solely by being musical. I'm grateful and don't feel above it at all. I got as close to music as I could by taking a job that many people might not take.

DeVoe's attitude exemplifies what I encourage: It's better to earn a living doing something musical than to have a nonmusical day job. Marly Hornik says she's done session work—backup or lead singing on someone else's track—to supplement her income. She got it by networking, adding, "It's not something I pursue actively but if it turns up, I'm happy to take it. It can pay decent money." Songwriters also hire singers to do the vocals on their demos. Get the word out that you're available. Lorraine Ferro has done that for years and says taking her first songwriting workshop was the driving force. When other people in the class heard Ferro singing on her demos, they asked her to do theirs. After a teacher asked if she'd do *her* demo, Ferro began doing them for famous songwriters.

One resource for getting side gigs is Musicians Contact Service (www.musicianscontact.com). For a reasonable fee, they provide a musician referral service, connecting individual musicians and singers with people who need them—mainly working bands. In order to do session work, you must be very good at singing or playing your instrument, including being able to learn a song quickly and giving people what they need on the spot. It takes a good ear. How do you get session work? Bobby Borg says you get it by *doing* it. He explains:

> *As strange as it sounds, I've noticed that people get session work from playing on records. I tried to play with many different people so eventually producers knew that I could cut the job. Producers go from one project to the next. My goal was to get to know as many as possible so when they needed a session guy or drummer to come in, they called me. You can become a successful session player by making yourself as open to recording as many up-and-coming artists as possible.*

Borg says it won't hurt to do the first projects for free in order to get your name out. Create a professional-looking flyer or brochure to make a good impression. Leave it in studios. Send it to producers. The more work you do, the more people will hear about you. Clare Cooper does session work for people she's worked with or through referrals. She adds, "It's taken a long time to build relationships and get to know a lot of people. I'm still working on it." Begin today! You never know who may know someone. Let folks know your availability. Ferro substitutes for performers through word of mouth. This can turn into steady gigs. She says, "Every session or band singer needs a sub once in a while. They don't want flack from the club or bandleader, so they have a list of people they trust to be good in these situations. I got lots of steady gigs through subbing for someone first, until either they left or the band was looking to expand."

A musician can also go on the road as a sideman or backup vocalist. It helps pay bills and develop more contacts. Anton Sanko says he always wanted to find a way to make a living from music so he could avoid a regular job. Being a sideman seemed like a romantic job to him. In college he became obsessed with electronic music, used his student loan to buy a Prophet 5 synthesizer, and got tons of work because few people had them. He kept buying electronic equipment as it came out and became known for specializing in it. His friends worked on Suzanne Vega's first record, and he explains, "I heard she was looking for a keyboard player. I auditioned by doing an arrangement for 'Luka,' which ended up being the version she used. I toured with her for a long time, produced some of her records, and cowrote with her for about six years."

Sanko advises, "Focus on doing something that's unique to you. You also need a personality that helps you get along with a lot of people—that's seventy percent of the job. Being in tight quarters on the road with people you hardly know is a breeding ground for horror if you can't get along. A nice thing about being on tour is you don't pay for anything." Borg was drummer for a band that opened for Warrant. When Warrant's drummer left, Borg was asked to sub. It was supposed to be temporary, but he was asked to join after the band saw how good he was. Borg played all over the U.S., Japan, and Mexico. He advises:

PROFILE

Anton Sanko was one of the first musicians to grasp the concept of sampling technology. He soon became a highly sought-after keyboard player and programmer, which led to touring as Musical Director and Arranger for Suzanne Vega. After years of touring and producing popular music, Sanko decided to pursue his original passion for creating music. He has since provided scores for Trimark Pictures, Shooting Gallery, Clinica Estetico, Lot 47, and First Look films, and in television for Harpo Productions/ABC, HBO, Discovery, USA, PBS, and the Learning Channel. He has also written and produced songs for popular movies such as *Philadelphia* and *For Love or Money*.

Invite as many people to your shows as possible, including managers, producers, etc. When you open for another band, get to know them. When a band opens for you, become friends with them. Every time you play, make sure people come to see you play. In the future, if these people need someone, they'll call you. Many people just go out and play their gigs without thinking about getting work in the future. You definitely have to use the job that you have currently to get further work.

Another avenue for session work is performing on jingles. Session singers and musicians are hired for recordings in the advertising business. Rachael Sage says when she moved to New York, she wrote many jingles, and did voice-overs and some singing for them. Sage made contacts by meeting tons of people and being friendly. You don't have to live in a big city to do jingles. Local businesses run TV commercials, too. Someone performs on them—why not you? Send your brochure to businesses that might do a TV or radio ad. Ask around. But you have to have THE GOODS—you rarely get the song beforehand, so your skills must be sharp. Eric Kaye, Creative Director/Executive Producer for The Lodge, says, "You have to be able to read cold and nail something in the studio within one or two takes. Not too many people can do it." Bernie Drayton, President of Three Tree Productions, hires session singers and musicians, and he advises:

You have to come in and sing in tune, in time, and interpret. When you come to me, you've got to sing that song like you've been singing it for six months—to get what the lyrics say, to have the feeling and attitude we want. I want you to do that in thirty minutes. If you're a musician, really learn your skills. There are many unprepared people—more than I've ever seen.

But it's worth a shot. Producers say there's a lot more money in singing on commercials than writing them. Drayton says, "Musicians get paid musician scale for playing it. If you sing, you get paid by SAG (Screen Actors Guild) or AFTRA (American Federation of Television and Radio Artists). If you're going to be in it for a length of time, you should be an AFTRA singer." How do you get this work? Many of the producers for advertising are on the Association of Music Producers website (AMP; www.ampnow.com). Kaye says:

To make it as a session musician, meet people who hire musicians. Develop your name as a hot musician and people will hear of it. Singers: Call all the music producers. Bombard them. Have a good tape, no more than ten minutes. Most reels are five minutes, preferably with thirty- or sixty-second snippets of various things. Always put on your strongest stuff, not what you think people look for—what shows you in your best possible way. If you're good at jazz, don't try to show you can do rock. It will sound crappy to those who do it all the time. Don't try to be versatile. Sell your strongest music.

How do you approach producers? Kaye says, "Send me a demo. It's tough to break in. Most producers use the same twenty or thirty guys." Kevin Joy, president of Joy Productions, says, "If you think you've got THE GOODS, call somebody listed on AMP. If you call first, they may listen. I listen to everything. I never know when I'll find that next terrific artist. If you're a singer, send what shows a variety of styles and your strengths—either snippets, a whole song, or a CD."

MUSIC PRODUCTION

Some indies produce other artists. Robby Baier accumulated lots of audio gear and put together a project studio in his basement, producing singer/songwriters and bands. He adds, "I get all my work through word of mouth and musicians I meet at music conferences. I love the work—it allows me to be creative, cowrite material, and invent arrangements. I'm honing my craft as an engineer at the same time. I charge fifty dollars an hour for my services." Producing is another of Lorraine Ferro's skills. She says, "Most people ask me to produce their projects because I was their coach and they trust my ear. When a student comes to me with a band rehearsal tape, I can't help telling them when I think they aren't serving their music or artistry."

You need to have a good ear to produce. Don't just go after this work for money. You need to be good at it! Clare Cooper produces through relationships with people she's worked with. She learned to produce by taking a production class taught by someone she admired:

We participated in recording and producing two songs by an artist [the teacher] selected, with her explaining every step of the way. I met lots of great

PROFILE

Justin Lassen wears many hats: composer, singer, remixer, producer. He's worked with dozens of celebrities, industry people, and companies. He's released albums independently and done studio work and production for dozens of artists. He says his remixing and producing has gotten him on the "good list" of most respected producers and companies in the film, music, and game industries. He's remixed for top artists, including David Bowie, Madonna, and Linkin Park. Lassen is getting a lot of PR in top magazines for his own music as he expands his career as an artist. He's toured Europe and is making waves.

musicians, some of whom I'm still in touch with. This gave me a solid foundation and raised my level of awareness when I recorded from that point on. By the time I did my own CD, I was comfortable in the studio and knew how to get what I wanted.

Justin Lassen released several independent projects before he became known for his remixing skills. Composer Robert Miles hired him to remix, and Lassen did such a great job that he ended up on all kinds of producer lists at various labels, management firms, and rosters. Remix jobs for top acts came in faster than he could accept them. He says:

In a few years, I did dozens of high-quality remixes for independent and major artists around the world. My remixes generally add about seventy-five percent original material and create an entirely new composition, while retaining the heart and essence of the original. I sacrificed a lot of the time to work on my own music to work on other people's music. To this day I have had to turn down many remixes because I can't handle so many gigs at once.

While he didn't choose to be a remixer, Lassen says that hard work paid off in many ways. People know the popular artists, hear his work, and the buzz gets around that his versions were produced at the highest levels—at times, better than the original version. His remixes are heavily talked about and pirated on the web. He gets fan mail and complimentary quotes and reviews from some of the industry's best producers, A&R people, publications, writers, labels, and artists around the world. He's used it all to advance his own career as an indie artist. If you want to pursue a production avenue, Lassen advises:

It's most important to make the client happy. I make sure to turn my work in on time as well. If they can depend on you, you can depend on them. Being reliable goes a very long way in this business of "talkers." Give the client something a thousand times better than what they expected and your buzz grows very quickly. Always turn in quality work that you are proud of—not generic demos and crappy catalogues of dozens of tracks.

WEDDINGS AND BAR MITZVAHS

Weddings and bar mitzvahs pay good money. Usually, you're expected to play covers and may even get a set list from the host. Many musicians scorn this type of work. But Ezina Moore says, "I worked for one year as a singer in a wedding band. It gave me an opportunity to keep my chops up while I worked on my original material." And it pays bills! Kevin Kinyon says that fees on his site range from $1,500 to $3,000 for a four- or five-piece band. Their average wedding pays about $2,000. That's a lot more than most bands make at a club.

Doing weddings are beneficial beyond just the money. Kevin Kinyon says, "It can make you tighter as a band. Bands can get to the next level simply because they are gigging a lot. It keeps you playing—pretty much the most important thing." Any chance to play for an audience hones your skills. It also gets you seen by a more varied group than usual. That can lead to something more. Bobby Borg says it made him a more versatile musician and drummer, and he got to play for all kinds of interesting people, like the Kennedys: "People gave me their cards. From that perspective, playing weddings was very helpful. It was also good to play lots of different kinds of music. As a result, more people found out about me and I started to do sessions."

CHARITY PROJECTS

While I believe that you should be paid to perform once you've proven yourself, getting involved with charities can be beneficial at the start. Suzanne Teng says her band started when organizers of a charity asked her to put one together and play at their concert. She says, "The community was fully supportive of my growth and invited us to perform at different events. It's really grown from there." Her career launched because she volunteered. What goes around, comes around! Beth Wood suggests you consider playing for free in some situations: "Benefit shows can be wonderful for word of mouth and exposure to new audiences. Most benefits handle publicity (free for you!) and draw a diverse audience, and most are more than willing to let you sell your merch so you won't walk away empty-handed."

Tina Broad says, "We performed three songs with the Malibu Ballet in 2002 at a charity gala for the Starlight Children's Foundation. It gives us a story to go to fans and press with, keeps the promotional momentum going, and helps keep our name out there." It's nice to give back when you can. Robby Baier was perturbed at spending cuts in school art programs and wanted to help locally. He and his band started a not-for-profit organization called STAR (Students Teach the Art of Recording; www.musiclink.com/star), which is committed to teaching recording at local high schools. They raised money, bought thousand-dollar recording studios for six high schools, and organized a tour to present it at an assembly concert. Baier says:

> Besides the great opportunity for the teens to record their own music in after-school programs with the school's studio, Melodrome was now a household name in all six high schools. We sold lots of CDs after each show, signed notebooks, CDs, T-shirts, etc., and had hundreds of new names on our email list. We started doing underage shows and noticed a big increase in

local following. It would be great if other independent bands did this with their high schools.

Go out and find your own cause. Some musicians donate a small portion of CD sales to a charity. Some charities even pay a little. Dorothy Potter loves writing for Songs of Love Foundation (www.songsoflove.org). You write very personalized songs for terminally ill children. The first five are free, and then you get $75 per song. It's not much money for writing and recording one, but if you have a home studio, you can make some cash while doing something worthwhile. You get the child's name and what needs to be included in the lyrics—their likes, etc.—and in return the child gets a CD with their personal song. I advise you to try this—it's a gift of love through your music! Potter says, "It's a beautiful thing. And my song-writing chops have been very sharpened by doing songs every month. I love music for healing. These are chronically ill children. Songs of Love is a foundation that is straight from the heart."

CHAPTER 15

Songwriting Options

There are many ways to make money from songwriting. When you know how to find opportunities, songwriting can be the most lucrative part of the music industry. This chapter has an overview of how you can make money from songwriting. The next chapter is devoted more specifically to how you can license your music to films, television, advertising, videos, and more.

PROTECTING YOURSELF

Why write songs if you don't protect them? They're your property, unless you give someone the rights to them IN WRITING. File copyrights for your songs. Beth Wood strongly advises making time to protect your creative works, explaining, "It is true that there is a common law copyright, but this does not carry the same weight in a legal dispute as a registered one. It is fairly inexpensive to register your works. You can register a whole CD as one project." The U.S. Copyright Office website (www.copyright.gov) has forms and instructions.

A song consists of the melody and the lyrics. The sound recording is the actual recording of that song. Jeanne DaSilva, who's represented songwriters for licensing songs, says, "Publishing relates to the composition itself. The master is the recording of that composition." If you write and record your own song, you own the composition *and* the master recording. If you record someone else's song, you own the recording but don't get songwriting royalties. In that case, you can license, sell, or transfer the right to use that recording to someone else, but DaSilva adds, "You can't grant them the right to use the composition. For that they must go to the original songwriter or representative."

Whoever creates the melody and lyrics owns the entire copyright. People may ask to put their name on your copyright for adding to the song. Producers often try to get a piece for their contribution. But arrangements and added music *are not* the song. Be careful about giving rights to someone not entitled to them. If you add someone's name to the copyright form, that person is an equal owner of the song, unless there's a separate written agreement stating the percentage he or she actually owns. I learned the hard way. Unable to play chords for my songs, I let the producer or engineer sign the copyright for helping. Two people signed for a small music contribution to my best song. Foolishly, I assumed they owned a small part. Wrong! Each of them owns as much as I do. I wrote the melody and lyrics, yet I only own one-third of the copyright! I'm listed as writing the lyrics, and the three of us are listed for the music. Yet ownership is split equally three ways because I had no separate agreement in writing. Don't share your copyright to show appreciation. Songwriting royalties are lucrative. A lawyer knows what's fair—be sure to ask.

Don't just assume that because you wrote a song and paid for the recording, you own the master. Wallace Collins, Esq., says there's a copyright in a sound recording that's separate from the copyright in the actual song. Protect yourself when you go into the studio. Producers and others involved in the recording can claim ownership of the sound recording unless you establish otherwise. When you work with a producer, spell out what he or she gets in a written agreement. Often, for a flat fee, the producer may waive ownership of the sound recording. A producer typically gets a royalty (an average of two to four percent) based on CD sales. Collins advises that you have an agreement in writing about who owns the master recording:

> There is a copyright in a sound recording separate and apart from the copyright in the underlying song. Just as cowriters of a song are co-owners of the song copyright, the collaborators on a sound recording could be co-owners under the copyright law. However, that is why most musicians and background singers are "work for hire" (pursuant to a written agreement), as are producers, even though the producer may also get a royalty. Each musician and background singer should sign a simple release or work-for-hire agreement. And there should be a document with the producer that makes it clear that regardless of what arrangement is made to pay the producer, the artist owns all right, title, and interest in the master.

Remember: in writing! If you collaborate with other songwriters, Lorraine Ferro advises having a written agreement between all parties. She says contracts for songwriting collaborations can be downloaded off the Internet or found in songwriting business books, and adds, "Use them, even if it feels uncomfortable. It feels horrible to me, too, but once it's signed, it feels great to get the work done and know you did a job that you are proud of AND you will get credit for doing it!"

Many people can represent your songs: music publishers, song pluggers, and people or companies that will market your songs for use in a variety of formats, including film, TV, advertising, and more. Don't be anxious to jump on an offer. There are many people who will sucker you if you let them. Bart Herbison, Executive Director of NSAI, says he's seen too many people get hurt badly by losing their common sense in pursuit of their dreams. He says:

> I know a trapped songwriter and artist who hooked up with the wrong person and signed a bad deal because she was eager to fulfill the dream. If only she had taken forty-eight hours and gone through the same exercises she would have gone through if she was going to buy a house: ask questions, get references, and check people out. If she had done that, she would not have signed this deal. It cost her ten years of her career and a portion of her income for the rest of her life. Make sure you know whom you're dealing with!

Most of the large songwriter organizations have people who you can call if you're not sure about what to do in such a situation. And make sure an entertainment lawyer reviews all contracts!

Songwriters often want a publishing deal to help them market their songs. Larger publishers require X amount of songs a year and have an exclusive on everything you write while you're signed to them. These publishers actively pursue avenues for the songs to earn an income. Michelle Bayer, the owner of Shelly Bay Music, says, "Mostly people get copublishing deals, which means that the major will copublish and administer—they handle all of the administration, like I do, but they also own fifty percent of it. That's usually in perpetuity. Rarely will you get a deal that reverts back to you in ten years." If the songs are already being marketed, some publishers, like Bayer, do what's called publishing administration, which is more about collecting money and handling all licenses for their clients. They register songs with ASCAP and BMI, and with the copyright office. Bayer adds, "I do all the paperwork that artists may not have the time to do or don't want to bother with, maybe because they're not around enough. I can also provide foreign collection because I have subpublishing deals all over the world. There may be money that they're not getting that I can get for them." A lot of the money is hard to collect yourself; using professional representation can help. Mara Schwartz, Director of Film, Television & New Media for Bug Music, a publishing administrator, adds:

> We take care of all the paperwork but the songwriter still owns their work. A traditional copublishing deal would give them a big advance, but then they would have co-ownership after that. Someone for Bug to help would have collection needs that they can't take care of on their own. They have songs on different compilations and things and have to collect from ASCAP and a label in Italy and one in Turkey. It gets them away from their business, which is recording and touring.

Publishing administrators don't market songs the way other publishers do. If your songs make real money from your own marketing efforts, a publishing administrator can take care of the biz end for a lot less money than a full publisher gets. Bayer says, "The difference with administration is it's usually a nominal percentage, maybe ten or fifteen percent, and I don't own anything for the future. If it's a three-year deal, after the three years everything reverts back to you and you can do whatever you want with it."

WRITING SONGS THAT SELL

I must repeat myself: It's *imperative* to have very well-crafted songs! Amy Kurland, the owner of Bluebird Café, warns, "If you believe you've written the best songs ever and shouldn't have to listen to anything else anyone has to say, you won't learn anything. You have to learn from all experiences." Jodi Krangle, the proprietress of The Muse's Muse, advises you to hone your craft to compete: "Your song has to stand out from the pack. There's always more to learn. If your songs are great, someone will be far more open to

---

PROFILE

Lorraine Ferro is a singer and an award-winning songwriter signed to EMI Publishing. She has written two multi-platinum No. 1 singles and won numerous songwriting awards. Ferro has sung live with and on many records for top acts, including Billy Joel. Her songs have been featured in many TV and film projects. Her self-released CD charted on *HITS Magazine*'s "Buzzin' Top Twenty" chart and John Shelton Ivany's "Top 21" amid artists who include Madonna. Ferro also teaches songwriting workshops, writes jingles, produces for other artists, and is heard regularly on national TV and radio spots, including as the voice of the "Sally Jesse Raphael" theme song.

accepting material from you in the future, even if you don't get the spot you went for originally. Songs need to be great or no tool to get your songs out will help you."

Jason Blume—songwriter, songwriting teacher, and author of the fantastic book 6 *Steps to Songwriting Success*, 2nd ed.—was signed as a songwriter with Zomba Music Publishing for 12 years. He says, "I never stopped benefiting from feedback. We get so close to our own songs that it's crucial to have a professional, not your girlfriend or mother, telling you how wonderful your songs are." There are services for critiquing your songs. Blume runs a good one, and many other places offer professional critiques, including NSAI and TAXI (www.taxi.com). Songwriting organizations also provide opportunities to get critiqued. Paul Corbin, VP of Writer/Publisher Relations with BMI, Nashville, says you can get feedback at your performing rights organization: "At BMI we're very honest in our thoughts and expression of the music and how it fits. It depends on how willing someone is to learn." Todd Brabec, VP of Membership at ASCAP, L.A., says, "We listen to people's compositions and tapes and try to make recommendations." Corbin advises being open to criticism:

> *It's hard to bare your soul in a song and have someone criticize that. Once you get over that, be as flexible and open-minded as you can be. If someone says that you shouldn't have something in a song because it won't work for radio, and you won't change it, you and only you will love that song. Being willing to change the lyric or shorten a bridge can really help you. Once you can get into a commercial rhythm, your songs can do quite well.*

Practice your songwriting and do whatever you can to improve your skills. Krangle describes the biggest mistake she sees:

> *A great many songwriters wait for inspiration to hit rather than simply sitting down and writing every day. Any writer needs to hone her skills on a daily basis, not just when inspiration hits. Write every day! The great majority of what you write will be crap. That's okay. Not everything has to be a masterpiece. But you're far more likely to write one great song if you've written a hundred than you are if you've only written twenty.*

Your songs must be THAT GOOD. David Ross (*Music Row*) says all songwriters feel they're ready, but they're often not: "Many producers or A&R people just want to go to brand-name houses. There is a pecking order in the process. Like a beautiful rose, you have to wait until it blooms—when your material is ready." Blume advises attending a song camp (many are listed in his book) or workshop with very qualified people. If an artist argues that it's too much effort to attend one, he responds, "If you are too busy or find it impossible to even spend four days, once or twice a year, then I question why you are doing this." Ferro says her first big step was attending a songwriting workshop: "That class made me a professional songwriter. I met my first writing partner in that class. We wrote as partners for ten years, and got our EMI publishing deals together. Next I made demos of the songs I loved. I spent money on learning and continue to do so!" Ferro took more classes at the Songwriters Hall of Fame with different instructors.

Look for books with good suggestions for improving your voice and other aspects of singing. One book with an interesting perspective about the relationship between listening and your voice is *The Ear and the Voice* by Alfred A. Tomatis (Scarecrow Press, Inc.). Another great resource for songwriters is MasterWriter (www.masterwriter.com), a collection of tools for songwriters that provides fantastic support with writing songs. This computer software has a huge rhyming dictionary; a dictionary with more than 35,000 phrases, idioms, and clichés; the *Roget's II Thesaurus*; and MUCH more, so if you're fumbling for words or phrases for your song, help is right in your computer. Its state-of-the-art database allows you to keep track of lyrics, melodies, and information related to songs you're writing. If you get a melody in your head, you can sing it right into your computer for safekeeping, so you can record all your melodic ideas. It also has a library of more than 250 tempo adjustable MIDI drum loops and full-function word processing. This is a fantastic resource for any songwriter, compatible with both Mac OS and Windows. Visit the website and try a free test drive!

So the real deal is, become as good a songwriter as possible. Tom Luteran, Creative Director at EMI Publishing, Nashville, advises, "Do your homework. Listen to the radio. Study the songs." But don't try to imitate what's selling or write according to a formula. Songs that make money are those that are fresh, with their own flavor. Just be aware of what ingredients work and create your own recipe. You MUST be true to you, too! Let your passion for music guide you. Krangle explains, "The songwriters who really achieve fame and fortune are those with a passion for it that transcends how much money they could make at it. They write because they *have to*." Lorraine Ferro says that way before she had a publishing deal, she defined herself as a songwriter:

I can't tell you how many writers call themselves "aspiring" songwriters, as though they aren't professional songwriters until some magical thing happens to them, like a hit song. Of course, that will never happen unless you believe you already ARE a songwriter worth having a hit song! When I defined myself as an artist/songwriter, I made any other work secondary to my writing sessions and gigs, not the other way around. I hadn't made a penny at being a songwriter, yet that's what I called myself, and I acted as such. I had three to four writing collaborations a week and wrote by myself, took workshops, and networked. It was that commitment to myself that helped get me my publishing deal.

MAKING CONTACTS

The songwriting community is a very supportive group—if you tap into it. Get out and meet people! Jennifer Marks says, "I went to performance rights associations and asked for help from them. I went to networking parties, cowrote with some amazing songwriters, and met some great people along the way." Lorraine Ferro strongly suggests:

TAKE A WORKSHOP! Don't sit home being bitter about the industry. Get into a network of writers who are working at their craft. Make friends and find collaborators. Get willing to become unattached to everything you write, in order to reach and move people. This is your livelihood, or that's what you want it to be, right? Work at it the way you would if you were already making a living at it.

Join local songwriters' groups to meet people and get feedback. Jason Blume says, "If you can get with people who are good at critiquing and willing to be objective about receiving critiques, they can be tremendously helpful." The appendix of his book lists the major groups in every state—there are hundreds of them—or search the Internet to find hundreds more. NSAI, an organization with fantastic resources for songwriters (see Chapter 9), has chapters in more than one hundred cities.

People teaching workshops might steer you to contacts. Some songwriter organizations have panels with pros speaking—go to all of them that you can. The Film Music Network (http://www.filmmusic.net/) has panels in several cities almost every month. Bring a CD and a professional attitude. When you meet pros at an event, they're more likely to at least listen to your music. Tap into your representative at ASCAP, BMI, or SESAC. Paul Corbin says, "Your rep is a good advice home. We know other people who we could refer you to." Todd Brabec adds, "We can refer you to publishers and record companies, and we have many different workshops." Your rep gets many requests, so wait until your songs are ready. They can also guide you to workshops and sources to help you improve your songwriting. Call your rep.

If you don't sing, find an artist to record one of your songs. Jodi Krangle agrees: "A good place to start can be an up-and-coming singer or band that no one has heard of yet. If someone gets famous singing your song, your songs could suddenly be in demand." There are companies that list people who need songs. Some require you to prove that you already have serious credits (TV, film, on a signed artist's album); they don't want to send wannabes to their clients. If you join the Film Music Network, they have a job bank with requests for music. TAXI sends its members many requests, too. *Music Row* has a weekly professional song-pitching sheet called RowFax: A&R people, producers, etc., ask for specific kinds of songs for their artists, and RowFax emails that info to their subscribers (you can subscribe on their website). Network to learn about other resources. Everyone has contacts and might share when they know you. Share yours, too!

WRITING FOR OTHERS

Writing songs for other artists can be lucrative. If your song is on an album that sells, you'll receive a royalty for every record sold. Even if your song never gets played, every song on the album collects the same fee. Jennifer Marks says, "I had a publishing deal and made money writing songs for other artists. I almost felt like I was stealing from them, as I enjoyed it so much." Jason Blume says there are many opportunities in country music but pop is more closed, so if you're not writing with the producer or artist, it's tough to break in. Artists for some genres, such as hip-hop or rock, are more likely to write their own songs.

Writing for others is a separate skill that Blume had to learn. He explains, "I was writing from my heart, for me, and what came out were songs that were only appropriate for me." But publishers need to pitch songs to many places. Blume's first big hit (recorded by the Oak Ridge Boys) was passed on more than 75 times before it got recorded. He says, "It needed to be the kind of a song that could have seventy-five different places to take it." Songwriting workshops help you learn how to write for others. Blume says, "I stayed in that place for five years before I realized the problem was my songs and I made the shift. I always thought it was because I didn't have the right connections or luck. But I wasn't writing the kind of songs that could be pitched to people who don't write their own songs." It takes time to learn how to write exceptional songs that others can sing.

Getting a Publishing Deal

Tom Luteran says the marketplace for songwriting is incredibly competitive now. There are fewer labels and artists, and you're up against the best of the best. So make sure your songs are THAT GOOD before approaching a publisher. Luteran says, "As a publisher for more than ten years, when I listen to a song, I listen for the sheer commerciality of it first and foremost. Whether I like it is not important. It's whether it's commercial or not. I pitch a lot of songs that I personally don't like, but that's my job." It's all about the song, not the singing. Jason Blume emphasizes the importance of "writing songs that are not good, not very good, but are exceptional. Then it's a lot easier to get one of those deals." When you send a demo to a publisher, begin with up-tempo songs. Ballads are still considered the kiss of death for an artist demo, and this applies to any situation where you're trying to get someone's attention. A livelier song stands out more. Put ballads later on your demo, but begin with a catchy tune that makes the person tap their fingers to the rhythm and want to hear more.

Major publishers sign staff writers. Luteran explains, "While they're under contract, we have the rights to everything they write." Publishers will pitch their writer/artists for record deals. But Luteran warns that if you don't get a deal soon enough, he can't wait indefinitely before pitching songs from your personal repertoire to other artists. A publisher has the right to place all your songs in income-earning situations, even if you want them for yourself. Don't get touchy about others singing "your" songs. Let them get placed! Luteran explains, "You can't think that you're never going to write another hit. You need to think this is the first of many." You can still record your song once someone else does. Blume says you need a great attitude and work ethic to get a staff writing deal:

> Staff writers get an advance against their own future mechanical royalties. If there are no future royalties, you don't have to pay them back but they won't keep you on. There is a quota. Mine with Zomba was fifteen songs a year if I wrote them by myself. If I cowrote them, that would be thirty. I never thought about quotas because I was writing so many songs—fifty in a year. That was my full-time job, what I wanted to do—writing one song per week.

Are you worried about making a writing quota? Luteran says, "If you have to consider a minimum commitment, you probably shouldn't be a writer. You should write because you love to, and it should pour out of you."

Staff writing doesn't mean you're actually on staff. It's an exclusive song-writing agreement. According to Blume, "It means that during the term of the agreement, any song you write is automatically published by that publisher, unless they choose to not publish it." How much of your song does the publisher get? Blume says:

> When you don't have a lot of clout and you sign a staff writing deal, you sign away fifty percent of your income. That can turn into a huge amount of money. People ask, "Why give away all that money?" Because half of a lot of money is much more than one hundred percent of nothing. Hopefully the publisher has opportunities to exploit your material in ways you could not on your own. Without my publisher, I can say that there is a zero percent

chance that I would have ended up with cuts by Britney Spears and the Backstreet Boys. Yes, I gave up a lot of money, but I made a huge amount of money that never would have happened otherwise.

Lorraine Ferro says that while she has a few multi-platinum singles that she's never seen a dime on, she'd do it again: "They have all my songs from that period and before in perpetuity, but that publishing deal opened so many doors for me." You may start with single-song deals. Blume says, "It's much more common when a relationship is developing between a publisher and songwriter for them to represent one song at a time. They can see how each other works. I published at least ten songs singularly before getting a staff writing deal." He advises you to attend a workshop where you know there will be publishers present. If you can meet them and get them your songs, Luteran advises, "Make sure the first couple of songs are different enough, yet still fit into their framework." Don't send clones of what's popular now; publishers already have those writers. The Music Business Registry's Publishers Directory (www.musicregistry.com) has most publishers and their contact info.

Cowriting

Many songwriters emphasize the various benefits of writing with others. Jason Blume says that with access to your cowriters' resources, in a sense you double your assets. If your cowriter becomes successful, your songs gain value. Or your cowriter may know someone who knows somebody with clout. Blume says, "It snowballs. Networking is crucial in this business. Collaborating is a wonderful way to do this." He's written songs—some of his best—that he'd never have written without someone else's energy and the chemistry between them. He recommends exploring new ways to write: "If you always cowrite, try writing by yourself. If you always write by yourself, try cowriting. I know people who had tremendous success collaborating via the Internet. With MP3s and such, you can collaborate with people all over the world."

PROFILE

Kyler England is a full-time singer/songwriter. She has shared the stage with many top performers, including Sting, Annie Lennox, and Liz Phair. She's won many songwriting contests, including the 2002 North Carolina Songwriters Competition and the 2003 Mid-Atlantic Songwriting Contest. England was featured on the 2002 Epic/Sony Compilation *Shekinah*. She's also been featured on NPR's syndicated radio shows "Women in Music" and "Here & Now," and she continuously tours in clubs and colleges nationally.

Writing songs with another writer can stimulate creativity. You'll each contribute to the song and motivate each other to come up with more. You can blend your individual styles into a song that neither of you could write alone. Paul Corbin adds:

> *Sometimes you may have trouble getting a song played because you don't "have a name" but your cowriter does. Or you don't have the experience but your cowriter does. Or your cowriter is the one who is best with music or lyrics. One of the big reasons to cowrite is not only to finish a song a little sooner, but also you have an automatic critique going while you're building the song. You generally have a better shot because you have twice the contacts.*

Blume suggests you first figure out why someone should want to write with you. He says, "It's like tennis: You want to be challenged. You'll write to a higher level with someone who is at a higher level if you don't get intimidated by that and let that get in the way of your creativity." He warns that your cowriter wants to "write up," too, and needs a compelling reason to work with you. What can you bring to the table? Connections? Phenomenal lyrics? Know your strengths in order to sell yourself. Blume says, "In Nashville, the best way to attract a writer is to have a great idea. Country music is a very lyric-driven genre. If you come up with a fresh and unique title or idea, you can find somebody who will want to write this idea."

How do you find folks to write with? Get active in songwriter groups and feel out other songwriters. Blume suggests attending workshops: "When you get your songs critiqued at a workshop, you are also auditioning your songs in front of potential collaborators who attend." There are websites for networking and interacting, like The Muse's Muse. Blume suggests finding your own market if you're THAT GOOD at songwriting. He explains, "Find the seventeen-year-old who has the image, voice, and look, but needs a cowriter, like the Matrix worked with Avril Lavigne. Find young bands and artists who are really serious about getting to the next level but may be a bit weaker in the writing department."

Have an agreement with anyone you work with. Blume advises that you establish from the beginning what the percentage in the split will be. How can you figure that out before you've written the song? He says from the beginning, he expects a 50/50 split, even if he ends up writing 80 percent of the song: "It's counterproductive to count words and notes. We can't know which line or note is the magic one. Be clear about how the demo will be handled. It's hard to know if you'll do a full-blown demo or a guitar and vocal demo when you haven't even written the song." Discuss these things up front if you want your cowriting venture to be a success.

SONGWRITING CONTESTS

Many indie artists find entering songwriting contests worthwhile. Jodi Krangle says, "I look at songwriting contests as a testing ground. It can usually get a songwriter some good critiques. Many songwriting contests offer detailed critiques with your entry. Plus, there are prizes that can be helpful to a songwriter's continuing career." Jessica Brandon, the head of Artists Relations for USA Songwriting Competition, says they had more than 32,000 entries last year. She adds, "It started with people with tunes in their heads (beginner songwriters). However, we have been getting professional songwriters as our reputation grows. We have A&R from all the big labels as judges: SONY, EMI, BMG, Warner, and Universal." Rachael Sage has won many contests and explains, "I have a Jewish mother who always says that if you don't enter, you can't win."

Most contests have prizes. Brandon says, "Our overall grand prize winner wins $50,000 worth of cash and merchandise—cool gear from Roland, Sony, and much more. Winning songs get radio airplay through one of our radio sponsors." Are these contests worth entering? Kyler England says, "I enter songwriting contests more because it's an honor and validation to be recognized, and it gets the word out about you." Jennifer Marks says, "I won a few and used those wins to my advantage in the press. When my second CD came out, I got a lot of attention from the story of winning contests, which was helpful for sales and gaining more press." Robby Baier adds, "It is good for the press kit, boosts your creativity and purpose, connects you to other winners, and offers promotion possibilities and prizes." Jennie DeVoe won the *Billboard* Song Contest and says, "Winning for pop was cool—it's the most popular category where radio is concerned, and it turns heads when you talk to someone about why they should listen to your music. It was very cool to get first place in a world songwriting contest, no matter what."

PROFILE

Jennifer Marks released her first CD at the end of 1998. She has performed since 1999 as a solo artist and has opened for national acts, including Howard Jones and Cyndi Lauper. Marks was the only solo artist finalist at the Coca-Cola® New Music Awards and did its national tour. Marks' music has been licensed for film, including the trailer theme song for *The Terminal*; on soap operas such as "As the World Turns"; and for promotions by corporations, including Maybelline® and Mattel®. She's been reviewed in top magazines, including *Billboard*, and recently signed a good deal with Bardic Records that gives her more fuel for her already running engine.

But there are entry fees, so be selective. And Sage warns, "You get prizes and recording equipment but have to declare it, so you may actually lose money. Be careful what you enter. If the award is $50,000 in prizes and it's stuff you don't really want, you'll still have to declare it." Like winning prizes on game shows, if you accept them, you must declare the cash value on your taxes. Prizes may not be worth that to you. Jodi Krangle says songwriting contests are good but don't overestimate their value. She explains:

> It may get you a decent critique on your song, some great prizes, and perhaps a mention on a website. These are nice to add to a songwriting résumé but shouldn't be mistaken for true songwriting success. They should basically be treated as an encouraging pat on the back. That's not to say that the prizes offered or the encouragement isn't worth the entering. I think songwriters have to be aware of what they can and can't expect from them. Occasionally, judges from contests may ask for single-song contracts if they really adore a song. But it happens rarely and shouldn't be expected.

Brandon says people should enter songwriting contests for exposure, not just for prizes: "If you make it to the finals of any category of our annual competition, it means that your song is more than just pretty good." Clare Cooper won honorable mentions from the Billboard Song Contest and Unisong. She says, "I enter them—you never know who the judges are and it never hurts to have your material heard." Lorraine Ferro's cowriters submitted songs they'd written together and they began to win awards. She warns, "There are a lot of contests that really are a rip-off—they just want to make money. But there are some that will help to further a career." She recommends the USA Songwriting Competition and the John Lennon Songwriting Contest, saying, "The people who win are of a professional caliber, and the judges are all legit. Both of them are résumé boosters." Ferro says prestigious contests are worth entering to get recognized by your peers, boost your confidence if you win, let you know you're on the right track, and potentially get you some press.

If you want to find songwriting contests, Krangle says, "The Muse's Muse has a contest listings section. A search on the Internet for 'songwriting contests' should also yield many pages." Jason Blume's book lists the best contests. Once your songs have been critiqued a lot and you feel they're THAT GOOD, try entering. A prestigious contest is the New Folk Songwriting Competition for emerging songwriters, part of the Kerrville Folk Festival (see Chapter 17). Dalis Allen, the festival's producer, says they get 600 submissions of two songs each. Thirty-two singer/songwriters are chosen to perform at the festival on Saturday or Sunday. There are six winners, but all 32 can win in other ways. Allen says, "A lot of venues and clubs come to the New Folk to listen. Even if you're not one of the six, you can still get booked." Everyone performing has a chance to get booked. Entering the contest gives you a chance to be heard at Kerrville, and it opens doors to getting booked in the future. Allen says there are many benefits to being there:

> *You come here to find that you're not the only songwriter struggling. There's a community of help, support, and affirmation. A lot of people don't like the terms "contest" or "competition." Many of our folks embrace all the people who've never been here before. New people can camp with them and learn from them; then they can move on and camp with someone else. It makes a New Folk competitors community and helps you make friends. Ninety-nine percent of the time, if someone comes out here, they come back.*

CHAPTER 16

Licensing and Other Music Income

There are many outlets for good music and talented composers. Bernie Drayton, a partner in Three Tree Productions, says, "There are many other options to being a recording artist: the producer, writer, arranger, and all aspects of it." Music Supervisor Glen Caplin warns, "Avenues to break and expose new music have gotten narrower. It's important to think about how to get your music into commercials, television, and films. It's a nice chunk of money in your pocket." Michael Whalen, award-winning composer for TV, advertising, and films, says, "My independence is one of my most important luxuries. Once I pay the bills, then I can make MY music." That's the indie spirit! Other sources of income from your music allow you freedom to pursue the rest of your music career.

Opportunities to place your music or compose for dollars helps you stay independent. Many producers and music supervisors who I've spoken to began by pursuing a career as an artist but love alternative ways to make a living from music. Mark Wood says he fell into composing for TV, movies, and other outlets: "I dreamed of being a rock star when I bumped into a filmmaker who needed music and gave me two thousand dollars. I wrote rock stuff for it—right up my alley—and got paid. It struck me that this is how it is done."

Explore all avenues! Nick DiMinno, also a partner in Three Tree Productions, says, "There's a synergy between advertising, film, television, and records. It's foolish to think of yourself as a one-trick pony [only doing advertising, or films, etc.]. It's smart to think in broader terms—there are opportunities if you look for them." Ted Suh, Chief Marketing Officer for 9 Squared, Inc.—a company that licenses music for a variety of uses, including ringtones—agrees, "There are tons of licensing opportunities for independent music in today's world. Many companies, such as video game developers, movie producers, and ringtone companies, are looking for talented artists without having to pay out the megabucks to sign them."

GETTING STARTED

Give yourself a better shot at getting your music into film, TV, commercials, and other avenues by being prepared. As I said earlier, treat it as a business! Michael Whalen advises, "The relationship with your client must be based on trust. Under-promise and over-deliver. Get it done faster than you say you will." That keeps the work coming! Mark Wood, who composes for a variety of outlets, says:

> Learn how to behave and handle yourself in a professional scenario where you're around businesspeople in suits and ties, so you don't come off as being a lame, stupid musician. A lot of the suit-and-tie people are scared that musicians are flaky and party all night. Clients think that you can't put together a sentence. That's been an interesting awakening.

Glen Caplin says a music supervisor has two roles. First is the creative process of choosing the source music that you will put into the film/TV show/commercial. The second part is the legal side—gaining clearances or rights to use the music. Music Editor Dan Evans Farkas says music editors also choose the music. He makes sure the editing is right and the music isn't fighting with the dialogue. He adds, "Music supervisors look at the forest, and my job is to look at the trees—to make sure that the music fits the scene." Music supervisor Jeanne DaSilva says before you approach anyone for audiovisual licensing, be prepared. She explains:

PROFILE

Mark Wood is an electric violinist. He started out wanting to be a rock star, was signed in the late '80s and early '90s, and sold platinum and gold records. He appeared on CNN and "The Tonight Show." Then Wood found his niche in composing for television. He has composed for the Olympics and won Emmy awards for his music. Wood also designs his own line of violins and has a music library of his original compositions that get licensed by a variety of producers.

Have your publishing organized—get your songs registered with ASCAP or BMI. Start an independent publishing company. Someone who isn't organized is a little scary to work with. In licensing, everything needs to be legal. Make sure that whatever you hand out—a CD, a website with your samples posted—includes clear information on how to reach you. You'd be surprised how much stuff I get with no contact information. Make it easy to read. Be very straight about who owns what, and where to reach the owners. I've taken things out of movies because I was uncomfortable about this.

If you use samples or a song that someone else wrote, get everything cleared properly. Music supervisors prefer music with NO samples. Evans Farkas explains, "The big problem with hip-hop music is that if you sample something, you have to clear it, which often is impossible. It might be possible to get it onto the record, but for a movie you have to go through the whole process again and the wheels grind to a halt." Mara Schwartz, Director of Film, Television & New Media at Bug Music, adds, "Many times somebody needs to replace a song at the last minute or needs a really quick turnaround. If they know that you own the rights to everything, they're more likely to use you."

Evans Farkas advises that if you have an instrumental track, make it available. Sometimes the lyrics are heard initially but they just want music when characters talk. He explains, "Many times a song is great but there's no way to get rid of the vocals. They occasionally re-edit a scene for a song—not often. When you're in the studio, make an instrumental version of your music. It makes it much more attractive and useful to the editor." When you record, do another pass without vocals. Have it ready in case you're asked for it. Often music without lyrics can be more marketable in these arenas, so you might as well do it while you're mixing.

Networking is the best way to make contacts when you want to license your music. Jennifer Marks' music has been used for soap operas, independent films, and by Mattel®, Starbucks®, and more. She says, "It is a constant hustle, and then you have friends or associates who pull it out for you." The more pros you meet, the more potential for contacts. Caplin says, "If you're cool and down to earth, I'm more likely to want to work with you. If you're very formal, buttoned up, and trying to be too 'this,' it won't help us create a relationship. Be yourself. You've got to meet people." Performing rights societies have departments dealing specifically with film and TV music. Contact them when your music is ready.

Have a great website. Music supervisor Jim Black says, "Websites are super cheap and a great calling card." He advises against emailing clips. Instead, set up a private web page (see Chapter 13) with clips of your music. Send the link to music supervisors and producers. Black adds, "I keep my favorite musicians and composers. I cruise through websites, check out their music, and if I feel it fits, I contact them for more information." He suggests making clips about 30 seconds long, adding, "Some music supervisors like to listen to a whole song because they don't know where the hooks will be. As long as it's on a website, full songs are great." Robby Baier licenses his own music. When I interviewed him, he was creating a database for music supervisors to search his files by tempo, key words, length, male or female vocal, etc. He explains:

> It is becoming increasingly difficult to compete in the marketplace due to the availability of inexpensive, high-quality recording equipment on one hand and the huge number of musicians and songwriters on the other. People offer their songs for no licensing fee, just to get a foot in the door. To compete, it is imperative that your songs are available ASAP, cleared and ready to go. This database allows music supervisors to enter my site via a password, at any time. They can download selected songs and shop them to their clients. They can send me an email with requests for the AIFF files (CD quality) to use for the production.

Audrey Arbeeny, Executive Producer of AudioBrain, says there are Internet sites that you can place your CD on: "Some sites are stronger and more legit than others. If you've got stuff, put it up there. People in advertising and other areas browse those sites." One that music supervisors recommend is Pump Audio (www.pumpaudio.com), a nonexclusive site that makes your music available for licensing, splits royalties 50/50, and takes no ownership.

Educating Yourself

The more skills you have, the better your chance of getting hired for something. Learn new technology! If you want to compose music for specific projects, knowing the technology increases your options. Arbeeny advises you to improve your computer skills, saying, "People who learn skills such as Pro Tools and how to edit on the computer have a better chance, especially if they write and mix their own stuff." Anton Sanko suggests, "Be a virtuoso on whatever sequencing program you use. Spend all your time learning it. When the time comes, the turnaround can be incredibly fast and [you can't waste time trying to figure things out]." He also advises watching many movies: "Pay attention to what the music does. Is it too much? Too little? There's always something to learn. I keep studying with somebody. It keeps me fit, like working out."

The hardest part of writing for others can be figuring out what they want. One of the most important skills is being able to communicate on a creative level. Sanko says if you want to score for films, you need to listen to what the director says and translate it into a musical idea. A client may have an idea in his head that he can't express, or she may not know exactly what she wants. Michael Whalen says, "Finding a mutual creative vocabulary with your client is crucial to the success of any project." Learn the lingo if you want to do music for TV or advertising. I asked Whalen to define some of the common terms used:

- A cold open *for a news program is the very first piece of music that you hear before the main theme. The music acts like a tease to draw in the audience, right before the news. It needs to be written in a way that is collapsible.*
- Collapsible *means that the same :50 (fifty-second) cold open that worked on Tuesday also must work on Wednesday as a :37 tease or Friday as a 1:23 piece. The piece must be structured thematically where people in the control room can dump out of it anywhere. This means writing tight short themes and using unique sounds.*
- A bumper *is the music that precedes a commercial and also leads back into the show. They are less common now but are still being used.*
- A vamp *is the end of a song that repeats round and round.*
- A prevamp *is a loopable piece of music that extends the beginning of a piece BEFORE the main theme starts.*
- In music themes or promos, *music and visuals which extend past the designated air length are considered* pad. *For example, if you write a :10 theme and it extends past when it will be faded on air to :20 or :30, that extra time is* pad. *For live news and talk shows,* pad *is important in case the on-air talent or director misses a cue. The* pad *becomes a badly needed fudge factor for those on-set.*

Get an education so you'll be prepared! These are all ways that your music can be used—more potential for increasing your musical income.

Music for Free?

Should your music be used for free? Michael Whalen says musicians are no longer treated as if they have any value: "We're told, 'If you don't take this job for no money, someone else will.' When you negotiate a deal, you have to assign a value to your artistic output. When you roll over and give your music away, you hurt everyone." Some say music can be used for free at first. Eric Kaye, Creative Director/Executive Producer at The Lodge, says, "Everybody gives free music to get a credit, but only at first." Glen Caplin says he did the first movie he worked on for free: "It was a Paramount movie that gave me the credibility to work on a Warner Bros. movie. Be willing to do things for the experience at first."

Decide if giving your music away for free will benefit you. Consider each offer individually. Arbeeny advises that you weigh the potential benefits. What can you do with the credit? Can you get press? Not all exposure has value. But having a history makes it easier to get paid opportunities. Set limits on how much you'll do for free. Michael Whalen says, "Once you've impressed someone and they like your demo, you have at least some leverage when they ask you to give them your music for nothing." Use it! Whalen warns that when they ask, "Would you like a shot at something?" it's a euphemism for "We have no money to pay you." Don't act too eager. Focus on the value of your music.

One way to learn the ropes and get your foot in the door, especially for advertising and video markets, is to work as an intern for a company that creates music. Caplin suggests, "Try to get work in a music production house to get experience and meet people." Eric Kaye adds, "Big name composers don't write all the music they're credited with. They may write out a sketch or melody and hand it to an assistant—a junior composer—to finish it." Sometimes if the bigger composer is busy, the assistant may get the gig. Consider approaching someone who works a lot and offer your services for free. This is an instance where the education and contacts can be very worth the free time.

THE SERIOUS BIZ END

Here we go again! If you want to make money with your music, learn about the different revenue streams and how you can collect on them. It's easy to get ripped off when exciting opportunities are offered. If someone wants to use your music, excitement can blind you to sign away the rights. Your desire to place music can overshadow good business sense. In that case, do it as a hobby. But if you want to earn an indie living, market your music as a businessperson. Michael Whalen says, "Don't forget that art is a business. Beethoven and Mozart had to pay rent and eat. So conduct yourself always in a businesslike manner: polite, honest, and clear. There is no bigger turn-off for a potential client than an artist who is a flake."

Learn what you're entitled to. Jim Black says, "Understand your contracts. Don't just have your lawyer do it. Know what you're signing. I've seen too many people who didn't read the fine print get taken for rides. Make sure you really understand everything." Glen Caplin says there are two sets of rights to negotiate: the master (the actual physical recording) and the publishing and composition itself. You negotiate the term of the license and the territory it covers. No matter what they pay you, don't give up all the rights! Caplin warns, "Don't sign an exclusive deal, which some people who want to use your music will ask for. That's foolish." Black agrees, "Don't sell your song one hundred percent to someone and lose all rights to it. All licensing deals are nonexclusive"—unless you give them all rights! Sometimes they want a work-for-hire agreement; that doesn't mean giving up everything. Todd Brabec, VP of Membership at ASCAP, says, "A work-for-hire is a legal contract where a television show obtains the exclusive copyright to a song. The writer's royalties are set forth in the contract." Don't just take any offer! Whalen advises not working until the contract is signed. He adds, "Don't be afraid to ask questions about your client, their background, and how their projects are funded. If it doesn't pass the smell test, act accordingly. Often a good business practice is simply acting in one's best interest and for self-preservation."

An artist is paid a licensing fee up front for the use of their music. It may be a small amount for TV, but there can be much more on the back end, since TV airplay earns performance royalties. Brabec says all music on TV is compensated for: "For TV it adds up to about two hundred forty million dollars. The people share that money: ASCAP takes fourteen percent and the rest goes out to the writers and publishers, fifty/fifty." Your share depends on how often the show is aired, and where. Royalties can be earned for years if the show has reruns or syndication overseas. Paul Corbin, VP of Writer/Publisher Relations for BMI, says you get paid based on the amount of exposure that your music gets compared to all others. An incidental theme on a small channel program won't pay as much as the theme on a major network show.

How do you keep track of royalties? Brabec says, "In television and film, everything comes in cue sheets, which are prepared by the producer of a television show or the network. It gives the songs being used on a specific show, and the writers and producers of that song." Whalen adds, "It is a listing of all the cues used chronologically, with the length, type of cue, composer, lyricist, publishing company, and PRO affiliation. They tell the broadcast dates and total number of minutes of your music used in the show." Make sure that cue sheets are sent to ASCAP and BMI. Whalen says they're crucial to getting paid: "Try to get it in your contracts that your clients have to give you cue sheets and air dates for the program. Establish good relationships with people at your PRO to help you file them properly." Michelle Bayer says if you have a publisher, they will take care of all this. Since TV shows get syndicated overseas, foreign subpublishers do the same thing with their foreign societies (see Chapter 19).

Film deals vary greatly. Music supervisors need music to fit their budgets and try to pay as little as possible. Indie films offer the most possibilities for beginners. They often don't pay much, but if you have THE GOODS, you can negotiate. Black explains, "Always try to get a little something to set a precedent. Who can't afford five hundred dollars for a song?" Indie film budgets are much more restricted than larger films. If they say they have no money, it's probably true—for now. But don't give them your music for free *carte blanche*. Instead, give them a license to use it at film festivals. Bayer advises, "I'd do a one-year *gratis* license for film festivals. These are usually worldwide. There's three festivals within a year that are relevant: Cannes, Sundance, and Toronto." Jeanne DaSilva agrees: "At a festival, the filmmaker probably won't make money. You can't charge more than a few hundred bucks. But if that film gets picked up by a major studio, you should make money." A film can attract distribution at festivals. If it makes lots of money, you should get more, too. Issue a license for film festivals only and negotiate your fee if the film does well. Black says some people do a step deal: They pay additional money at specified intervals based on how many people see the film. Bayer adds:

> Do the festival license for free and build in various steps. For example, if the box office is three hundred thousand or one million dollars, you get five hundred dollars. If it hits two million, you get another five hundred dollars. A lot of independent films don't have the budget, but if all of a sudden the box office is three million, they may have money to give you later. You're sort of working with them, hoping it turns into something in the future. The more people who come to see it, the more money the filmmaker gets and therefore the more money the filmmaker has to pay later.

Don't let your desire for someone to rep your music cloud your good sense. Some people offer shady deals. DaSilva warns you to be careful. She's seen songwriters get ripped off and advises not to sign with a company where you don't have approval rights. Nor should you give a company power of attorney to make deals in your name. If you're offered a contract for audiovisual licensing, read the fine print and have an entertainment attorney review it. DaSilva advises, "Make sure the company cannot do things without your knowledge. I call my clients if someone wants to use their song. They sign the paperwork. Make sure you have to sign any deal that grants the right to use your song so you know what it says." DaSilva advises not giving any of your publishing rights to the licensing company. She knew an artist who granted one licensing company 25 percent ownership of her song in perpetuity—not just for licensing, but for everything. DaSilva adds, "The artist signed the deal because it sounded cool. Not even an agent gets that. People think, better something than nothing. But you can ruin your career before it starts." Choose your reps wisely!

FILM AND TV

Licensing music for movies and TV is a great revenue stream for indie musicians. Kyler England says, "My main income, other than CD sales, is from placements on TV." Why would they use indie music? Most indies take less money and own their songs—a fast deal. Danny Benair, the founder of Natural Energy Lab—a music marketing company representing labels and artists for film, TV, and advertising—says, "The quickest buck will probably always be television. The turnaround is quick. If they want something, they need it in about a week."

Music supervisors need legal clearance to use music. Music is added after a film or TV show is shot. They need it fast. As an indie, you can clear your songs quicker than a signed artist. There are many opportunities if you're good! Indie artist Tor says, "Since I moved to L.A., I've scored more than twenty television shows and twelve films." Michelle Bayer does TV and film song placement with her partner and his company, Sugaroo!. She says the independent film business is the most open to exposing other independents, adding, "Sometimes independent films turn into something big or are critically acclaimed. That's a good start for an artist. There's lots of television with low music budgets, so they're interested in independents. A lot of television folks like being cool enough to break somebody unknown."

Mark Wood says, "The music I do for film and TV is fairly lucrative. It can take months of selling my own music to make the money I get from a show or a film. So, I balance it." Tor got his first opportunity scoring and composing for an independent film through people he originally met at his day job. Tor agreed to do the film and only take half the money up front. Since it was his first film, he agreed to do extra demos if they weren't happy with his work and gave a money back guarantee, because he had faith in his ability. They loved his music and he quit his day job. Tor adds:

I quit for something I would make little money on, simply because I realized I couldn't do anything that did not fill my soul anymore. That was a huge turning point in my career. I told the universe that the money I was making had no relevance in my life, other than paying rent. Immediately after I did that I got another job—a really bad movie. But word travels out here.

PROFILE

Tor Hyams is a singer/songwriter whose career expanded into creating music for TV, film, and sports events. He's worked with and produced many talented artists, including Lou Rawls, Perry Farrell, and Deborah Harry. He created *A World of Happiness*, an album of original children's music performed by a roster of celebrities from the fields of music, film, and television, and dedicated to disseminating messages of kindness and compassion to "children of all ages." Proceeds are contributed to a group of charities that benefit children.

Eventually I got a job on a television show doing theme stuff. Then I literally made fifty to eighty calls a day for about two years to movie and TV people.

Tor is a good networker. He called and called: "I was severely, charmingly persistent and I started to get more jobs." His first license was for the show "Homicide." They paid little up front but he got more than $15,000 in ASCAP residuals. Tor says he works hard to make sure his stuff gets tracked, adding, "There's no substitute for residuals like prime-time network television because of ASCAP royalties. You make so much money on the back end that the up-front money hardly matters."

Many artists agree that networking and high visibility is key. Be friendly to everyone! Tina Broad says BROTHER had an episode of UPN's "Twilight Zone" written around one of their songs—the show's executive producer is their friend and fan. They also did a cameo on "ER" after the casting director's friend saw them street performing. Eric Kaye wrote to the producer of a PBS series who was an alumnus of his school and got his first break. He says, "I made lots of demos and he gave me a shot. Eight years later, it's been good for one or two PBS documentaries a year." Kaye didn't give away his music for free; he demo'd to show what he could do. His work could only be used if he was hired. Alex Woodard says, "It's a lot of networking. Sending someone a song doesn't mean they'll use it. But they may play it for someone who plays it for someone who wants it. Something will happen if you believe in what you do and it appeals to people." Tor advises:

Spend most of your time networking. People get many songs that may be better than what I produce, but hardly anybody has made as great friends with these people as I have. In L.A., there's always a party. You meet people and keep getting invited to stuff. These parties aren't fun, they're work. The people who get you jobs are not the executives. It's always the assistants—the receptionist—people who are usually ignored.

Kaye advises, "Slowly build credits. Meet as many people as you can." Kaye met some soap actors when he wrote the music for a soap stars workout video, a job he got through his bass player's wife, a personal trainer who choreographed it. Through the soap people's circle of friends, Kaye met a producer who ended up producing for "Dawson's Creek" a few years later. Kaye says, "I got three songs on 'Dawson's Creek,' all from writing music for the soap stars video. I'd say that ninety percent of jobs are through personal connections as opposed to how good your reel/demo is."

Kaye says New York and L.A. have the highest concentration of people: "You're much more likely to run into a producer, etc., in a bar. Ask everyone you know if they know a director or producer." Go to events featuring pros that use music. Robby Baier met music supervisors at music conferences who placed his songs in films and TV shows. He says income from licensing enables him to play the music he wants, without having to mold himself for labels: "The more film placements I get, the more opportunities offer themselves." And, he reminds us, royalties are great: "Gigs only pay once. A TV show pays you every time it gets re-run." Audrey Arbeeny advises, "Events where people speak are the easiest place to get access to them. There are many. If you can't afford to go to a conference, volunteer your services and get in free." When she speaks on a panel, she accepts music to consider for future needs. The Film Music Network has great panels with industry pros; songwriter organizations do, too. Those who speak are more open in these settings.

Do you feel excluded because of where you live? Keep track of conferences and who speaks at them. Track them down on the Internet and approach them, even if you didn't attend. If you join the Film Music Network, you can listen to their panels online. Jennie DeVoe didn't let living in Indiana stop her! She advises finding the names of music supervisors of TV shows and sending them your music:

> It may get buried, but do all you can to talk to the person and let 'em know it's coming. I've sent stuff out and not gotten a call until they wanted to use a song—two years after I sent it. The more you send, the better your odds. If you can accomplish song placements in shows, it shows that you're worth a listen and turns a head as you try to achieve your next feat. Plus, you make money in the meantime to pay your electric bill and buy peanut butter.

Some directories list music supervisors. Jim Black recommends the *Film and Television Music Guide*, which lists almost everyone connected to film and TV. The Film Music Network has a directory on its site for members. Glen Caplin says, "It's okay to email and ask if we're looking for new music. It's a wonderful way to keep in touch with people." Dan Evans Farkas suggests, "Email with a link to a web page with music. It's like a résumé: This is who I am, this is how to reach me, these are the styles I write, and this is what I've done. The smaller the film, the more likely we are to try an unknown. Often we look at independent artists when we're in a hurry." Michelle Bayer suggests sending an email to ask if they're interested in receiving your material. They may turn you down because it's not what they need. If they say no, try another. Audrey Arbeeny advises:

> Call a production company like mine. Make a deal with somebody who is reputable and has contacts. Say you think your music may be good for a cer-

tain show and can they take it in for you. Go to smaller producers and pro-
duction companies and try to freelance on projects. Many people won't take
unsolicited music. Being a musician myself, I do. Send someone something
interesting instead of calling."

Bayer recommends making your material as professional as possible: "You don't need elaborate artwork, but it shouldn't be a cassette tape with songs scrawled on it. It should look and sound professional. There are ways to do it without it costing that much money." Evans Farkas likes standard jewel cases, not thin ones, so he can identify them on a shelf. Indicate the genre, and have contact info—a website, email address, and phone number—on the packaging and disk. Evans Farkas adds:

Include the duration of each song, publishing info, your society (BMI,
ASCAP), and anything we need to do our final music cue sheet. Music edi-
tors often do the first pass of the final music cue sheets and then the music
supervisors fill in the blanks. Everyone throws out CDs if they don't have
information on them. Write a letter that looks professional, like one drafted
by a lawyer or at least a really great secretary. It's all about being very organ-
ized and professional. Note which tracks you think are the best. If there are
samples, let us know that they've been cleared.

Caplin warns, "Here's the cold hard truth: I'm always super busy, with a million things to listen to. I try to listen to what's sent, but it isn't possible. If it isn't from someone I know, I may not listen." Caplin doesn't need a full press kit. He'll read a one-sheet and look at press. Anything that provides a story will make him want to listen to it: "I may not listen to the CD but I'll usually read the paper. Describe the record. Give an idea of what it is about and anything that makes it special—such as people we might know who were involved—that may make me listen to it. Sometimes if the packaging is good, I'll listen to it."

Follow up without being a pest. When people whose music has been used by music supervisors call too often and won't hang up, they stop using the music. Evans Farkas recommends asking how often someone wants you to call. He adds, "Ask, 'Can I email or call you once a month, or keep sending stuff? Maybe check in a few months?' Feel the person out for how often to contact them. Don't call more than once a month."

How can you get repped by companies that place music in TV and film? Danny Benair of Natural Energy Lab says, "It has to be something that I think we can work. Sometimes I think a song is great. Other times, somebody fills a gap with a style we don't have." Sometimes he turns down good songs because he has too much of that genre. Bayer says Sugaroo! represents the roster of artists on about 24 independent labels, so they don't represent as many indie artists. They also avoid too much of one genre. Bayer says, "If somebody is different from what we have, or so phenomenal that we know we can help them, we would sign them." A deal with Sugaroo! is generally for one or two years: "We do the license, take a percentage, and everything else is yours." Benair says people find him through his website and word of mouth. Press kits aren't important; he'd rather get a concise sampler of your music. "At the end of the day," he explains, "for most licenses it's going to be about the song, not the look." Benair says you can also direct people who might place your music to a website or send an MP3 file (always ask first!). He adds, "If you hear about a movie being made and think you have a perfect song for it, contact me. If you know about something, let us know."

To compose for TV, learn what people need. People call Suzanne Teng for work on movies and TV because of her reputation as a flutist and percussionist. She says, "I go in and play music they've written. They've usually got an idea of what they want." The late Larry Kamm, former Coordinating Director and Creative Consultant for the YES Network (Yankees Entertainment and Sports Network), said, "Music is a supportive part of the broadcast—thirty-five to forty percent is original on large shows. Writing for sports is a different world, unlike writing for anything else." Arbeeny, the on-site music supervisor for several Olympic Games, says, "People watch sports for many reasons: camaraderie, unity. It brings out people's aspirations." Sports music is emotional. Arbeeny adds, "If you understand the emotions of what's going on, try to articulate that into sound." Kamm explained, "Everything in sports is *people*. Keep in mind when you're writing that people have stories. We also look for sound effects for sports. You need five-, seven-, ten-second stings." They need music, not lyrics. Kamm advised, "Write music so it's easy to edit. As you write, think about ways it can be looped or shortened. Composers that do, sell more music."

At the same time, as Michael Whalen advises, "Don't try to sound like others. What will set you apart from others is that you sound like yourself." He says when you write a theme, don't give them just one piece of music. When Whalen did the theme for "Good Morning America," he gave the music supervisors four CDs with different variations of music and moods, explaining, "No one arrangement of a theme can survive all possible uses. From elections to wars to a trip to the moon, the setting of themes emotionally is VERY important for their longevity on the air." If you're good at composing, Arbeeny suggests you check out cable shows that use music.

Or, find people making independent films. Bayer says, "People who work in the independent world have a heart for independent musicians as well." Caplin says there are always scoring opportunities for student and indie films: "Go after small filmmakers. There may not be much money, if any, but if you believe the filmmaker could go somewhere, go for it." Evans Farkas agrees that independent films, especially small ones and those made by college students, want music in their movies and can't afford it: "They don't have an organized group picking music for them, and it's easier to work one-on-one with a young director than it is to get into the door of someone well-known." Jim Black suggests, "Go to the places where they teach film. Those kids come out of school and work on projects. It's a teeny, teeny business." Develop relationships now. Today's students are tomorrow's prestigious filmmakers. Anton Sanko met Jonathan Demme when he worked on a music video and says, "Demme was unknown. We became good friends and kept in touch. One day I told him, just as a friend, that I was burnt out on pop music and would like to write for films. He asked me to do a documentary he was doing. It took off."

Caplin says filmmakers work with the same people from project to project if they like them, and advises, "If you meet young filmmakers who you think have talent, get with them when they're young. If they go somewhere, you'll go with them. Go to places like SXSW Festivals and Sundance to meet young filmmakers." Kaye agrees that you have to get out and meet as many people as possible:

> Film festivals are a fantastic way—even the lesser-known ones. You never know who may be there. It may be their first film and they could turn into a major director. You can go to a podunk film festival and meet a future Academy Award–nominated director. They're a great way to meet music supervisors, producers, directors, and people just starting out who five years from now may be big. People who are just starting out often like working with other people who are just starting out to develop a relationship over time.

Kaye goes to Sundance every year. He recommends having CDs to give out whenever these types are near: "CDs are the equivalent of business cards for a musician. Nobody wants to see a résumé. They just want to see what you can

---

PROFILE

Eric Kaye is Creative Director/Executive Producer for The Lodge, a music production, design, advertising, and licensing group. After putting his dream of being a rock star aside, he developed a very successful career writing songs and music for a variety of outlets. He's written music for many TV shows and films, and his music appears on more than 100 commercials for clients such as Mercedes, Coca-Cola, and AT&T. Now he's again putting more energy into playing with a band, the Strines.

do." He's being asked more often for DVDs so they can see what the music looks like against a picture. Kaye advises, "Take some video from TV and score your own music onto it with a note saying it's not real but it's a sample of you scoring a picture." Jeanne DaSilva advises getting involved with organizations at a grassroots level—any film festival organizations, film production organizations, Women in Film and Television, film schools like NYU—places where people in film congregate. She says, "Go to their events or advertise to them." This avenue is worth pursuing if you want a full-time career.

ADVERTISING

Advertising uses original music, too. First make sure yours is ready. Nick DiMinno says, "If you don't feel someone will hear your best music, don't put it out there. I can't stress this enough. When you put something out that's not your best, you do yourself a disservice." Producers need music tracks more than they do songs with vocals. Your biggest competition these days is major labels. They've learned the value of ads for promotion and sometimes try to break an artist by offering music to a producer for commercials. Glen Caplin says, "Commercials have become the new independent radio. They have become a good way to break new music. Look at Dirty Vegas: That track went platinum and radio didn't pick up on it until the commercial. Fatboy Slim broke through commercials." Audrey Arbeeny says:

> I think there are more opportunities than there used to be. I see the demise of the big music-production-dinosaur houses. They controlled everything in advertising, had on-staff writers, and locked out the independent person from getting into the commercial industry. Home studios are better now, equipment is cheaper, and ad agencies look for less expensive opportunities to get new artists or to have fresh writers in. It's a huge area of opportunity.

Many producers began as musicians, so they will at least listen to new people. Do you think you must move to a major city to do commercials? Local businesses everywhere hire people for theirs. Kevin Joy, President of Joy Music, says while aspiring to be a rock star, he was heard playing live and hired to do commercials for local businesses in Syracuse, New York. After several jobs in advertising and a record deal that didn't work out, he started his own production company. Joy still submits his own songs to publishers and advises:

> If you're songwriters and want to get into this business, keep writing good songs. Try to get someone to place them. You can't go right to an agency. Go to music producers. AMP (Association of Music Publishers; www.ampnow.com) represents music houses that do most of the major

music for advertising houses. If you're a songwriter or act, get to a music producer. If you do underscores, it's good to affiliate with a music house. Don't eliminate music houses if you're a songwriter. Contact them. They may be able to hire you on a per job basis.

The AMP site has a page with contact info for most production houses. When you interact with them, show your personality. DiMinno says, "My business exists on relationships. If you have two equally talented people, the guy who has the personality and has fun will get the gig every time. Make them laugh a little." Contact them all! Joy says he listens to everything that comes in. Bernie Drayton says, "Call me on the telephone. I try to listen to everything. Send it short—no more than five minutes, with one-minute to minute-and-a-half cuts. If you can't get it in that time, you're not doing it. Send it on a CD—I don't have time to download files." Understand what producers need. Joy says, "They're not looking for jingles anymore. They want it to sound like it has nothing to do with the product—like a record." Drayton says songs for commercials have the same format as regular songs but in shorter terms. The optimum length for a commercial on TV is 45 seconds. He adds, "I don't want to hear somebody's jingle. I want to hear what you do musically. I can apply that to whatever I want to do in a commercial."

Drayton says writers get paid the least—a fee. There's a little paid by ASCAP, BMI, or SESAC, but at a much lower rate. It still helps pay bills. Joy says, "There's a need for incidental music—underscored stuff that you can't buy a record for—and a good demand for music to evoke a mood in a commercial. It's a good way to still be creative and stay with music." He adds they sometimes prefer an indie who's making waves: "An unsigned band with a huge following that's under the radar screen is considered cool." Sometimes a commercial has a tight budget, so producers look to indies for cheaper music. Michelle Bayer she's been asked to provide music because a national commercial "only" had $20,000—a lot to you but not to a name artist or big record label.

If you have time, see if a production house can use your help. Sometimes they hire musicians. Often it's unpaid, but the lessons are worthwhile. Talk to local businesses and ask who handles their commercials. Maybe someone will be interested in giving you a shot. Bart Herbison, Executive Director at NSAI, says, "Songwriters can earn a living doing production work and still do what they love." Check local newspapers. What businesses advertise? Herbison adds, "There are many things out there. Every car dealership in America will buy a jingle from you if they like it." Joy advises, "Keep writing. Be as unique as possible. Eventually someone will hear it." The more people with access to your music, the more chances of success!

VIDEO GAMES

Todd Brabec says, "Video games are being widely used as a source of income for writers. It's a great area for new and upcoming bands and writers. There are a lot of games and they sell millions of units." Video games offer opportunities, but it's hard to break in. Jim Black says, "Video games can be a lucrative market, but they've become more like film. There are music supervisors for games. Don't go directly to the companies—there are gaming supervisor books out there. It's become a sizable industry." Search them out. He adds that there's more money in composing for games, but that market is completely oversaturated.

The fees for use of your music in video games are a lot less—they even try to get it for free. Publisher Martin Pursey, the founder of Bonaire Media in the U.K., explains, "They want tracks for their games but will not pay because they see it as a promotion. It isn't promotion! It's self-gratification if you put a song on a game without being paid. If they are willing to pay for it, do it. If not, walk away. Why should they get your music for nothing? Have self-respect!" Gaming supervisors often want hits for their games. But like in advertising, some use new, hip acts that are making some waves.

Study games first to know what kind of music works. Composer/Sound Designer Steve Horowitz writes for games and warns, "If you don't like games, don't write for them. People who do this spend a lot of time playing games. You need to be a gamer." Try playing a few games to see if it's for you. Michael Sweet, Creative Director of AudioBrain, specializes in games and elaborates:

> Both the ability to write, and to realize the implications of having to write, a score that can go from section to section in an instant is at the heart of the matter. It is important to listen and understand how game scores work, interactive and adaptive branching, dynamic sound effects, etc. After you understand how they work subjectively, then think about how you might build a game score and add your unique style to it.

Learning technical skills gives you an edge. Sweet explains, "For game audio, a thorough knowledge of MIDI and audio sequencers, as well as how to build instruments for samplers, are probably the most important technical hurdles. Things like audio compression, conversion, and file formats are also helpful in gaining an advantage in writing for games." If you get serious about writing for games, check out G.A.N.G. (Game Audio Network Guild; www.audiogang.org). Its members are composers, sound designers, voice-over directors, game designers, producers, and others in the interactive entertainment industry. It's a good place to network. They have panels and online resources with the latest info on many areas of this field.

MUSIC LIBRARIES

Music libraries provide music that's less expensive than getting original music from an individual songwriter or publisher. Mitch Coodley, President of Metro Music Production, says, "A music library is the sound equivalent of having a stock photo library. A person or company can rent music, one song at a time or one production at a time. They don't own the music, but they pay for the right to use that music for their specific project." Libraries have gotten more popular in recent years. They allow networks to access a larger variety of music. Producers turn to library music to provide fillers and pieces of music to fit into tight budgets. Stewart Winter, composer and the cofounder of VideoHelper, a music library, says:

> Production music is created specifically to be licensed. Libraries give producers a less expensive alternative. There are tons of varieties of production music, which in turn gives them a wide variety to choose from. Legally, it's a lot easier to use production music because it's ready to be licensed, as opposed to using a song where lawyers have to hammer out a price. Production music is about one one-hundredth of that price.

Joe Saba, cofounder of Video Helper, says libraries have become an increasingly significant part of the media landscape. With a 100-plus channels of cable television, producers don't have time or money to hire people for custom work. Saba encourages, "There are more opportunities to place your songs with libraries. If you build a catalogue, you can develop a royalty stream. You can be at a bar drinking and your song comes onto ABC. You make fifty bucks, so the next round's on you!" Libraries don't pay a lot for each usage, but it adds up once you're in the loop of a good library.

How do libraries work? Coodley explains:

> If someone is a constant user, they usually take the whole library to have it on hand. A very occasional user gets it off the website. They'll find a piece and ask the cost to license it. They give me their credit card and I send them an AIFF to do a one-off. It ranges from the very occasional that we get from websites to everyday clients who use music constantly and need access to the whole library. Then there are people in between who say that they need all the harp strings we have. We either work on a needle-drop basis or an annual blanket basis. A needle-drop is one use of one song—it's the equivalent of having an LP and dropping the needle. So technically, if someone uses that piece at the beginning and then at the end of a video or a program, that's two uses even though it's the same piece.

When you write for a library, you don't have a project. It's pre-scored music. You need to study what works best. Saba advises putting yourself in the shoes of someone you're trying to sell music to. Don't think, "I have something good." Think, "What can they use?" He says many libraries have niches, so if you enjoy writing a very specific type of music, you'll probably find a library for it. Saba emphasizes the importance of being really great at making music. He wants music that's in-your-face, attention-grabbing, and different. Coodley says you need a superb ear for your production and engineering skills: "It's rare to find people who do both. Library music is very sophisticated, extremely well-composed and crafted. It has to last for a long time. If you want to make a living with it, your pieces must have staying power."

Why place music in a library? Coodley says that most of it can be done in your spare time if you have a home studio, and explains, "It's out there for-ever, potentially making money, circulating in the world. People have the opportunity to use it. When they do and it goes on the air, you'll collect ASCAP or BMI royalties." The earnings from library music are more often from TV airplay, which makes them all yours. Winter says, "We can pay a licensing fee on a blanket basis to use your entire library for a certain amount of time, or license each cut individually for a set fee that's based on the library. There isn't a nationally instituted fee in this country." Saba advises, "Keep one hundred percent of your writer's share. I've seen the owner of a music house take twenty-five percent of anything that comes out of the show." Winter adds:

If it's a work for hire, make sure that you still own your composer's fee. They'll tell you that they own publishing, which is standard. But for per-formance royalties, you should be assigned the composer's fees. Some libraries say that you keep fifty percent of the composer's fee and they keep fifty percent. That's becoming kind of regular for many larger libraries

PROFILE

Joe Saba is President of VideoHelper, a boutique production music library. He got his professional musical start right after college in 1993 as the keyboardist for Fabulon on EMI Records. When Fabulon stopped playing together, Saba partnered with Stewart Winter. Working at ABC, they wrote music almost for fun. When they realized they could actually make good money at it, Saba thought, "Screw the major labels!" He is much happier making the music he wants to make for a decent living with library music, without a French stylist buying him clothing.

because they work with a producer who helps them fine-tune it. I don't think that's terribly nice, but it's done. Make sure to keep your composer's fee. Don't sign a buyout agreement. You'll lose complete rights to the music!

As in any biz, some people take as much as they can get. It's your job to protect yourself! Saba says it can be lucrative if you're patient: "Sometimes royalties take a year or two to come in. But once you have a few cuts out, you can have a stream. If you're trying to get a band off the ground, you can have one or two thousand a month coming in. The range is incredible." He advises checking out the Production Music Association (www.pmamusic.com), a not-for-profit organization whose members work to raise the profile and value of production music. It's a great resource for composers.

If you want to place your music in a library, Saba recommends finding one that fits your style. He says you'd need at least ten to twenty songs to approach a library. Winter adds, "For each cut in the demo, you want thirty seconds to a minute." He warns that you shouldn't submit long tracks: "If you don't have us by the first five seconds, we go to the second track." If you don't grab them with the third track, it won't happen. Winter prefers getting CDs rather than tracks by email because it's handier to listen to again. Coodley looks for production values and the concept. He says you have to understand what underscore music does:

> *Even if the vocals have been taken off a song, it sounds like a song. Sometimes I get calls for a song. But as background music, which is what library music is, the sound of an instrumental song isn't always what is called for because there's usually some kind of mood or dramatic element that people are attracted to, which works for the picture. So if I get a new writer's demo, I listen to hear if they understand what drama is.*

Research music libraries. Winter says, "There are tons of libraries. Just Google them. Libraries usually take outside submissions." Saba says, "The Production Music Association has a list of its member companies, all of which are respected libraries that have been around. That would be a great starting point. . . . If you see a library is doing music like yours, send your music with a note explaining why it would fit with them. It can hurt if you send music that doesn't." Audrey Arbeeny, who has a sports music library, says libraries use good, general music. She advises not giving them your best songs. They will take exclusive rights, so don't give them music you might want to use for something else. But if you enjoy creating music, write some just for a library.

Mark Wood has been writing music for many years and has his own library. He explains, "I love to write sports music. I wrote for the Olympics and ESPN, and all the sports networks call me to write music for them. It's my forté. After about fifteen years of doing that, I have hundreds of compositions that I have the rights to, so I can release a music library on the side." It's hard to start a library these days. You need a big catalogue and many contacts. Saba says, "Starting a library starts with good music that someone will find useful." It's easier if you have a niche, like Wood does. But check out the competition first! Coodley explains:

> You'd need enough music to call it a library and be able to tell clients that this will fill a niche. One disc won't do it. You have to present your music as a catalogue even if it's small. You could probably get by with only a few CDs. You would let clients know about it through phone calls, advertising, getting listed in trade journals, and going to trade shows. National Association of Broadcasters (NAB; www.nab.org) is probably the biggest. It's very difficult to start a library without serious money behind you. Libraries that started recently started pretty big. They do a lot of expensive packaging and send free CDs all over the world. So it can cost a few hundred thousand dollars if you want to do it right.

ALTERNATE MARKETS

There's music everywhere: telephones, elevators, airplanes, etc. Ted Suh says, "Technology drives new and innovative ways to deliver music and for people to utilize it. Whether it is through a portable MP3 player or as a cell phone ringtone, technology drives the new markets." AEI Music Network has been licensing music to companies for years, including for airlines and stores. Someone working for AEI saw Alex Woodard in a club, got his CD, and did a deal. Through AEI, his music has since been used on Abercrombie and Fitch soundtracks, and in restaurant and retail establishments from Vegas casinos to Home Depot. Danielle Egnew says Pope Jane's music was also licensed by AEI.

Tina Broad says BROTHER has a great creative relationship with Robert Cromeans, the maverick Scottish hairdresser and artistic director for Paul Mitchell. They play and compose for him when he puts on theatrical fashion shows. Suzanne Teng's music is regularly licensed on yoga compilations and in yoga and acupuncture videos. Teng says she's very involved in these communities, so people know her music: "People are aware of our music because it's reviewed in a yoga magazine. That press helps." Find appropriate markets for licensing your music.

Some corporations make compilation CDs for promotions. Michelle Bayer says, "Sometimes stores like the Gap have compilations and often have totally unknown artists included with name artists." They do pay for the use! Some companies even take the artists on tour. If you see a compilation, do what you can to track down who put it together and get in touch—they might make another. Or, call the corporation and ask what company creates the CDs.

Todd Brabec says ringtones are huge now. What are they? Suh explains, "Ringtones are thirty-second snippets of music that alert you to incoming calls on cell phones." Brabec adds, "When someone downloads a specific composition, the artist gets money. That's negotiated with the music publisher. If the ringtone costs two dollars, the artist usually gets about twenty cents of that. So each time that the ringtone is downloaded, the artist gets money. If you have a big song, millions of people download it onto their phones. You can make a lot of money." Suh prefers songs with commercial success. He explains, "It has been proven that these songs produce the most downloads. Whatever is hot on the air will sell well as a ringtone. We definitely want a wide variety of music, but ten percent of our catalogue makes up ninety percent of our sales." The best way to approach a ringtone distributor is with research. Suh advises learning which companies put real marketing dollars behind their ringtone portals. He explains:

These are the companies reaching out to all niches. Once you know more about this industry, contact the content managers—the people who decide what content will be sold through our distribution channels. Content managers are sent demo tapes all the time, so please have a unique approach for pitching the content manager on your music.

Whatever avenue you want to pursue, first learn as much about it as you can. Learn the technology that drives these markets if you want to compete in them. Suh agrees, "Technology is presenting new and exciting opportunities for musicians, as well as creating niches for them. You have to educate yourself on the technology and the business models that surround this evolving environment for selling music." Ask experts all your questions. That's how you learn, and it also lets the inside people know what you want to do. The more your music is out there—because you're performing it live, you have it all over the Internet, you're getting reviews, etc.—the more your chances that people who license music will hear it. You never know who'll find you if you get your music out there!

CHAPTER 17

Performance Opportunities

I can't say enough about the importance of performing live. There are many places to perform for good money and also sell CDs and merch. This chapter is an overview of many types of gigs that I've found, how to get booked, what each type looks for, and how to be creative in finding places to perform for money. You can create many variations once you're aware of the possibilities. Marly Hornik says, "We'll play anything if we can make money from it." That's the indie spirit!

CLUBS

There's a huge assortment of club venues. Some websites list them and offer opportunities for acts to open for each other in their regions. *The Musicians Atlas* is touted as THE source by many acts. Michael Johnathon says, "You can earn two hundred thousand dollars a year playing those small rooms for singer/song-writers. They hold lots of fans." Speech says, "Throughout the country, there's a string of clubs that fit anywhere from two to eight hundred people standing. That's literally where hip-hop people find themselves at." Start with smaller clubs and work up to larger ones, like Whisky A Go-Go in L.A. Gena Penney books for it and says it's mainly a rock 'n' roll club. She looks for a band's potential. For a chance to play there, Penney says she wants a picture, an excellent three-song demo, and a short bio with where you've played and with whom: "I just want to see what you sound like, look like, and where you've been." Penney also does a showcase once a month for unsigned bands. She sees every band and picks what she thinks are the best ones—she tries to book six acts. She emails everyone she can in the music industry, and the showcases can get a good turnout. Because she's so strict about her choices, people expect to see excellent bands. Penney advises being polite when approaching anyone. She says, "Some bands come to a promoter and get cocky. That makes people in the music business sour. We're all human beings! These people come up with these attitudes out of nowhere." Make your attitude courteous and professional!

Ask other artists for suggestions. Many clubs expect the bands they book to have a following. Don't moan about not having one—build it! Some clubs will help if they like your music. John Taylor, Entertainment Director at Tootsies Orchid Lounge in Nashville, says acts with no following can still play to people because buses arrive with tourists to hear good country music. Some artists perform four, five days a week. He adds, "We give everyone who comes into town a shot. You must have a good voice, sing in key, and have decent pitch. We help developing acts with their stage presentation. We do auditions on Saturday and in the morning. Many kids come in and we get them up onstage. They play for tips. People *do* tip." Taylor advises sending a promo package. For him, it's all about the music—the songs. He likes individuality. Several major artists broke at Tootsies.

Performing Covers

Many artists are happy paying rent by doing covers. Depending on your genre, there are opportunities for regular gigs in supper clubs, bars, etc. Clare Cooper says she got her first one when she saw a piano player doing songs she liked to play when she went to a club. She asked about auditioning, and now says:

The timing was right: He needed a sub to work Thanksgiving night. I subbed a few more times. When a regular shift opened, it was offered to me. As I became known, I met people who hired for other clubs. It was all cumulative. Also, I'm very adaptable and open to playing in a lot of different styles, and I'm a good sight reader and accompanist, which is important for piano bars. I play mostly covers, but I can sell my CDs at the gigs, and I'm fortunate enough to have built a small following who request my originals.

Many musicians scorn doing covers. But doing them can pay bills and improve your skills. Sarah Mann, a booking agent with The Music Garden, says that playing covers is very, very lucrative. She explains:

Usually, bands make much more money playing covers than originals. Musicians can make a very good living strictly playing covers, but often they struggle playing their own material. In the Southeast college market, the average show pays between fifteen to thirty-five hundred dollars, depending on the popularity of the band. Some of the top cover bands can make up to seventy-five hundred to ten thousand dollars per show.

Do covers sound better to you now? Mann says several types of private parties book cover bands: "The college market is a very large portion of our business. Fraternities and sororities book a lot of bands, and pay very well. High school proms, country clubs, corporate events, balls, weddings, and high school reunions also book a lot." To break into this market, do your homework to find agents who book bands. Pay attention when cover bands perform. What songs work? Ask bands and venues what agents they use. Mann says:

> Most private party buyers use booking agents. It's beneficial to the band to sign exclusively with an agency. The right cover set list is vital. The band has to play covers that the crowd wants to hear, not what they want to play. It must be songs that are very popular, that people can dance to. A good picture and a demo are also key ingredients for a successful cover band.

Open Mics

Open mics help you get started and create new fans in places that you were unknown. I Googled "open mic" and got 3,600,000 links. Search to find appropriate ones for your music. Forge thinks open mics are a good way to start building a core fan base. He explains, "You have to show people that not only can you rhyme to yourself in a studio, but you can also engage and excite the crowd. You need to learn the art of rhyming in front of people and overcome nervousness." There are open mics for many genres of music. The Bluebird Café in Nashville has one for singer/songwriters every Monday night. While artists audition to play there on other nights, anyone can perform on Monday nights to show their stuff. Preech says that people just starting should use open mics to get their name out. He got started by doing street battles and open mics. It helped him stand out from other rappers. He explains:

PROFILE

Little Egypt is a hip-hop act that began in 1995. Members **MC Forge** and **Visual Poet** put out their first vinyl record in 1999 and have played at colleges and festivals on the East Coast ever since. Now they tour nationally, opening for name acts including Mos Def and Fat Joe. In 2001, they were invited to tour Poland after Polish radio picked up on their record. They've licensed a song to PBS and are working on more opportunities.

I didn't care if you were DMX or a signed artist, I would battle you and make sure you knew I was here. I battled everybody and anybody. I did shows and mix tapes. Wherever there was a mic and another MC who thought he was good, he caught the business. On every block in New York, there are five people who claim they can rhyme. To be the man in this game, you have to do a lot and eliminate a lot of people who think they're rappers.

Listening Rooms

Listening rooms are becoming more prominent across the country—a blessing for musicians and fans. Jennie DeVoe says they're places and venues where the evening's highlight is music, not the beer or pickup element of the scene. It could be a coffeehouse, a private home, or a bar or venue that is a club—usually nonsmoking. A club may even be a listening room only on specific nights. DeVoe explains:

When it's promoted as a nonsmoking listening show, the ticket buyer is aware there will probably be seats and no chitchat through your show. You can make a place a temporary listening room or go to places that stake their reputation on being listening rooms. When I started, it was easy to fall prey to bar band pitfalls. Telling your audience to buy beer and taking set breaks gets old. You realize you can draw a crowd because of your original music or because you induce a party scene and sell beer for the owner. You can do both, but the challenge for me was getting people to come based on my original music. If you want to move people with your music, stake your reputation on doing a mostly original show—hope you are worthy of a silent listening room. I love throwing in covers we do well, as a bonus to the show.

The Bluebird Café is a legendary listening room. I attended an audition in Nashville. Four times a year, singer/songwriters line up on a Sunday morning to perform for one minute. Owner Amy Kurland says she listens for the song. She'll turn down great performers if the song isn't there. Those who pass the audition get a slot about six months later on a Sunday night to do three songs. A songwriter plays Sunday several times before getting another slot—if they cut it. I asked people waiting to audition why they did it. They talked about the legend of the Bluebird and its history. Some audition many times. Most people I spoke to were in awe of the club. Kurland explains why it's so popular:

We didn't want to be a nightclub or singles joint. We wanted to have real music. Because of this, we got good musicians to play here. When we said no smoking, people cheered. We keep a clean bathroom and have safe parking. The Bluebird is an essential element of the music business process in

Nashville. Publishers and record labels have locked doors; the Bluebird welcomes you to give it a shot. You have the chance to play for people and meet people. Some of them have keys to those other locked doors.

The Bluebird is considered THE PLACE for songwriters for a reason: Kurland is very selective. Many of Nashville's top stars got their start at or played the Bluebird, including Garth Brooks, Faith Hill, and Alan Jackson. What does she look for? Kurland says:

I want to hear good songs and the best presentation that a songwriter can give. I don't care if they can't sing. It is important that they know the lyrics. I want to hear a universal idea—things I can relate to or that are interesting to me—something solid and sensible. I don't want to hear mush. There are too many people singing about "I love you" and "It hurts that you don't love me." You need more than that. I want a song that makes me want to cry, or laugh, or reminds me of my own life. That's a great song.

If you want to learn more about the Bluebird, Kurland wrote a book—like a scrapbook of its history. You can get it off the website (www.bluebirdcafe.com).

COLLEGE MARKETS

The college market offers lucrative opportunities for those who work it. Colleges book a variety of entertainment for different campus venues. Artists' opinions are mixed, but everyone agrees the money is good. Forge says, "Colleges pay us the most—more than clubs." Eric Lambert, Executive Director of APCA (Association for the Promotion of Campus Activities), says the less you charge the first time, the more you'll probably get. He adds, "For solo acts, the average introductory price is eight hundred to twelve hundred. You can't charge too little; you're touring. You can get stuck at that price, too. You can ask for more the next time, but people will refuse to pay it. Don't price yourself below seven hundred dollars." Beth Wood has had several schools hire her multiple times, which isn't the norm. She says she's learned to take her job very seriously and takes pride in being professional: not showing up late, calling when she's supposed to, and trying to remember everybody's name in the student activities groups. She adds, "It sounds like common sense, but if you are kind, professional, and friendly, people are more likely to hire you again."

The college market has its downside, too. Nancy Oeswein, President of the award-winning Auburn Moon Agency, a college booking agency, explains:

There are pluses and minuses to the circuit. Audiences are very inconsistent: You might have three people one night, two hundred the next. While you reach your audience in terms of the future record-buying public, it's not guaranteed that you're building a fan base. There's not a high rebooking record. If the school really likes you, they may have you back in a year, most likely two. Some schools have you in a nice, high-end auditorium. In others, you play in cafeterias or a designated multi-use room where they set up chairs and have coffeehouse programs. Some set up a stage outdoors. It varies significantly.

Musicians get hired to play in cafeterias, auditoriums, dorms, and other spaces. Ezina Moore says sometimes you have a few hundred people and sometimes three who are trying to eat or do homework. Sound systems range from a boom box to an awesome PA with an engineer and huge production staff. Lambert warns that unlike clubs, colleges are not usually technically efficient groups and may have no clue about your sound and light requirements:

You need to have stuff to bring with you sometimes. Unlike a club that will advertise and publicize everything for you, colleges don't do this. They expect you to send them table tents and posters. The person who books is a student: They're working and they have school. You have to be able to work with a myriad of different situations. Your material has to be flexible. If you book yourself into a homecoming concert and the mellowest you get is a cover from Cake, that's a problem. No one can dance to that. Be careful when you book the gig that they know who you are and what you're playing. If they say it's called Hard Rock Night, go ahead and jam out. If they're hiring you for the President's Banquet, know what they're expecting to hear. Student activities departments work differently from campus to campus.

Adam Richman, who does 100 to 150 college gigs a year, says, "I supplement my income by selling CDs, stickers, T-shirts. It depends on the school and if they've come in their pajamas, without money. I've always been able to sell to a percentage of the audience." Usually you get some expenses covered, too. Forge explains:

They have the budget to pay expenses without too much negotiation and trying to get over on you. You don't have to deal with separate promoters. When dealing with clubs, there are many more dynamics, including being worried about the bar and your draw. Going to a university is easier because your target audience is right there. They have big concerts and smaller weekly events. We try to target concerts because we want to be associated with the names who perform. Sometimes you have to play in cafeterias. We will play anywhere. When they bring in a headline act, we look to open for them.

Oeswein warns that while it generally pays well, there's a lot of competition in the college circuit. She explains:

> People hear that the college circuit pays well, but it doesn't pay out for every-body. Probably five, ten percent of artists competing in the college circuit make a living out of it. There's probably another twenty to thirty percent who do well enough for it to be worthwhile. The other fifty percent of artists drop out. It takes time to build an audience. There's a big investment for artists. If you're one who does break through, it can be a really big payoff. Not all artists are a fit for colleges. The band market has been soft in the past few years. Often they look for cover instead of original acts. Colleges think in terms of what will fit with Homecoming Week or with Parents/Siblings Weekend. Many artists try to find creative ways to market themselves. Some colleges have Women's History Month programs, or something unique that fits, such as celebrating gay/lesbian issues. If your heritage is different, such as Asian or Latino, you have your own months to do specific programs for. The market has an abundance of what they refer to as "coffeehouse acts." They'll do a coffeehouse series to fit a venue. Many times, they won't be able to handle the production of a larger act, but they can have a direct input and a microphone on stage and bring in a solo or duo act.

Solo or duos often work best. Many artists pare down for the college circuit and save other venues for a full band. Make it as easy as possible for colleges to book you!

Forge says that in 1999, he and Visual booked shows in the colleges they'd attended—being former students gave them leverage. To book new colleges, they each tackled half the country and went to college websites for the contact info of whoever is in charge of the college activities board. He explains:

> We send a letter via email. They always request a kit. It's best to send the music as well as a video, so they can see prior shows. We've tried to choose clips from the names we've opened for. When you start out, you may not get a lot of money. Now we get at least two thousand dollars per show. At first, we realized that if we got three to five hundred dollars per show but opened for [big name acts], that could be used for publicity to spread our name. You can't go into negotiations at the beginning thinking they'll pay your rent.

Visual adds, "It's a juggling act. Sometimes you take a gig that pays less but you have a chance to reach many thousands of fans and to perform there the next year." Moore says she called schools and did mailings. She went to music conferences and found CMJ's annual conference, catering to the college markets, especially helpful. Moore says, "Meeting people face-to-face helped me get on college radio. I gave my CD to college radio people at conferences." This led to touring in colleges. College booking policies vary. Often they book during one semester for the following one. Visual says, "Schools differ. Some book a month or two in advance; others book in November for April. You should talk to them six months in advance." Oeswein adds:

> I get calls from independent artists telling me they made twenty calls to schools. What are they doing wrong? I ask if they made twenty calls to the same school, and they say called twenty different ones. Sometimes what it takes is twenty calls to one school. No one's getting rich on any side of the college circuit, even in the agencies. I'm more interested in what feeds my soul than what's feeding my bank account. I think I'm the rule, not the exception, in the college circuit.

Many colleges do what's called "co-op buying." Schools in the same region work together to book the same act on consecutive days. Richman says schools they play sometimes book the same act over a certain amount of nights for a cheaper price. Usually the act offers a price for three gigs over five nights or five gigs over seven nights. It helps the artist get exposure. The college covers Richman's hotel accommodations and, for an isolated date, his travel expenses are covered as well. APCA has a cooperative buying program. There's a big meeting where the other schools say that they want the same artist, and they all work together to bring artists in during the same time frame for a discounted rate that all agree on.

Oeswein says independent artists who do very well in the college circuit are usually represented by an agent. Some schools only do a few shows a semester and have a tremendous turnover. They rely on agencies they trust to screen artists carefully and only send appropriate ones. It's hard to get representation. Wood says, "By chance, I knew an artist who was looking to get out of college touring. She worked with a good agency, so I sent them my music. It was very good timing because they were looking for a female artist." Oeswein says that when she looks at artists, about 55 percent of what she looks for are things such as the lyrics, performance, ability to captivate an audience, and even image. The other 45 percent has nothing to do with the artistic side. She explains:

> When I'm having an interview with someone, I have to feel that they'll work hard, be professional, be reliable, and show up on time. I'm willing to do some hand-holding—it's my job. But there's a limit to how much I'm willing to do. I am your agent and friend; I am not your mother. I make sure that anybody I take on understands it's a partnership. We communicate clearly,

understand each other's expectations, and make magic together. We'll help expose what you do to a whole new audience, but only if we work together.

A performance video helps, but Oeswein recommends not investing in one your first year in the college circuit. Once you get agency representation, someone can help you put it together. It's critical to have the right kind of video and presentation. She explains:

Many people make the mistake of investing a lot of money in a video that isn't good for the market. No one's going to get in the door with me if they don't have really good lyrics. The whole package has to be there. You have to have something to say. That's true for the overall market. People want things that are meaningful. They also want good musical skills, good vocals, and a good manner onstage. You have to be able to engage the audience—to talk to them. One of the wonderful things about this market is that it demands the artist be able to engage the audience. You won't have audiences with people throwing things across the bar and things like that.

Many artists go to conferences hosted by organizations like NACA (National Association of Campus Activities; www.naca.org) to make contacts in colleges and find agents. If you showcase, people who book for colleges—agents and student activities reps—can see if you've got THE GOODS. The trouble is, artists say NACA is very expensive, and lately it's hard to get a showcasing slot even if you're willing to spend the big bucks to do it. APCA is a smaller competitor. It doesn't have NACA's clout, but it's cheaper. Lambert says, "I'm an entertainer and I know how it is to try and make it in this business." He wants to give indie musicians a less expensive alternative, so APCA doesn't charge submission fees. Membership is $199 and very worth it, even if you don't attend a conference! Lambert says:

NACA's directory only covers its associate members (artists, agents, and schools that are members). Our directory has every school in the country that does activities programming. Theirs has about eleven hundred schools, and ours is closer to twenty-eight hundred. You don't have to be a member of

PROFILE

Adam Richman is a singer/songwriter. He was in his teens when he asked his parents for his college money to use for recording a CD instead of going to school. Richman went after the college market and now does 100 to 150 gigs a year. After I interviewed him, he signed a deal with Or Records.

APCA to be listed, but all the member APCA agents are listed. You also get performance reports, our magazine (in hard copy, eight issues a year), a marketing book series, etc. We update our list monthly, which you can download as it's changed.

You have to submit music and be accepted to attend an APCA conference. But if you get a booth, you also are guaranteed a showcase, unlike NACA. APCA is also a lot smaller. The colleges tend to have smaller budgets, and Lambert won't showcase anyone who gets more than $2,000. Oeswein says while APCA is much smaller than NACA, it's helpful for an independent artist. There will at least be some agents watching you showcase, and you'll be seen by student activities people. Oeswein adds, "What will get my attention a lot faster than sending me one of the six or seven hundred CDs I get a year is someone who is actually at the conference and takes the time to meet me." Richman broke into colleges through NACA. He purchased a booth in a regional conference and learned about it:

> I went to the conference with my CD in a CD player and tried to make friends with people. After I established a rapport, I played my CD and let the music speak for itself. When the music piqued their interest, I sealed the deal with competitive pricing. I booked a good number of contracts on site. Then I was immediately approached by three agencies that work exclusively in the college market. I chose one. I did the same thing at two other conferences. I stood in their booth, played my CD for people, and booked seventy college shows.

Richman says personality helps a lot. He believed if he could get them to listen to his music, it would sell itself. His challenge was to lure them to his headphones. He did so with good personal skills. Students liked his music and his competitive pricing. If you take a booth at any conference, Lambert recommends having a banner that is no more than eight feet wide and no less than two feet from top to bottom, in full color, and gives a quick visual image of you: "If they go past your banner, they should know exactly who you are and what you do." Have a one-page brochure that you can make on your computer. Lambert recommends having 20 to 30 professional press kits in a nice binder, and a CD to give to schools that are truly interested. Don't include prices. Lambert also advises:

> Become a better businessperson. A lot of people put money into it and then just wait for schools to come to them. You have to make a professional image and sell yourself. If you come to an APCA conference and do great business but don't follow up, you've wasted your money. You can't just sit back and

expect everything to happen to you. People will think you didn't want to do it. You have to stay in touch with them. The college market demands that you be a businessperson.

Frat parties are another good source of college income. A good repertoire of party music is needed. Often you play to hard-drinking students. It's not for all acts. The money is good—some artists get at least $3,000 for a party. To pursue this direction, promote your gigs in fraternity and sorority houses. Give out CD samplers. Quiz everyone you know to find former members of a frat. Ask them to write letters of recommendation, or better still, if you're an alumnus of a fraternity, call your chapter and ask someone to recommend you. Once you get in, word can spread. National houses tell chapters in other schools about good acts.

Not everyone likes playing colleges, but many acts supplement club touring with college gigs. Playing colleges enables many to pay their bills while still playing venues they love—those that don't pay much but generate a bigger following. Richman agrees, "If you're an independent act without money to help keep you on the road, playing college shows balances it out. Many bands try to book four college dates over a month tour because they know that night will supplement their money over the next week of club touring."

CHILDREN'S EVENTS

Some musicians say good money can be made playing for kids, depending on your music and how adaptable you are. I once met a rock musician who played in a private nursery school to entertain his girlfriend's students. The kids loved the songs he improvised. Word spread and other schools booked him for good money. While he still pursued his rock music, he made a CD of original songs he'd written to entertain little ones, and sold many to parents and bookstores. These opportunities can supplement your income.

While he also plays concert halls and colleges, Zak Morgan earns a good part of his living performing at libraries and schools. The Internet helped him find gigs:

I looked up a town and searched for public elementary schools there. You get the phone numbers. No matter what type of venue you want to play, it's all very accessible on the Internet. I made lots of phone calls, sent material, and even outlined an article about myself. I made a list of people in a region where I wanted to play and called to ask permission to send material. I checked up ten days later. People won't give you a gig if you don't ask for one. If you're willing to make the phone calls and put in the hours, you'll separate yourself from ninety-five percent of other people.

Morgan also does showcases, which he refers to as a "little commercial" in front of potential presenters of a show. He explains:

> Find out who does showcases in your region, where you can go and play for ten minutes. People watch, and if they like you, they book you. I've walked out of places with forty or fifty gigs. They're for all kinds of music. Ask arts councils where they are. Some sponsor you or pay part of your fee. For me, there are elementary school teachers or librarians, but colleges come, too. Theaters from towns and neighboring states also come and look for talent.

Jennifer Marks has toured high schools to promote her new release for Bardic Records. She says, "The kids have been amazing. It will be very helpful for building a fan base." Suzanne Teng gets many gigs in schools by referrals and word of mouth. She says, "Now that I'm a momma, I've done more work with kids and I'm going to get even more involved. We perform, and depending on the age group, we do demonstrations or have hands-on activities." Many people find it's good to have something besides a performance, such as a talk or a demonstration of your music. Some musicians create programs that help school-aged kids, such as talking about not doing drugs or developing confidence.

FESTIVALS

Festivals offer great opportunities for income and to get your name out, if your music is suitable. Most cater to families. Visual says they pay and feed you well. He adds, "Sometimes we profit as much from selling CDs and T-shirts as from the pay for playing." MANY artists agree. Beth Wood says:

> I find festivals very lucrative. They offer the chance to perform for hundreds of people who might not have heard you before and a chance to reach a diverse group of people. Most festivals are happy to let you sell CDs. Some even set up tents with volunteers to help you. Festivals offer a guarantee (a commitment of a specific amount of money no matter the turnout—or the weather), so you can count on that paycheck.

Sometimes you must prove yourself before they pay well. Mary Gauthier says most opportunities to play a festival are worth taking, explaining, "When they give you a break and your name won't draw anyone, just do it. You'll have the opportunity to be on a bill with bigger names. Use it as a résumé builder. Almost always, you sell lots of CDs." DJ Minx says she played at Detroit's Electronic Music Festival on opening day. She didn't know what to expect and says:

When I started to play, the crowd slowly grew. Policemen, firemen, CNN News, homeless people, children, and people from all over the world were dancing and coming to life to this music. When I was done, I did interviews, took photos, and tried to speak to everyone who wanted to talk with me. I began to tour more after the festival.

The Kerrville Folk Festival—at 18 days long!—is one of the most prestigious. Dalis Allen, its producer, explains, "We are a songwriters' event. People come just with a guitar and perform. We've had Judy Collins, Shawn Colvin and Peter, Paul and Mary. The music has to be original and excellent." Allen says that while people may not have heard of all the performers, they'll come anyway because they assume if they're playing Kerrville, they're probably good. She emphasizes, "We are a songwriters' festival, so I look at the song, their performance of the song, and also variety. For the festival, it has a lot to do with the response I feel to the song." Allen accepts packages only during October and November. Include a photo, a one-page bio, where you've played, and your music style. Allen is interested in some personal info in your bio that tells who you are, where you grew up, and what influenced your music. She adds, "Be concise and simple, at least in the first go-round. Stick with it, but don't be a pest. You want to make sure people hear your name but not overdo it." Allen is much more likely to book someone she's heard live than just from a CD submission, so she tries to go hear artists—if you tour in Texas, let her know. If Allen likes your music and will be traveling to your city, she'll contact you to see where you're playing. A good way to break in is through Kerrville's New Folk Emerging Songwriters Competition (see Chapter 15).

Check festival websites for details. See who's played them. Do you fit in? Forge found festivals online and sent each a letter. Mary Gauthier mailed her CD to every festival promoter she could find. One heard her on the radio and gave her a shot. That's why it's so important to work hard to get your name and music out there. Once you have a good performance at a festival, word gets out. Christine Kane believes that being on the road, opening for people, and meeting promoters attracts opportunities. Beth Wood suggests contacting local convention & visitors bureaus to see if a city has festivals. She says it's like building a résumé: Once you play some, other festival directors are more likely to hire you. She explains, "A festival director once said that if you play well at a festival, get a quote from that festival director to put in your press kit." Festivals book way in advance—note submission deadlines. Rachael Sage adds:

We apply to an enormous amount of festivals. There are forms to fill out. You can submit digitally on their websites or submit pitch letters. Others have very specific rules. Look at submission policies for everything. Some start up to a year in advance. Others are in the fall and you apply in spring. Build a database and note all the little factoids and policies. You need to organize and amass information without being overwhelmed—have it organized at your fingertips.

Start researching now. Artists say they plan a year in advance. Target specific regions, so you're not jumping around too much. Everyone advises bringing lots of merch. If you're good, it sells. Announce your mailing list. Some festivals have many thousands attending, so you can increase your following substantially if you rock the show.

HOUSE CONCERTS

House concerts—concerts that are commonly held in someone's living room—are very popular. The host empties the living room, brings in chairs, and puts the word out through flyers, newspapers, and email lists. Usually, two sets are played with a break in between, allowing lots of time to interact. You get most or all of the door. Beth Wood loves house concerts. She explains:

House concerts can be very lucrative. Often the cover charge is a "suggested donation," usually ten to fifteen dollars. People are generous. Audiences range from twenty to sixty people. Lots of folks buy CDs. Hosts usually have a list of regulars who promote the show. They usually put you up for the night. I suggest attending a house concert first. It is a different kind of performing environment that takes practice to get used to. There is usually no sound system, so it's a different kind of singing. Lots of folks gather around in close quarters—you don't have the usual barrier between performer and audience. You also connect between sets and after the show. I enjoy the environment because it has a laid-back, intimate feel, and people are there to listen! The worst scenario at a house concert is that there are not many people, in which case you have a little pocket money, a free place to stay, and nice people who are interested in your art.

The cover charge is considered a "suggested donation," because for tax purposes it's a party, not a business. Most people respect that and pay up. The people hosting house concerts are like patrons of the arts. Many cover the cost of putting on the party and give the artist all the money. They're usually smoke-free and intimate. Suzanne Teng says she's done quite a few through referrals: "Someone organizes it and we play at their house. We have one fest we do regularly: A man has a nice pool and cooks a meal. He organizes the whole thing, charges to come, and takes some for food. He goes all-out." In 2000, Pat DiNizio created his own interpretation of house concerts, which he called the Living Room Tour, by putting the word out on the Internet. He let fans know about it with a press release and says it was a successful venture:

> Within weeks I had ninety bookings in the homes of fans across America. A few months later I drove across the country several times by myself doing a solo acoustic tour of living rooms. I wanted to get away from the concept of a band and all that goes with it for a while. It was an enriching, rewarding experience in terms of me putting forth new music and making friends with people I had never met. I knew them from the phone or Internet. Then suddenly, I appeared at their doorstep with my PA and guitar and played all night for them. Some people pay my fee outright. Others pay my fee and also charge the guests. Most people willingly provide a room for the night. It cuts down expenses and makes the evening more special—it becomes more of a family situation. Some people do this every month.

There's a network of homes across the U.S. that host house concerts. Many are listed by state at www.houseconcerts.com. Do a Google search on "house concert" and you'll find many enthusiastic patrons that sponsor them; I got more than 11,000,000 links. Beth Wood says there are several ways to break into house concerts. One is to organize them yourself. Or, encourage fans to do them. She advises going over specific details in advance so everyone knows what to expect:

> Usually you play for the door, so be SURE of everyone's expectations about the money. Sometimes performers and hosts agree to take smaller expenses out of the door. It is essential to hammer that out beforehand. Another way to break into the circuit is to play as an opener. Many house concerts are happy to have a short opening set, as long as the headliner trusts you. Hosts on the house concert circuit usually want to hear you live before they book you. If someone is considering you, let them know when you are playing a show in their area. Also, many series hosts attend

the Folk Alliance Conference—it's helpful to showcase so you can play in front of these folks.

Phyllis Barney, President of Folk Alliance, says that some musicians use the house concerts circuit as filler nights. She explains, "They're good if you're trying to space things out between weekend gigs. It's a good network because people are in touch with each other. They have the chance to see each other and get to know a regional area first, then begin to branch out. House concerts are listed on our links and in the database." House concerts don't work for all music. DiNizio says, "They're friendlier to traditional folk and bluegrass artists that come with an acoustic instrument." Singer/songwriters do very well, too. DiNizio brought a PA system because he's a rock musician playing acoustically and he likes how it sounds—most performers don't use one. Bring lots of CDs, DiNizio says: "If people feel what you say musically, they want to take part of you home."

Send fans who want to do a house concert to www.houseconcerts.org to learn how to host one. Most hosts do one a month, so they're very selective and want musicians with a buzz. DiNizio says you need some publicity before trying to book house concerts, so put the word out that you want to do them. The hosts running it should guarantee at least twenty attendees. Alex Woodard's house concerts are booked and promoted through his street team. He says these living-room shows are more intimate and fun: "I charge ten bucks and give them a CD. Usually I sell more CDs and more than twenty people show up. I sell lots of merchandise, too. It's all about word of mouth." Woodard sometimes does shows with no guarantees for very active street team members, to thank them for support.

In addition to the typical house concert circuit, sometimes people hire artists to play at private parties and barbecues. If your music appeals to a college-age crowd, find students willing to have you play at a house they may share. Underage students are a lucrative market since they can't go to clubs to hear live music. They can invite many friends, charge admission, keep a portion for beer, and give you the rest. Let folks know you're available for all types of house concerts.

BUSKING: PLAYING IN PUBLIC PLACES

It takes balls to play in public places. Hamish Richardson says BROTHER spent years on the street, "Never exclusively, but consistently." They busked from Australia to L.A. and warn you to be prepared if you want to busk. Richardson says:

> *It's do or die on the street. If you can't build, hold, and win over your audience every show, you don't eat. You learn to think on your feet, embrace the*

spontaneous, and quickly get to know what works and what doesn't. It's delightful, particularly once you crack a formula for what works for your act. We have so much fun. But it is tough. Tough and fun.

Some cities, like New York, have formal programs for buskers to perform in the subways. Dorothy Potter earns extra money by busking in the subway in New York on her own. She says she does it on *her* schedule, and used to do it three times a week. She explains, "Busking is great. I'm a platform player. I set goals. A busker I know stays in the subway until her bill is paid. I go with just a guitar. An amp is a pain if the police come and tell you that you can't be amplified. I go down for two hours and come up with forty to sixty bucks."

David Ippolito is a veteran of outdoor performing. In 1992, he didn't want to play in bars anymore. He bought a mouse amplifier, had a microphone duct-taped to a stand, and went to Central Park, hoping to make lunch money. About nine people stood around. He left quickly. The next week he spotted the place where he plays now, and he set up his stuff that Sunday. After an hour, there were about 250 people on that hill. Ippolito invited people to sing along. He's played for about 500 people at a time ever since and says:

Every Sunday, I play to seventeen-year-old girls, thirty-year-old women, forty-year-old men, fifty-year-old couples. They all sing the same music. They've showed up every weekend for twelve years now. It's a little field of dreams right in the middle of Manhattan. Nobody knows about it, except for a few thousand people. Friends help me. In twelve years, I never ask for money. My guitar case is open and just sits there. I make a living doing it.

When New York City came down hard on the musicians, Ippolito started getting permits. But Potter says it's perfectly legal to perform in public if you don't use an amp—it's considered freedom of expression. She explains, "They can't tell you not to sing in the subway. There is nothing illegal about getting money for it. It's a public space. For them to tell me I can't sing, or other people that they can't toss money into my hat, would be an invasion of liberty. This has been through the courts." Ippolito says many musicians ask why *he* does this and *they* can't. He answers:

You can do it, too! Just do what I did: Show up. When they tell you to stop, smile, pack up, and disappear like a drop of water on a hot rock. Then come back and play. When they write a ticket, pay it. When they confiscate your equipment, go to court, get your equipment, and go back. If that's what you know you want to do, follow your heart and you can do it, too.

Some performers and performances are spontaneous. Ezina Moore always travels with her guitar. She says she was once on a very delayed flight when, after sitting on the runway for hours, people got angry. A flight attendant asked Moore to entertain. She was shocked but performed until they took off. She sold 20 CDs and got $50 in tips from passengers. Canjoe says he frequently does impromptu performances in public restaurants, on city sidewalks—even once at the baggage terminal at LAX airport. He says:

> *If I am traveling by air, I frequently get stopped by passengers and security and asked to perform. I've been pulled over by state police a few times for speeding and given side-of-the-highway shows for them. Once there was a major traffic accident that snarled the interstate for hours. I did a side-of-the-road show and sold several CDs and canjoes. I once performed for one of our state senators and a state trooper when the senator had a fender bender in front of my house. I sold canjoes to both of them.*

. . . AND MORE!

There are endless possibilities for gigs. Read Jeri Goldstein's *How to Be Your Own Booking Agent*, which has tons of info on gigs that aren't in clubs. Resort hotels book entertainment. Cruise ships are great gigs for jazz, cabaret, and other genres that appeal to those who take cruises. Call ship lines and ask to whom you should send material. European cruise ships offer great opportunities, too. I Googled "cruise ships" and got more than 4,000,000 links, including cruises for rock and pop. Alex Woodard played The Rockboat, an annual four-day floating concert. He explains, "They rent a Carnival® cruise ship, get great bands, invite fans on board, and play every night while the ship sails. My stage manager at SXSW was involved with the company that started it. Enough people called on my behalf, so they brought me on as the only artist from west of the Mississippi."

The more exposure you get, the more possibilities come your way. Woodard says showcases bring paid gigs. If your music is happening and you create visibility, alternative gigs will come. Rachael Sage got a residency at Starbucks:

> *Everything is just people—your relationships. I went to Starbucks all the time. They saw me with a guitar or keyboard and got to know me. A guy who worked behind the bar began managing and booking artists. I gave*

him my CD and he said I could play any Friday night I wanted. He later booked me on a pilot program tour of Starbucks all over Florida.

While she only did it once, Sage found the experience worthwhile. Take risks! Beth Wood has a passion for sports and often sings the national anthem at major sports events. She explains:

I got to audition for the Texas Rangers through my brother, who worked for them. For the Dallas Mavericks basketball game, I called the front office and asked for the promotions director, the person usually responsible for booking the anthem. She told me the process: Send a recording, audition live, etc. I love doing the national anthem. I have a passion for hearing it sung in a traditional manner (which most teams want). It's a win/win situation: I go to games for free, and thousands of people hear my name and hear me sing. The Texas Rangers have asked to help them judge their national anthem tryouts the past two years.

Corporate conferences also offer many opportunities. Ezina Moore asked everyone she knew to keep her posted on events at their companies and she got booked into an assortment of events by being so proactive. Call and ask! Many companies hire entertainment for holiday parties, company events, and openings. They use a variety of music. Research to find appropriate conferences. There are more details on this in my book *The Real Deal*, and Jeri Goldstein gives a lot of info in her book, too.

Another way that Dorothy Potter supplements her musical income is through hospital gigs. While some organizations get musicians to perform in hospitals for free, many pay at least something. Hospital Audiences, Inc. (www.hospitalaudiences.org) is one that places musicians into paid gigs. Fees aren't huge, but if you don't have to travel far, it's more income for you. Potter says:

PROFILE

Canjoe John builds, sells, and plays the canjoe, a one-stringed musical instrument with one tuner key, ten frets, and the string pulled through a 12-ounce beverage can as the resonator. CanJoe Company is an internationally recognized business with national and international sales. Canjoe has sold more than 10,000 canjoes since 1994. He has played with many great artists, such as Bill Monroe and Little Roy Lewis, and recorded his first album in 2000. He continues to play fairs and other venues, and gets lots of publicity for his unique talent.

I may go in for an hour and get seventy-five bucks. The most I've ever gotten for doing one was three hundred dollars. When you're a working musician, you learn to mix the big gigs with the small gigs—that's how you earn a living. If I get one hundred and fifty to two hundred dollars to show up, it's great to fill in my schedule.

If you want to see the world, try U.S. military tours. AFE (Armed Forces Entertainment; afe.afsv.af.mil/Tours.htm) has six circuits throughout the world: Europe, Caribbean, Pacific, Mediterranean, Balkans, and Southwest Asia. Tours range up to six weeks. AFE coordinates and purchases all commercial air travel. They don't pay salaries, but each person gets a $150-per-day honorarium, including departure and return days. You're expected to pay for food and accommodations, but they'll help you find cheap hotels—and sometimes even get you a room for free—and you can eat in base dining halls for a reasonable price.

Some artists make a good living playing church functions. While Christian music works best, churches are open to performers with good music that has a good message. If you create an appropriate talk to go with your music, your chances of playing churches get higher. Lost And Found makes their living through churches. George Baum says the duo began by playing anywhere folks let them: a church dinner or youth group meeting, then at a Christian camp. In 1980, they released their first album, with no goals—they just liked playing music. Baum says:

In 1986, we decided to try something crazy: We rode bicycles around the perimeter of the United States, playing concerts along the way. Over the course of three hundred and forty days, we rode about eight thousand miles and played two hundred seventy concerts at churches, colleges, high schools, and camps. We [mostly] stayed with families, arranged by hosts. Michael had just graduated from college and was looking for something interesting before entering the field of public policy. I had been working in restaurants, playing in bands on weekends, and was looking for something interesting, period. That year, we supported ourselves selling our album from 1980 and accepting offerings that the hosts would occasionally collect.

In 1990, Lost And Found decided to make music their full-time career. Building on contacts made during the bike trip, they developed small regional tours. Eventually, they got invited to play at youth gatherings, which helped get exposure to larger groups. Baum elaborates:

By combining our bike trip exposure with youth gathering opportunities, we unknowingly created a cycle of churches and youth gatherings. This is how we've been able to make a living since 1990. Some situations are more beneficial than others. One of the most helpful things to play is a national denominational youth gathering. These events are a means of gaining national (albeit limited) exposure. By definition, a national youth gathering brings together folks from all over the country. Consequently, when we go to any state, there are bound to be some folks who have seen us at their denomination's big gathering. Then they bring friends who have not seen us before, the word spreads, and concert attendance grows.

Baum says Churchnoise (www.churchnoise.com) is helpful: "Churchnoise members gather together several times each year to discuss their various successes and challenges in trying to make a living, independent of Nashville and all things corporate." One of the main benefits of joining is access to the website, which provides concert notification. Listeners can sign up on the site for any or all of the performers listed and receive email notification about a performance in their area.

Cultural arts and civic centers also offer opportunities for performing. Phyllis Barney says those who book for cultural arts centers are invited to the Folk Alliance Conference. The *Billboard International Talent & Touring Directory* lists many of them. If you showcase there, you could make contacts. The Association of Performing Arts Presenters (APAP; www.artspresenters.org) is the big national organization for these venues. Presenters come from all over to view showcases at the annual conference and book artists. Christine Kane has done showcases that landed her shows in the arts market. She's opened for people in various theaters and has been asked back as a headliner. Kane adds:

The arts market has national and local conferences and showcases. It's an enormous world unto itself and is geared way more towards theater troupes and one-person shows, etc.—not so much a singer/songwriter thing. It's a little surprising that I've gotten showcases—I have no idea why this particular door opens for me and others don't.

Often, those who do the most legwork get the gigs.

CREATING YOUR OWN VENUE

Capitalizing on his huge fan base, David Ippolito has rented halls for indoor concerts for more than six years because he can't play the park in winter and doesn't want to play bars. He found a 225-seat theater in downtown Manhattan to rent for $400 plus $50 for the sound guy. While on the subway to the first concert, he told people about it and hoped they'd show. A friend collected $20 at the door. It sold out. After doing a few shows there, another musician suggested doing shows uptown. Ippolito said he couldn't afford to, so they did one together at Merkin Concert Hall. They continue doing concerts there with a full band. If you want to put on your own concert, Ippolito advises:

Renting a hall is a big one. If it costs fifteen hundred dollars to rent one and you've got fifteen hundred and twenty dollars in the bank, rent it anyway. Worry about the twenty dollars later. Put up a sign and hope people come. You're doing your own thing—grassroots. Your other choice is to complain that you can't get a concert, that nobody knows about it and nobody's going to come. I hate sounding like Nike®, but just do it.

Many artists take the initiative of renting a venue when an acceptable one won't book them. If you have the fans and a way to attract them, you can make good money. Bobby Borg took the initiative in college: Instead of waiting for club owners, his band set up its own club. They rented a house and threw huge parties. They arranged for fans to travel back and forth from colleges and charged admission to hundreds of people. Borg adds, "We became better known for throwing those parties than playing at clubs. The band lived upstairs. It provided us the chance to make money, get word out about the band, and sell CDs." That's what it's all about!

CHAPTER 18

Putting Together a Domestic Tour

Touring is a big revenue stream. Dean Seltzer says, "Seventy percent of my income is from playing and thirty percent from merchandise sales." He earns a full-time living. You can, too, if you're willing to pay your dues by working your way up. I've gathered as much info as possible to help. Zak Morgan says if you stay home practicing, you'll be a better player but won't become a better *performer*—the key to indie success. He advises:

> Play as many gigs as you can. Performing is not just showing how good a player you are. You have to connect with the audience and entertain them. The more shows you do, the better you get. It's like an athlete: A quarterback in the NFL will never develop unless he's on the field. You must be in the trenches. At first I took gigs that didn't pay well, just to cut my teeth. Gradually you get better, and people call. Learning how to connect with an audience is just as important as learning to play your instrument.

Being a good performer is a separate skill and must be developed over time and with practice. Once you feel comfortable with it and the audience response increases, try to perform in new markets. This chapter will tell you how to start building a tour that works for you. Get your music out there!

LESSONS FROM THE ROAD

Play live as often as you can. Even for little money. Even if it *costs* money at first! If you love playing your music, don't worry about money—it will come as you grow as an artist. Gigs give you exposure, help create a fan base, and get you invited back for bigger bucks if you prove yourself. It's critical to build a following of fans that buy your stuff and support you in general. You CAN build a large following—IF you have THE GOODS. Always have an email list handy for fans to sign. Ask club owners for a slot right after someone with a big following, and set up quickly. Many will stay around if your music speaks to them, and they'll support you. If your music doesn't motivate fans, improve! Complaining about how few people come to hear you doesn't do any good—becoming a better musician and performer does.

Rachael Sage advises being open to all performance opportunities: "I received that advice and took it to heart. I had a fear of leaving New York and going out, but as soon as I let go of that and put it out into the universe that my goal was to connect with an audience that would connect with my music, gigs started coming. I'm still doing it." Prepare for bombs. Most artists have them at the beginning, when a lack of experience shows and people react badly. Playing as much as possible will help you improve. Mary Gauthier explains:

> Everyone starts out pretty much the same: nervous, self-conscious, no stage skills, and the songs aren't quite there yet. I had to get good before I could get paid. I took a lot of getting beat up: being ignored, playing for empty rooms, opening for people and not having the crowd respond. You have to fall flat for quite some time before you get good at it. The only way to get tough is to work those muscles out—the emotional muscles you need onstage. They don't get strong just because you want them to. It's like going to the gym: You need to work them out onstage.

I asked successful touring indies for specific touring tips. These are things you usually learn from bad experiences, or don't learn at all. Almost everyone advises being prepared for *anything*. Ezina Moore says, "You have to stay organized and be prepared with a Plan B for when things go wrong. For example, I did a gig where the contract stated they had a PA. I always request that the model type be listed in the contract rider. We get to our sold-out gig and they have none. So forty-five minutes before a show, I have to rent a PA and figure out how to use it." Beth Wood advises writing details down, explaining:

> If there is a good coffeehouse in Chattanooga, make a note so you'll know where to find it next time. After a show, write down the venue staff names so you'll remember. Before you leave, write down how many CDs you sold

and how much money you collected so you don't forget. Putting things in writing also helps if you book way in advance: By the day of your gig, you may have forgotten the details you agreed on. Ask questions if you are unclear on anything when making a deal. It is better to ask a bunch of questions to clarify your deal now than to be surprised by something later on.

You can whine when things go wrong or you can be proactive. Robby Baier suggests taking spare gear with you, especially capos (little units you clamp onto the guitar to change the key)—they always go missing. Matt Allison advises making sure to have an adequate quantity of CDs and merch for the tour. If you run out, have someone at home ready to FedEx stock to your next tour stop. He adds, "Running out of merchandise can put a real dent in your potential earnings." DJ Minx advises, "Always take your CDs, vinyl, etc., on board the plane with you instead of checking it. Chances of the airline losing your luggage are slim, but that could make or break your tour!" Be prepared on the biz end, too. Danielle Egnew says she's learned that touring is not just about music. It's also about administration and organization, marketing and sales, and communication. She explains:

Touring teaches you to be a clear communicator. There is nothing worse than showing up to an out-of-town gig and finding you have no place to stay— when you thought you did! Don't tour until you have planning and marketing strategies down, or you'll set yourself up for failure. If you don't have a clear strategy, you'll end up sleeping in your car and your low blood sugar will catch up with you after five days of the three-for-a-dollar 7-Eleven® corndog special. A struggling, starving artist cannot do a decent performance, and doesn't smell so terrific when five-days-old recycled socks walk into a club. That artist cannot realistically uphold their end of a tour: to provide quality entertainment to all venues they have contracted with. You have

PROFILE

Mary Gauthier is a singer/songwriter who tours the world often. The *New York Times* called her third album the No. 1 Independent Album of the Year, and *Rolling Stone* gave it four stars. Gauthier performs all over the country, in Canada, and in Europe, where she began with a licensing deal in Holland and worked her way into Germany, Italy, France, and Scandinavia. After five years of independent success with no need for a record deal, her win/win situation attracted a deal from Lost Highway Records (Universal) that would advance her already established career. She signed after our interview.

ONE CHANCE *to make a first impression. If it's not professional, there are hundreds of thousands of other artists that club can book. And they will.*

Create a tour budget. You can't just tour with no thought to expenses and expect to earn a living. Businesses create budgets. You must, too! Gregory Abbott advises becoming knowledgeable about the economics of touring: when and how much you get paid, costs of travel, cartage, hotels, etc. He says:

Know the personnel you'll need, both in front of and behind the microphone. Ultimately—secondary to getting your music exposed—learn how to turn a profit. Profitability is what enables you to continue doing that which you love to do. All this need not be a grind. The education is not only interesting but enjoyable. Its potential for enhancing your quality of life is limitless.

Learn how to use the Internet and other sources to save money on travel expenses. Jennifer Marks says, "Hotwire is the bomb! You can get great rates on good hotels instead of staying in a Motel 6." What kind of expenses should you budget for? Manager Tina Broad says:

We pass along accommodation, meals, backline, production, and engineering costs to just about every client, big or small. This usually means we're up for flights, ground transportation, the usual staff costs (paying our drummer and local guest players), gas, tolls, per diems, and incidental costs like replacing lost cables, new strings, batteries, shipping merch out. These are all costs specific to each tour, but we also pay insurance premiums quarterly.

Pay attention to the little things that can make each stop on your tour run more smoothly. Forge recommends spreading out the driving as much as possible. He says, "Driving takes its toll—break it up. On a ten-hour drive, switch every two hours." Beth Wood suggests, "Chewing on sunflower seeds keeps you awake while driving." Baier advises, "Get there early so that you can relax before the show." Wood recommends observing the golden rule: "When you go to a new club, be friendly. Learn the staff's names. Remember the sound person's name—he/she is your friend. Write this information down so you'll remember it when you go back. If you are nice, people are generally excited about booking you again." Be ready to self-promote. Forge says it's key to understand that you're marketing yourself whenever you can, so don't be shy about self-promotion. He explains:

Put your name out. Have you gone to a show with an amazing unknown artist and not known their name? I make sure that at least one of us has a

T-shirt on that says our name. After the show, we tell people we're selling CDs. Do everything in your power, without being annoying, to put your name out. During an interview, say your name a few times. Those little things make sure that you aren't ignored or overlooked.

Michael Johnathon believes in creating the illusion of success, as he's done with his "WoodSongs" radio show. If people have to wait on line to get into your gig, or get turned away, they'll want you more. So Johnathon recommends doing venues that are smaller than what you could fill. He explains:

When you know you can fill seventy-five seats, only go to fifty-seat rooms. Let it go around the circuit that you're filling the room, filling the room, filling the room! When you can fill one hundred and fifty seats, stay in the hundred-seat rooms and keep filling them. "WoodSongs" is a good example. I stayed in that little studio with people being turned away after waiting in line. Then I went to a hundred-and-forty-seat theater. That packed out fifty-seven weeks in a row. The bone is, it's so good that you can't get tickets. Let's be honest, it's only one hundred and forty people in a media market of two million. It's not a lot but it feels like a lot. Now we're in a four-hundred-seat room that fills up every Monday. I'm going to stay there, turning people away, until I'm ready to go to an eight-hundred-seat room. It works.

We've all seen people line up to get into a club where there aren't hundreds of people, but making them wait creates the illusion of a big crowd hungry to get in. See what illusions you can create, and then grow into them in reality.

Band vs. Solo

The more people in your act, the more expensive it is. I know signed acts with five or more musicians who couldn't get tour support from their label because there were too many to send on the road. The number in your act should be part of your budget. Do the math. A full band behind you might make you happiest, but at what cost to you? George Baum advises, "Keep your band as small as possible—the more people in the band, the more you'll have to charge to keep them going."

Many venues that pay expenses won't pay for everyone. Howie Statland says, "I just did a tour of the West Coast by myself—almost three weeks of shows every night, singer/songwriter–style. I have a band but couldn't afford to bring them." As I said earlier, some acts alternate touring with a band and touring solo, choosing appropriate venues for each. Marly Hornik hires two or three musicians. She says it's easier to get paid with a band because more venues will book an entire band to come. Singer/songwriter venues tend to be coffeehouses, not bars, and don't make as much profit. She explains, "It's a lot easier for a bar to say it'll give a percentage of the cash register total or a guarantee. You can make a lot more money that way. It's also more fun musically for me, but I played solo for years before I was ready to play with a band." Many musicians have day jobs to pay their back-up musicians, but that won't enable you to make a full-time living with your music. Take this into serious consideration before you start to plan a tour.

Should I Move to a Major City?

Many artists who don't live near one of the three big music cities (New York, Los Angeles, and Nashville) strive to move. Should you? My answer is a big fat DON'T! It's much harder to break into one of those cities than into a smaller town. "Music cities" are competitive, clubs are empty if you don't fill them, and it's very hard to get press. Instead, work your own region. It generates better opportunities to enhance your career. Be the star in your region and move out from there. Beth Wood says she made friends with guys in a band from North Carolina who offered her help. She quit her day job and moved there. She says:

> I rented a room for VERY cheap, and wrote and played a lot—anywhere and everywhere that would hire me. The Southeast has many towns strung together up and down the East Coast. I moved to a small town near Asheville, a very supportive artistic community. In a sense, I made a strategic move from trying to get ANYONE to notice me in a giant pond filled with big fish, to a smaller, friendlier pond where I could get heard more easily. I'm not saying that would work for everyone, but it helped me a great deal.

There are more opportunities and less competition in smaller markets. Danielle Egnew says Pope Jane started in a Montana town with bars and clubs that pay cover bands to play on weekends. She approached clubs and asked if they'd book Pope Jane to play all night, like a cover band—only they'd play all original music. Egnew says:

> The clubs and bars were excited about having an all-female band play all origi-nal music, all night. They didn't care what music we played as long as their bar tills were packed at the end of the night. So we packed their bars, being the only all original gig in town, and sold lots of CDs and T-shirts. It gave us a chance to write more than eighty songs, just to cover our weekend obligation, and play them live to see what people liked and disliked. More artists would benefit from seeing obvious opportunities around them, rather than obstacles, and make it

into something that pays off. No one suggested to me that I hit up cover band bars to do an all-night original show. I just figured, hey, where there are people drinking and wanting to dance, we can provide music—and get paid to do it!

Publicist Jim Merlis says, "Certain towns are a bit easier than others. Any town where people go to become famous is harder. You're more appreciated when you go to other markets. People in New York are more jaded because they see so many musicians." The cities Merlis refers to are harder to make money in without a huge following. Many musicians refer to these markets as "pay to play." They invest more money in promoting the show than what they make, or they have to presell tickets and maybe even pay for them in order to do the show. Gena Penney says if you get booked to play at Whisky A Go-Go, you're required to sell tickets. She says there's a big difference between pay to play and presale: "Pay to play is giving somebody money and they get onstage and do their thing. If you're just going to buy all of your tickets and don't have people to sell them to, I don't want you to play, or your money." Penney requires preselling to ensure an audience, not to get money. Wait until you have a decent fan base before approaching clubs that do this. Tackle smaller markets before trying to break into larger ones.

WRITTEN AGREEMENTS

To make money as a professional, get all touring details in writing. To make sure things run smoothly, EVERYTHING needs to be established in writing in advance. Each musician has his or her own perspective, so I've included several. Ezina Moore says:

I never do a show without a contract, period. I get everything in writing, down to the model of PA system that they have and the name of the engineer that runs it. I require a deposit for every show and a monetary guarantee for each gig, no matter how small the venue. I require the venue to pay for advertising in the local music paper. My band is on salary, so I have to cover expenses. When I go into a club, I look at it as a joint venture. We are both in it together, so expenses and profits should be shared.

Moore says unlike many complaining musicians, she always gets paid well. Her confident manner makes promoters take her seriously, and she gets what she asks for—in writing—or she doesn't accept the gig. Jennie DeVoe says that a simple one-page contract, clarifying all expectations of both the purchaser and artist, is best. She advises getting a nonrefundable deposit if at all possible—it keeps clubs and festivals in check. You must protect yourself!

Marly Hornik says either the bar has a set schedule and fee and you can take a slot, or they'll ask you to come up with a price. Think carefully before blurting it out. She advises:

> Take into consideration what night of the week you're playing, how long you're playing, whether or not there's a cover charge, how many people really go to the bar. I have to get guarantees when I take my band on the road. I try to be sensitive to the fact that a lot of these people are trying to keep venues that host original music open. Many places are closing. The audience is shrinking or spreading out over other activities. I try to be sensitive that these people are trying to keep that music alive and are taking a risk. They're on your side.

Hornik says most venues pay expenses. They almost always get a meal and often hotels: "Venues that host music regularly are used to dealing with touring bands, unless they usually only have local acts and you're an anomaly." Danielle Egnew says:

> We have been put up in hotels at the venues' expense. Some offered meal stipends in their restaurants. I have watched bands split hairs with clubs over receiving a guarantee up front—and they lose gigs. Most live music clubs don't have the money to front a band cash until the night the band plays and the bar makes the cash through the door. A touring band needs to be a smart business. But one that marches into a club making demands will catch a boot in its hind end, out the door. They'll not hesitate to stop doing business with divas. I can't stress that enough. Attitude nets an artist nothing but burned bridges.

Remember, ask and ye shall receive! Ask for everything, and then negotiate for a fair agreement.

Don't expect email confirmations to protect you as much as a real contract! It must be signed with a pen, not with your send button. Egnew says most big

---

PROFILE

Dean Seltzer had his last day job in 1996. Then he began by playing solo acoustic in ski resorts around the world. He got more serious after he returned from Europe in 2000, putting a band together and releasing an album. Seltzer has opened for top acts including Dwight Yoakam, Puddle of Mudd, Robert O' Keene, Pat Green, and the Baha Men. He plays a variety of clubs and even the rodeo.

festivals, clubs, and colleges send their own contracts. Pope Jane faxes the signed contract first and then mails it—only an original copy is binding. Visual says it's good to have your own contract ready if a venue wants to book you: "We have our own contract because some schools ask us if we have a standard one. I found it online on a website. It serves us. When we do a bigger show, with bigger universities, we add a paragraph." Tina Broad says BROTHER developed its own performance contracts and uses them wherever possible. The group has standardized its requirements in terms of backline and hospitality riders, so they go into most touring situations on their own terms. She explains:

> We've entrenched things like a minimum-six-foot table and appropriate lighting for the merch operation; clean towels; bottled water; high-carb snacks; full meals; types of rooms (e.g., doubles, nonsmoking); brands of amps for backline; minimum acceptable technical specs. They sound like small things, but when they're attached as riders to our contracts, it means fewer things for us to have to think about. Make sure technical and hospitality riders are appended to the signed contract so that you have some recourse if things aren't right when you get there.

Broad says they also make sure to invoice a booking deposit that's due in no later than thirty days out from their performance. It helps with cash flow. For example, when they're traveling to a gig where they pay for flights, they're not shouldering all costs till the full performance check comes in. Written agreements are the best way to ensure that you get what you need to perform your best.

IF ONLY I HAD A BOOKING AGENT!

Please, get real! Nobody will discover you if *you* don't make it happen. There is no fairy god-agent. Everybody wants an agent because they don't want to do the work it takes to get booked. But agents don't want acts who haven't done it themselves already. National ones won't touch an act that isn't playing nationally. Regional ones want artists who've tapped and conquered the markets within approximately a 300-mile radius around their hometown. Acts often aren't booked just based on having good music. People who book artists also look for your experience touring, your press, and most of all, a good base of fans who love your music. Getting all that takes time. There are no shortcuts around hard work and diligent phone calls. Please don't expect easy tips in this chapter. Making money touring is definitely doable, but YOU have to make it happen. I provide the tools, but YOU have to get off your butt and get busy. It takes patience to do it yourself at first, because people won't jump to help you.

Press will come if you persist in putting your name out and keep in contact with them. Fans will come if you've got THE GOODS.

It all starts in your local market. Create your hometown foundation before you get on the road. Kyler England says, "I started performing in my hometown of Raleigh, North Carolina, while in college. Building a fan base in your hometown is really important before starting to tour." Danielle Egnew agrees:

> To begin a tour, you must be able to develop your local marketing and promotional skills by playing for a few friends or in a local bar. The [skills] that go into throwing a living-room gig are the [same ones] that must be in place to book tour gigs—except tour gigs are on a much more organized and larger level. Make a deal with local clubs to promote your own night. Take the money you'd spend on hotel accommodations, food, gas, and equipment, and make some professional, terrific, 11x17, four-color printed promo posters to make you look like the most together, most amazing artistic act in town for your local gigs, and pack them. Pour your energy into where you are. Your local fan base will tell you a lot about your music and what you're trying to accomplish with it. Then use some of that money and record a tremendous album and get it pressed, even if it's in a limited quantity. An artist doesn't need to go two states away to do any of that or to get paid for playing. Plus, you'll learn a lot about what it takes to promote a show financially, which leads to an education on how to support the marketing for a tour.

Beth Wood adds, "Even if you have ambitions of conquering the world with your music, it is very important to develop a presence in your local music market first. Your home base can be your proving ground." Hamish Richardson of BROTHER says he and his brother Angus nervously approached a few pubs in their hometown that had live music:

> One or two owners took a punt on us and we had our first paying gigs. Long nights, unforgiving rural Aussie pub crowds, and we'd end up with about thirty bucks each. We got a bit of a reputation round town and started getting invites to venture to surrounding towns. Rugby nights, weddings, college bar nights—building a reputation was what it was all about. We did our own songs, mixing them in with covers—it was definitely a cover scene. We started making a few forays down to Sydney, three hours away, and finally decided to make the move to the big smoke. "They'll be back—three weeks tops," our old guitarist remarked to a friend. That was a lifetime ago.

Conquering your hometown helps get you out of it. You may have to hustle for the first few gigs—or even for years. Some artists whine about not making money from playing live. Are you one of them? Whining serves no purpose except to put you in a worse mood.

Be creative when you book gigs. Unless he's on the road with no choice, Alex Woodard almost always try to play places that DON'T charge a cover. He explains:

> Usually, I get paid off the bar and everybody's happy. For example, it's hard to get paid in L.A., but I have a great room that I play in Hollywood where I make good money off the bar. It's a venue with shows almost every night. But I don't charge a cover—the room maintains a good vibe and everybody's happy. I make most money off of shows and merch. On a good night I'll pull in four hundred bucks from the house, and another couple hundred in merchandise.

IF you have THE GOODS, or something remotely close to it, fans will come to your gigs and you'll start bringing in money. If they don't come, figure out why. Meanwhile, push on! There are times when your music isn't right for your market, or you live in a city like New York that's saturated with musicians. If that's your case, start touring elsewhere. Jennie DeVoe says she didn't have a clue ahead of time about the music business:

> I got a couple guys together, bought a PA, and started doing bar gigs, collecting fans, and slowly building my name. We did some covers until eventually the originals were well-known. I staked my name on my original songs. The motivation is still passion. The first steps are having a product to peddle—your songs, your voice, your performing abilities. You only have a few times to prove to a bar owner that you're going to capture an audience, make it grow, and perpetuate a need for you to come back. So a band better have something to offer before they get a gig, or it could do them in. Work a market until you own it. Then work a few more and start building your name.

Once you attract a following, you'll make money. Until then, use each gig as an opportunity to rehearse your live show. Robby Baier says, "I look at touring as a way to get tight as a band, get the songs out, and have a good time." Get as much feedback as you can to improve. It takes time, but it will gel when you get to a higher level of musicianship and performance. Baier explains:

> In Boston, I attended the Club Passim Campfire series and got into that scene. Northeast Performer magazine did a cover story on me, and I was able to book club gigs. I swapped with other performers. I offered gigs in the Berkshires and Northampton for gig opportunities in Boston.

Baier continued to get gigs by networking. He progressed to New York City and recently toured through the Northeast. Dean Seltzer began by calling Chili's and playing some acoustic shows there. Then he approached ski resorts, starting in Steamboat Springs for one season, then playing resorts around Denver and finally in Europe. Seltzer says:

> I called over to Sweden and just asked around at ski resorts. I didn't have a lot of contacts before I left. I just had a feeling, and a guy said that if I was good I could come over and play. I was doing solo acoustic stuff. I came back from Europe in March of 2000 after playing music at ski resorts in Sweden and realized that I couldn't build anything without a band behind me. So I put one together and started playing gigs. At first it was disconcerting, because I couldn't get musicians to play with me without gigs, and I couldn't get gigs without a band. For a long time I booked gigs without knowing who would play with me at that gig. If a great lead guitar player agreed to play with me on a specific night, I would tell him to keep that night aside for me and then I would try to find a gig to play. The first year was really tough.

Touring is work! It won't be handed to you. Mary Gauthier says you have to push people until they say *no:*

> That's hard for musicians to do. Most of us aren't sales people. But until they say no, it could be a yes. There's a fine line between annoying somebody and getting the no you need to move on. There's got to be a no or a yes. Often the no tells you to quit knocking on one door and move to another.

Michael Johnathon says with certain promoters and bookers, he understands from the beginning that he's talking to someone who really doesn't care about the music. You have to be prepared to talk to them in ways they understand and to give them what they need, not what you want them to need. He explains:

> Most bookers don't listen to the album. They just want to know the bullet points. You have to understand the needs of the person you're talking to, whether it's a club owner, a coffeehouse, a college school booker, etc. Their world is not music, playing guitar, or traveling the world singing. They don't get your world. Their world is the phone, piles of mail with CDs they can't listen to, and artists relentlessly calling every other day, being a complete pain in the ass. When you figure out what they need, really calmly and really briefly give it to them. Usually, they're so grateful to talk to someone who's making sense that they'll work with you out of gratitude. It starts that way, but when you develop your reputation, eventually you just work off of it.

FINDING GIGS IN OTHER REGIONS

So you're ready to book a tour? Get your press kit ready to send and exercise your finger to make it strong for making phone calls. Jennie DeVoe says:

> Getting into new markets takes a few good tools. A good press package is key. You have to earn your press package in a market. Once you have a story and a following in one or more markets, begin some detective work about clubs in other areas that you want to play. Start calling, and send your package to those places. It's good to have a relationship with someone over the phone so they know your package is coming and will open it.

Preech played beaches, biker weekends, and Jones Beach Greek Fest by doing lots of research on the Internet. He adds, "Sometimes you have to open up for free, and then you get invited back to play. That's how you get people to see how great you are." Israel Vasquetelle says the Internet has made finding clubs in other regions one of the easiest things in the world. He explains:

> Anyone who is in tune with their community should know about at least a few places that give opportunities to independent artists. The Internet is one of the best tools for anybody trying to get their name out there. It's definitely about networking. Someone halfway across the country or world can find out about another artist and ask them to tour together. If you live in New Jersey and want to play a show in Florida, go online, do a search on "Florida hip-hop," and you'll get a hundred different links to venues, artists, group websites. Contact them, build a relationship, and you can work together, share information, and open for each other.

Rachael Sage advises putting out what you want to happen: "You plant seeds. Apply to a hundred festivals one year. The next year you may realize you should apply to two hundred. You just learn." I agree with planting seeds. When you work to get your music around, things can blossom from the effort. Someone might remember you later when an opening act drops out of a tour. You may hear from someone you contacted a year before who held onto your material because you'd made a good impression. When you approach people, prepare to embellish what you have as I discussed in Chapter 3. If you don't have a manager, identify yourself with your company name as I suggested in Chapter 4. Even if you don't have a company, invent a name and use it. Ezina Moore did all this and says:

> *It was so easy! You gotta have a* Musician's Atlas. *I called clubs in whatever city I wanted to tour and asked them to book me. I pretended to be the manager. I mentioned that Ezina Moore has sold eight, ten, and now fifteen thousand CDs—that got their attention. Before the eight thousand sold, I told them that Ezina Moore was just on "Jenny Jones"; that she was the next—whoever was big at the time; that she was just signed to a million-dollar record contract by Soulful Warrior Records [Moore's own label]; that Ezina Moore was Miss Black USA (I never mentioned what year). Sometimes they wanted to hear the CD; sometimes they just asked the genre and told me when they had openings. I asked about their PA system, if they had a sound person, the capacity, and what they charged at the door. Then I negotiated a fee for myself and established a deposit amount.*

Many musicians recommend *The Musician's Atlas* to get started. It's easy to use and lists many clubs by city. Howie Statland says, "I found most clubs at first from using a *Billboard Guide* and *The Musician's Atlas*. I made phone calls, sent emails, and worked my butt off." Gena Penney says if a band with a good track record is touring through L.A., she'll consider them: "I'll try to put them on a strong night when I have four or five other bands that I know are going to be bringing a lot of people in. It's hard, though. If they don't have anyone to come and see them here, I can't do it." If the band is willing to promote itself well and is arriving a week before the show, she might give them 25 tickets to sell. She explains, "If you sell someone a ticket, that's a commitment. It's not like handing someone a flyer."

One of the BEST places to find gigs is to go to the websites of other artists who have music similar to yours. See where they're playing and contact those clubs. Dean Seltzer says, "I paid attention to the pulse of Texas music to see where the big bands played. Then I searched out those clubs to see if they were interested in having me play." Mary Gauthier says she started a database on her computer of places that had booked similar artists:

I was in Boston at the time so I started hammering names and numbers that were in Boston. I looked out towards the greater Massachusetts area. Then I went to Vermont and Rhode Island, then farther away. I go to Musi-Cal (www.musi-cal.com) and Pollstar (www.pollstar.com) and there are all the gigs in the whole country right there.

Artists' websites often have links to one of the sites Gauthier mentioned. Music-Cal is popular for indie artists with lots of gigs. Instead of listing dates on your site, you're linked to Music-Cal. Rachael Sage looked online to see where her peers were playing, and tried to get out and join with others. Take it a step further: Jennifer Marks says, "I often looked at where musicians of similar styles had been, and then just followed their paths." Literally try to book the same tour route as an artist who's similar to you. This makes putting a tour together so easy! Call the venues in the same order listed on the site and talk your way into a gig.

See if you can partner with other acts to split touring expenses. Howie Statland says, "Once I did a tour with a friend. We rented a car, booked a tour of the Midwest, and did it together. He opened up for me. We both pitched in financially and both made money from that." Or, for acts with a higher profile, Mary Gauthier advises, "Try to get in as an opening act. Call the main act and send a CD. Follow it up and follow it up until they say *no*." Many touring bands use local acts to save money and might let you open for them in your own region. Jennifer Marks says, "Doing openers is often an easier way to build a fan base." Check listings websites to see what acts will be in your area. Contact their managers, agents, and tour promoters, asking to open for them. You sure won't get it if you don't ask!

Contact people who handle live shows at venues such as amusement parks, theme parks, SeaWorld, etc. If they like your music and you develop a good relationship, you might open for top name artists. Why would anyone want you? Economics. You'd do it for free, or very little. That's okay, since you can sell CDs and merch, and it adds credibility to your press kit for other gigs. Call the Chamber of Commerce in any city in a region that you're touring. Ask if they have any city-sponsored events that include live music. Send a package. Live musicians perform at most New York City street fairs. Parks bring in live music. Find out who books those types of events. Go ahead and call!

So much of this is about networking and building relationships. If Matt Allison can book tours of the U.S. and other countries from his home in South Africa, there's no excuse for not getting yours off the ground—IF your music is ready. He explains:

Touring is all about networking. I became friends with like-minded artists and they helped me book the U.S. tour. I met other artists who enjoyed my music online, on message boards and in chat rooms. We hit it off. They offered to book shows in their states and offered up their homes as well. Some became my closest friends. The money made on tour was purely through donations and selling CDs at shows. I played in New York, New Jersey, Connecticut, Texas, and Oklahoma for two weeks, and two in the U.K. The expenses and income balanced each other out. I didn't come home with stacks of cash but managed to keep myself going and pay my bills. It was a very productive "trial run" for the two-month U.S. tour I did in 2003.

Before Lost And Found began their bike tour of the U.S., Michael Bridges sent letters of recommendation to more than 1,000 churches along what the duo perceived to be the first third of their route. They got invitations spaced in a fairly workable pattern. They sent out additional letters as they went, and got recommendations from contacts they met on the first few legs. Baum says:

We might meet a pastor in Houston who is on a committee that organizes a statewide youth gathering. He or she invites us to that event, where we meet a pastor from Dallas, who invites us there, where we meet a youth director who is on a committee that organizes a national youth gathering. We keep track of people who casually mention they might want to book us somewhere. We often joke to other bands to get a piece of paper and a pen—to make a career of this, that's all you really need.

Ask, ask, ask. Almost everyone knows someone! There are plenty of opportunities if you look for them. Baum and Bridges began by doing it themselves. It worked so well for them that they've had someone on staff booking gigs and more since 1995. Networking is a tool you all have. Use it!

PROFILE

Howie Statland is a singer/songwriter/guitarist who signed to RCA in 1996 with his former band, Thin Lizard Dawn. He left the band in 2000 and recorded two records independently as a solo artist. One became the score to the independent film called *Low Flame* that he wrote and directed based on his music. That caught the attention of renowned composer Philip Glass, who attended a screening and invited him to collaborate on a score for another film. Now Statland has a rock band, NYCSmoke, which has been reviewed in top magazines including *Billboard*. He has toured across the country.

GETTING ON THE ROAD

The thought of getting on the road may be daunting to you. It can mean leaving the comfort of your fan base and taking risks. A key to success is going back to markets until you conquer them, or have been there enough times to know it's not working there. No matter how few people come to a gig in a new region, do a great show and book another gig there. That's how most artists break into new regions. Word will eventually circulate if you're good. Marly Hornik says:

> Convince promoters in other markets that working with you is a long-term investment. Maybe the first time you'll only bring twenty people, but down the road if you keep working hard, you may be able to bring a lot more. I have a really nice press kit with reviews in the New York Post and magazines. Music promoters and venues appreciate that and get psyched to see that you have it going on.

Working the press in every market helps greatly. Being persistent in a market can pay off. Be patient as you SLOWLY build your following away from home. Jennie DeVoe says:

> Touring is a harder juggling act to keep in the air than gigs in your hometown. It's like starting over, so try to apply things you learned in your hometown. One way is to hook up with and open for a huge draw in the cities you're going to. Or, go into a town with your own name and begin anew. I do it both ways.

Try to be organized as you book. Don't jump all over the region. Zak Morgan says, "Get the hang of booking it logically in terms of geography. Draw a circle on the map and find all the clubs, schools, or libraries in that region, and then call them all." Have some sort of logical order. Jennifer Marks says she saw other musicians making a living and started booking her own shows outside her hometown. At first she only made enough to cover expenses. It takes a while to start making money by touring. Christine Kane found it a slow process. She began when a local singer/songwriter friend had to cancel a weekend of shows and called her to fill in for him. She says:

> I told him I didn't think I was ready, but he insisted I was. So, I did the weekend. I had such bad stage fright that I made myself get on the phone that next Monday and book some more shows at local coffeehouses so that I couldn't cop out because of the fear. I continued to make booking calls and expand my driving radius. It came down to just pushing myself really hard to continue making the calls, because I really wanted to do this for a living.

Howie Statland says, "I'll land a really good gig and then plan a tour around that." Work your way out from one city or region. Keep the gigs evenly spaced. Once you get one, keep calling venues in the next market over until you get one for the next day. Be friendly and sound confident. The calls get easier to make if you practice. Marly Hornik says:

> I got to a point where it was scarier to sit around not doing anything than it was to get on the phone. I go to Google and look for venues. I'll search for "Cleveland nightlife" and try to find venues. I go to www.onlinegigs.com, where you can get gigs, festivals, and colleges, too. I look at a map to plan a route—that's really important when booking. You shouldn't drive more than four hours from place to place. It's awful if you're just driving. My first day is a really long drive to get to the area I need to be in, and then the rest of the days are only one- or two-hour drives, for a week.

Onlinegigs.com is a subscription service that virtually automates the administration of booking and promoting bands. For a small monthly fee, it offers a huge directory of industry contacts and the ability to track correspondence with them, print labels, issue contracts, automatically update any website with gig information, automatically generate a tour itinerary with directions, and issue press releases to local media in those markets. Now you have fewer excuses for not getting on the road! Kyler England adds:

> I had to take a full-time job to make ends meet, or get on the road and gig like crazy—a simple choice. I researched venues in towns I wanted to play, mostly places with family and friends to give me a place to crash and help promote the shows. I found venues by checking other singer/songwriters' websites to see where they played, as well as asking friends who toured a lot. I stayed fairly close to home at first, mainly playing in cities between New York, where I was based, and Raleigh, North Carolina, my hometown. I tried to get good opening slots and small guarantees. On my earliest tours, CD sales were the biggest proportion of my income. These days I play a mixture of club and college dates. College gigs are a great way to make sure your tours will be profitable, as they offer substantial guarantees.

One gig can lead to another. Dean Seltzer's first gig outside of Austin was a rodeo kickoff in Houston. He got it because someone who saw him perform recommended him. Somebody else saw him at the rodeo event and asked him to play a bar in Houston. You can work that kind of stuff! Sometimes you must sacrifice at the beginning by doing free gigs to get exposure, but the exposure can be invaluable for future possibilities. Jennie DeVoe advises finding a balance between getting exposure and getting paid well:

> You can ask for any amount, but be realistic. I will open for a national act for almost nothing—the trade-off or benefit is, I gain exposure to their audience. Exposure is priceless, so prepare to weigh the pros and cons. It depends on your worth in each situation. Maybe you can ask for twenty-five hundred dollars because you are going to be worth it. Maybe you do a gig for free because you are going to gain exposure, and if you ask for too much money for opening for a national, they will move on to the next act, who will do it for close to free.

Marly Hornik warns, "No matter where I go it's always a big dance with the promoter to negotiate how much money and time." DJ Minx began by playing at parties for little or nothing just to get her name out. She says it helped:

> By taking on these gigs, I'd be featured on flyers with producers and DJs from all over the world! People thought if I was good enough to play with big names, then I must be a good artist! I also passed out mixes of my performance the week after I played—that helped a great deal! Many people became familiar with my company, Women On Wax, and started contacting me to request my DJ services. Agents promoted me and my talent to find more clubs for me to play. They then shared the flight and accommodation costs so that it's easier on everyone's pockets. That got me more and more gigs around the globe. I learned from friends there was a minimum amount that you should expect to be paid, so I'd accept no less than I earned within the States and got just what I'd asked for.

Don't expect touring to be an exciting party time. Evan R. Saffer of FIXER says:

> We play gigs midweek, drive all night to another city, sleep for an hour or two and drag our asses to work. The cycle continues. We grow stronger in the process, until one day soon the music will win this evil war. We always thank fans for their support at our live shows and through our website, and for buying CDs and merchandise to keep the machine rolling.

Jonathan Williams of the Hoodz Underground gets booked all over the U.K. When he has dates for a release, he contacts all the promoters so they can at least pencil in future shows. If they turn him down because they have little money left after booking a main and support act, Williams gets them to put his group on for just expenses. He says:

These acts attract more people, and local fans would remember that big hip-hop night that had the Hoodz on. I start by getting shows closer to home first, where we already have a following, and go farther afield after the release has had all its promotion, airplay, etc., and is known more nationally. Our aim was to get gigs supporting larger acts, which happened in 2002—supporting Blak Twang, a pioneer in the U.K. hip-hop scene. He had a single in the British Top 40, so the event was packed. Showing other promoters the flyer with us supporting Blak Twang led to us supporting other established acts. At first I only took shows supporting acts with large followings, even if we had to do them for free. This helped to quickly build our own fan base. We gave it our all at shows, so crowds left with good comments. I used all the flyers showing who we opened for to attract other shows.

Make sure you don't run short of products to sell. CDs and other merch can support you on the road. Get everyone possible to sign up for your email list, including the city they live in. Matt Allison devised an easy way to collect names:

Having people crowding around a merch table to sign up for the mailing list is counterproductive, so I made up individual flyers. It includes a good photo of me, some review snippets, my CD artwork, my web address, and a mailing list slip at the bottom. I had the printers perforate the mailing list part so it can be torn off and handed in at the end of a gig, leaving folks something to walk away with. Some people want me sign something but can't get a CD straight away, so I sign the flyer with a personal message.

If you've got THE GOODS, more people will come to your shows when you return to a market. Word spreads when people like you. Keep in regular touch with fans. Make them feel appreciated so they come back—with friends. Beth Wood advises remaining humble and realistic when breaking into new markets:

You can't expect to make a jillion dollars your first time in a town where few people have heard of you. The venue is giving you a chance—make the most of it so you can come back and build a following. You might have to play for tips or for fifty bucks your first time. You may open for someone with more of a following. If you do your best and get those names on the mailing list, those folks might bring friends to see you next time you come.

CHAPTER 19

Tackling International Markets

There are many opportunities to make money in international markets. A big and wonderful difference is that music lovers in other countries are often much more into music and respect it as an art. They'll support you forever if they love yours. Artists that tour internationally get hooked on the enthusiasm at shows, and they're blown away by how much product they sell. Audiences fill up large clubs and don't talk when you play, even if they don't know you. Rachael Sage says, "Europe has been the most amazing experience I've had. It's rewarding to create a connection, even with a language barrier. Many listeners are incredibly attentive: They'll come to you after the show, quoting lyrics and asking about them. Most people in the States aren't like that."

Europe is lucrative for those willing to work VERY hard. Dorothy Potter says music is an important aspect of everyday life there: "People will pay for it. I get more money from pubs that take fifty people than from three gigs at [a big club] in New York." She's now in Europe eight months a year. Justin Lassen says he tours Europe because people are open-minded to new music, explaining:

*Europe is a COMPLETELY different music industry. Acts like Nine Inch Nails, Backstreet Boys, and *NSYNC opted to become successful in Europe before America because it works. Companies in Europe say, "What the f**k* *is wrong with labels in the U.S.? Why aren't you signed yet?" U.S. companies only see me as a producer, not an artist. I think my work in Europe will do a lot for my career, even back in the U.S."*

I'll give an overview of the music scenes in major international markets—European and elsewhere—and then I'll tell you how to work them.

WHAT MUSIC WORKS WHERE?

Many Americans see all countries as "overseas." Think "international markets" instead. Don't lump them all together. Each has its own music taste. Research and target those most appropriate for your music. Check international charts to see what sells—*Billboard* has them, and you can search the Internet for more online. You might be surprised. I didn't expect country music in Europe, but country artist Lisa O'Kane carved out a career there and says, "It's huge! They love country music. A venue in Switzerland made up a special dance for me. They love all kinds of country music and particularly like Americans. I'm lucky to have such a captive audience when I'm there." I talked to international labels about what sells best in different countries and share their answers with you here. Don't forget that genres not mentioned here have potential, too.

Peter Wohelski, Project Manager at Studio Distribution, which distributes both here and in international markets, says most countries are still big on dance music. Internationally acclaimed DJ Pete Tong says that the dance music scene in Europe is "lavishly healthy, particularly in Eastern Europe." He adds that in the U.K., where he's from, "The scene is in good shape due to its diversity, and all forms of and music are working." Jim Tremayne, Editor of *DJ Times*, adds:

> *If you're a DJ or producer working with music for the dance floor, you have to look at it as a global marketplace. If you make really good dance tracks, you can license them to any number of countries in Europe and get paid twelve times for one record as it sells through various distributors in Europe and Asia. If you're thinking that you've got this great dance track and you have to get it on this mix show in a local area, you're thinking very small.*

Musicians say the countries that seem most open to a variety of American music are Belgium, Holland, Denmark, and Germany. Their radio stations are most likely to play your music—if they like it—but most other European countries are open to great music, too, especially if you market it in person. Henri Lessing, Managing Director of Media Records Benelux in Holland, says anything people can dance to—from club to underground to very commercial to disco—can work well. Johan Hendrickx, Managing Director of 2 Brains Entertainment Group, a record label, management company, and booking agency in Belgium, says right now, American R&B is very big: "It is a scene that grows every day—hip-hop and R&B." He adds that indie music sells well.

Thomas Degn, Label Manager at NiceandFirm with Bonnier Amigo Music in Denmark, says a wide range of music sells in the Scandinavian countries where his company distributes. Borje Lindquist, President of Liphone Sweden, says pop music is big there, and adds, "Hard rock went away for some years but now it is coming back." Jorma Ristila, Managing Director of Stupido Records in Finland, thinks about half the popular records there are in English. All kinds of American music, especially Beyoncé, sell well. Heavy metal is very popular, too. He warns that Finland is a small market and may not be worth pursuing, but larger companies like Bonnier Amigo Music also distribute to this market.

Alex Lasmarias, International Assistant at Discmedia International, says music in Spain is very mainstream: "If it works well in the States or the U.K, it will work well in Spain, especially mainstream things like pop. Dance music is still big, especially electronic music. People like to go to clubs. Spain has many DJs." Lasmarias says that both vocal- and music-driven dance (house and techno house) is popular, as well as alternative rock, blues, country, and metal. Lasmarias is encouraging: "The Spanish market is not the best market, but it is an interesting one. People love music. Spain is a country that artists should consider as a chance for them."

Ricardo Ferro, A&R at Zona Musica in Portugal, says that many people speak English there. House music is big, and vocal dance music does well there, too. Mario Limongelli, General Manager for NAR International in Italy, says that rock and pop do best, but many other genres work as well. Poland is a market that's opening up. Hip-hop has become very popular, and Jan Kubicki, head of A&R at Magic Records, says, "We do a lot of club music that's vocal- and artist-driven, mainly with pop bands." It's a market that can be lucrative for American music. Visual agrees: "A big highlights of our career was headlining a tour in Poland for people with a real respect for hip-hop as an art form."

Michael Baur, former COO/CFO of Edel Music AG in Germany (considered the major label of Europe), says kids love hip-hop but they burn their own CDs. The dance market has fallen more than any other. What is the strongest indie market there? Baur says, "Rock and heavy metal bands are very strong. Pop is very much a major label business; marketing pop is a lot about money." Andy Burhenne, Marketing Manager for Metal Blade Records in Germany, agrees that the metal scene is still doing very well. He says, "We don't have problems with CD-burning. Metal fans want the original CDs in their collection."

Jazz is much more popular in Europe than here. Matthias Winckelman, Managing Director of Enja Records, a jazz label in Germany, says, "Here, there's much more radio station coverage and better awareness of jazz. But it's not what it used to be." Winckelman says radio play is down, and opportunities are scarcer as the number of bands increases. He adds, "Germany and France are the most important countries in the world for jazz because of the acceptance of jazz as an art form in these countries. It's beginning more in Italy and Spain. Things are getting better, but it's a slow process." Winckelman says an American jazz artist still has a better chance in Europe than in the States. Gregor Minnig, Director of A&R/Vice President of ZYX Music in Germany, mainly releases dance music and jazz. He says, "Jazz always does well, but not necessarily in huge quantities. It depends on the packaging—how you deliver music to the customer."

Steve McClure, Asian Bureau Chief for *Billboard* magazine, says there isn't just one Asian market: "The conditions vary from market to market in terms of size, maturity of the market, and stylistic preferences. Hong Kong and Taiwan are so-so. Japan is highly developed, the second largest music market in the world." Keith Cahoon CEO of Hotwire, Inc., a music publisher based in Tokyo—he also ran Tower Records in Japan for eighteen years—says, "Japan is very open to all kinds of music. They like indie/college radio rock, heavy metal, hard rock, jazz. A lot of different genres do well for independent music here. For specialty music like jazz, Japan is really strong." McClure says the over-65 demographic is an untapped market for music like easy listening and jazz. Of course, dance music is big. Yuko Suzuki, Manager of Business Affairs for Avex Inc., a dance label in Japan, says, "Dance music that works well is more musically driven. Trance and Eurobeats are very popular." McClure adds, "Techno has come here from the U.K." Wohelski agrees that the Japanese are avid music buyers. He exports lots of hip-hop to Japan—all kinds. Speech's hip-hop music rocks in Japan. He loves that they just see it as music: Radio plays Marvin Gaye along with Arrested Development or 50 Cent. Speech says, "To them it's black music rolled up in one. They're exposed to many different types of music in one show." The Japanese market is worth pursuing. McClure says, "The independent music sector is probably the only part of the physical CD business that is thriving there."

The Australian market can be conquered if you're willing to make that long trip to the other side of the world. Few countries have more opportunities for playing live. Phil Tripp, the founder of entertainment company IMMEDIA!, says that Australia has always been big with independent music because they're so far from the rest of the world. IMMEDIA! publishes a comprehensive directory for the Australian music scene—all the info you need to tour for only $50. It's updated regularly, and you can get it from the website (www.immedia.com.au). What genres work best in Australia? Tripp says:

Probably what we politely call rock 'n' roll, because music here has been brought up in a pub environment. Bands really have to entertain and kill it. The music that excites people live is what sells. There's a lot of folk music. Country music is surprisingly big here—not all of it done American-style. What really sells here is rock. We've also got a very big dance scene: electronica, pure dance, house music, beats. Raves happen a lot—we get a lot of outdoor raves in the middle of nowhere.

Research international markets. Learn as much as possible about the markets you want to break into. Cahoon advises, "The more you know about the market, the better off you are. Many people don't spend time learning about the market." It isn't easy. For example, McClure says, "Japan has a real problem with English." Most music websites are only in Japanese. He adds, "Do your homework and check out the music scene. If you want to have any degree of success in this market, you have to commit. You can't just dump your product off. Work, work, work! This is a media-saturated country." Give yourself an edge with your research. Find a Japanese friend—I'm serious! If you find someone who speaks Japanese, they can translate the information on websites for you. See if you can find a college student who'd do it for a few bucks. McClure says there's a definitive Japanese-language publication about the music market called *Music Man*. If you do go to Japan, McClure advises having the other side your business card printed in Japanese. You can get them done as soon as you arrive in Japan if necessary. He says, "It's worth it down the road. In Japan, twenty to twenty-five percent of prerecorded music sales is made up of non-Japanese repertoire." Do this in any market that you're planning to put work into.

Learn about customs of different countries. Lisa O'Kane says, "Always be respectful of the people whose country you're visiting. It's a privilege to be there. I follow the saying 'When in Rome. . . .'" Club owners know other club owners and can recommend you if you ask. Make good impressions from the get-go! Learn key words in the language of a country you're after. McClure advises, "Don't be loud, obnoxious, and brash. Confrontation gets you absolutely nowhere. And if someone is hemming and hawing about doing something, take it as a *no*—they won't actually say *no*." You'll know if they're interested. Many people in foreign countries prefer you take the hint rather than having to reject you.

Pay attention to time differences in foreign countries. Phil Tripp says, "If you call us at six o' clock in the afternoon, we're asleep. Before calling Australia, check what time it is here. Don't call on Friday because it's Saturday for us, and we're off work." If you call Australia on Sunday night however, it's Monday. If you're not sure of times, check www.timeanddate.com for the time and date anywhere in the world.

SONGWRITING BIZ

Songwriting is valuable in international markets. Publisher Martin Pursey, with Bonaire Media in the U.K., says, "If you're a good songwriter with material that is commercially viable, you can get it out here through films and games first. Royalties range from one hundred to one hundred thousand bucks." Cahoon adds, "There are many opportunities for TV commercials, games, and many other things in Japan." A publisher helps generate income from songwriting—and helps protect it, too! Kim Frankiewicz, Vice President of International at Universal Music Publishing Group, U.K., says, "Publishers can help you earn money outside of just selling records. Outside of America, there are lots of countries in which you must have your songs protected. Without a publisher, you must go into every single territory to get your songs registered and copyrighted, and to collect the money. You can do it yourself or hire people to do it for you."

If your CD sells in other countries, you might not know if the songs earn income in the many smaller markets. Publishing administrator Michelle Bayer says, "If we did the deal here, I could, through my subpublishers, go in and collect for you in Europe, which is where you might be losing out." She says if you have a local publisher, it would collect the money first. While ASCAP, etc., would collect your share either way, a local publisher watches out for your interests and speeds the process of collecting your royalties. But there is other money earned that may not come through. Bayer explains:

> It's called "black box money," a term they use for miscellaneous money from digital recordings, the Internet, and many other things. They sort of lump it into a box, and only local publishers can collect that money. You're always at more of an advantage if you have someone locally to collect it. You can't collect black box money yourself. You'd need a local publisher.

While universal rights can cover all territories, the publishing company will also represent songs in selected ones only. Frankiewicz says an indie artist with good songs can get a publishing deal. Publishers can bring your music to record labels to shop an artist or licensing deal. They make money if your record is put out. Steve McClure says, "In Japan, publishers take a very proactive role in trying to set up label deals, much more like the European model. A lot of people from the States don't realize that. You can really get a publisher to go to bat for you here." Songs earn money from the same avenues that they do here.

Matthias Winckelman says Enja Records also does publishing for jazz: "We look at the potential that might be there and try to place copyrighted music into films, archives, TV, and many other things. We publish for many people not connected with our label." Publishers look for great songs. Pursey says, "Genre doesn't matter. It's about the song. If you've got a great hook for a great song and can develop it, that's all you need." Because Bonaire Media is small, Pursey can work with a songwriter to develop a song so it's more marketable. Frankiewicz says when looking for a songwriter to publish, she considers personality and drive, too: "If somebody is not working it with us, I'd rather not go with that person."

Songwriting royalties are worth much more overseas than in the U.S. Pursey says, "It's based on sales as opposed to a flat rate—a percentage of the dealer price—a lot more than in the U.S. That's why you should pick your publisher with care." Cahoon agrees: "The per unit sales is generally higher. Japan has fixed pricing. Depending on the release, royalties are based on a percentage of retail price, so mechanical royalties can be good here. If things go right for you, publishing can be quite good here." Performance royalties are also much better in these markets than in U.S. Pursey adds that broadcasters in the U.K. have a blanket deal for synchronization: "In the U.K., someone cannot use synchronization without paying for it. You don't have to give your music away."

Finding a publisher is similar to finding a label deal. Frankiewicz says these days it's usually through an introduction because publishers receive so much music. They look at things quicker when it's from someone they know. But people in international markets are more accessible. If you tour, get radio play, get press, etc., and people like your music, ask who they know. Because foreign markets are small, the pros know one another. Don't be afraid to ask. If you get your music out there on your own, someone can steer you to a publisher. Pursey says songwriters can send him a link to a webspace with music samples. He advises, "Never send material attached. It will be deleted." Pursey adds that the Internet has opened things up, making it much easier to approach people anywhere in the world.

MUSIC CONFERENCES

MIDEM (www.MIDEM.com), an international music conference at the end of January in Cannes, France, is the largest gathering of industry professionals from around the world. It's expensive—both the registration fee and the cost of staying in Cannes. But if you want to attend a conference with a HUGE assortment of movers and shakers from the music industry—8,000 to 9,000 people of almost all nationalities—start saving! I've attended large music conferences but found MIDEM much more overwhelming, frenetic, and exhausting. It takes days to get through all the booths, and there are panels on a variety of interesting topics. MIDEM feels like a high-end marketing marathon; everyone is there to do serious business. Many head honchos probably never even enter the Palais des Festivals, where it takes place. Instead, they hold court in the lobbies of top hotels or in restaurants. Considering the cost of MIDEM, there are a surprising number of indie musicians in "attack mode," handing out CDs and flyers that advertised their products. They throw CDs at anyone who'll take them, like at U.S. seminars where attendees push their CDs on everyone. But many industry folks only meet with those who've made appointments in advance. Some even refuse the materials artists offer them. Lisa O'Kane says she made appointments ahead of time:

> It was one busy week at MIDEM. I met with several record companies whom I've corresponded with over the last year as a result of those meetings. I was asked to perform at the SONY cocktail party one evening. It was great to network with heads of companies and was a tremendous educational experience. I have established invaluable relationships. They know who I am now. The trip was an investment.

Here's what I learned that will help make MIDEM more productive for you. First, you can't just go and expect to find people. Most probably won't meet with you because they book appointments weeks or months earlier. If you make the investment, register months early: You'll save money and get a cheaper hotel—early bird specials can save hundreds. Once registered, you can access their online directory; it's updated often. Many big companies register early, so you can get their info and contact them in time to get appointments. The MIDEM online database is searchable in different ways— by what the company does, by genre, by country—any variety you want. You'll get a huge book with all the contacts at the conference. Many people pay all that money just to have this directory, with almost 9,000 contacts to help you break through in international markets. I advise arriving a day early, to sleep and acclimate yourself. It would be VERY helpful to rent a cell phone, because it's frustrating to leave messages when people can't immediately return your call. It also helps when you're meeting someone for an appointment and there are dozens of others in the same area also looking for people they've never met. Pay attention to this advice: Attending MIDEM is an opportunity that merits doing it right.

Rachael Sage says with a six-album catalogue, it was time for her to connect to overseas distributors. She'd already toured Germany four times. At MIDEM, she and her team met many potential contacts; she was still sorting through them when we spoke months later. She got to distributors and other contacts by being very aggressive about walking right up to people. She explains:

We see their name tags or overhear their conversations with someone else. We're not shy. Plus, being the loudest, most eclectic dressed person on-site helps. The more glitter I had on, the more friends I seemed to make. I don't draw a line between being the artist and being the label president. I just put myself out there. My label manager and I cover different terrain. She's much more right-brain, financially oriented—the business side of things. I'm looking for creative opportunities to get my music out and to work with like-minded people—artists, distributors, touring and promotions companies.

Sage says they made appointments with companies that put together tours to find an agent in Europe, and they came away with some interesting possibilities. They also ran an ad in the directory: "We thought, we're going and spending all this time and money. It was cheaper than putting a promotional item in the bag." It helped: They still hear from people. Go to MIDEM with a plan. People hang out at key bars at night—chat up everyone you can. Sage says she just ran into people with potential to help her. She even met a woman who organizes festivals in the U.S. Don't go unless you believe your music would work in international markets—AND, it's THAT GOOD. If you go, pack extra vitamins, a smile, lots of material, and balls! Sage says, "It was good to put ourselves out there. I'm sure we'll go again next year."

An alternative to MIDEM is Popkomm (www.popkomm.de), which takes place in Berlin and offers opportunities to showcase in a variety of venues. Katja Bittner, Director of Popkomm, says, "The German music market is very much concentrated in Berlin." There's a big focus on artists and music, and a variety of panels for different topics of music biz and technology. Popkomm is trying to create a bridge between music and commerce by including the film and game industries. Bittner adds, "We have a great club festival. The club scene in Berlin is one of the most exciting in Europe. We take applications from unsigned artists and try to find a space where newcomers can showcase at the club festival. It is also an opportunity to get an overview of what the international market offers."

Bittner says club and concert managers help decide which showcases are appropriate for each artist. Having your own label or a following helps. The more you have going on, the better the club you might play. Apply on the website—you can choose the language and find contacts appropriate to your music. Bittner says April is a good time to start. Why attend Popkomm? Bittner says you can make international contacts, meet distributors, and learn how to work with crossover marketing activities to promote your music. She adds, "We have the decision-makers: people who are able to make deals and talk about solutions and new distribution rights. The spirit of Popkomm is to have business be very casual in a very nice atmosphere. It will be a lot cheaper then MIDEM."

GETTING A RECORD OUT

You need a CD to work international markets. Some people look for distribution, but most find licensing easier. Henri Lessing advises, "Get together with a label and try to create something. The label will help you get on tour and to the right spots. You need the right partner and your music must be right for the market. Just like in the U.S., you need lots of live performances, press, and a label behind you." If you get a tour together, you'll be in a much better position to approach a small label to help you. A label will give you support in its markets with press, radio, and even clubs you couldn't book yourself. But just like in the U.S., you need to create a buzz first. A great resource for international contracts is Showcase, a music business guide listing record labels, publishers, venues, booking agents, and a lot more in many foreign markets. Order it at www.musicregistry.com.

For an American artist, getting press or booking a tour can catch a label's interest. Begin by bringing CDs on your tour and selling them. If audiences like your music, they'll buy a lot more than people in clubs here. Phil Tripp advises sending CD inserts to a manufacturer in the market you're working to save money. But don't do it until you've already toured and have an idea of what you need. George Baum says now that Lost And Found tours regularly in Germany, they send a master and artwork to a German friend who gets CDs pressed for their tours. Dorothy Potter says she has a relationship with a CD duplicator who works with her: "We began by taking fifty CDs, and sold them. When they were running out, I emailed for another box. I can do limited numbers for very cheap. They cost just over a buck, and I sell them for fifteen to twenty euro there. I can get fifty more CDs fast."

Distribution

Unless you're prepared to do serious biz in international markets, don't expect to get distribution for your CDs. Distributors in different markets say they'll only rep you if you're touring, getting media coverage, and can prove that you're determined to work it properly. They advise having someone local run your biz there. That can get pricey if you only have one album. If you can find other indies who want to work the same markets, you might hire one person to run a cooperative venture between you. Otherwise, try to get a licensing deal, or do it yourself.

Keith Cahoon says a lot of music gets imported from the U.S.: "You can find almost anything that's available in the United States in a record store in Japan. Tower and HMV have very deep catalogues—as good as, if not better than, any stores in the world. And there are lots of independent specialty stores that carry very specific genres." Large U.S. distributors don't sell internationally but, Cahoon adds, "A lot of one-stops export to these markets. If those people are aware of your music, and you have press in the U.S. or Europe, you can make some inroads here." If you have a one-stop distributor in the U.S., ask if they export.

Alex Woodard created his own system when independent international stores tried to order through his website. A man in Spain wanted to carry his record, but he didn't want to send 20 CDs to Spain without knowing if they'd get there safely. So, he offered an alternative. Woodard's songs were already on a website with downloadable MP3s for industry people. He sent the man the insert booklets so he could download the music, burn CDs, and put them together to sell. The retailer sent a check after selling twenty and asked to buy more. Woodard says, "That is a different way of using technology to sell records. He gave me about ten bucks a record. So I've never had an international deal, but I sell CDs there."

Licensing

Licensing your CD to a foreign record label gives them the right to manufacture and release the record in all parts of the world except for the U.S., or in whatever territories you want. A lawyer can help you to negotiate a fair deal. The label can help you get media coverage and guide you through the process. The support system a licensing deal can offer in international markets makes touring easier and more effective.

Mary Gauthier says a friend played her music at a record store in Amsterdam and some customers asked who it was. They then called Gauthier and asked for a copy. After hearing it, they ordered ten CDs, sent payment a few weeks later, and eventually ordered larger quantities. A salesman for a Dutch record company heard about Gauthier's success and contacted her for a licensing deal. She says that cracked open the whole of Europe, one region at a time, and adds, "The record company did a sublicense with different countries for my record. I gave them the rights to do that. Then the subli-

---

PROFILE
....

Lisa O'Kane is a country music artist based in L.A. who got her career going in European markets. Her friend sent her first album to a European country publication, *Country Music People UK*. She became the spotlight album and got a five-star review spot in their magazine, which led to other reviews and radio play. Three years later, her album is still playing all over Europe. O'Kane's first tour of Europe was at the beginning of 2003. She's performed in Holland, France, Spain, Switzerland, and Germany, playing venues from small clubs to ancient concert halls to large festivals. She released a new album in the U.S. in 2004.

censee would bring me in for a press junket and we would start the thing over again, each time."

Music itself plays a much more important role in getting deals in foreign markets, but adding media fuel to a great CD increases your chances. Lisa O'Kane hired publicist Martha Moore to help get media exposure, and the airplay and press reviews led to her record being licensed in Scandinavian countries. Speech's first solo album was with EMI Worldwide. It did so well in Japan that he continued with EMI there when the company closed in America. Speech says, "We also license our music to other countries. We searched out labels that might be interested in the product." Compilations are popular in many foreign markets. Forge says Little Egypt has been on compilation albums in Poland, Germany, Brazil, Canada, and Australia—mostly after being found through the group's website. He adds, "They usually license one of our older songs and pay us up front." Sales on Little Egypt's own albums increase when the compilations are released.

Matthias Winckelman says at first Enja had mostly American artists. Now the label signs a lot more Europeans. He advises, "We get about twenty CDs and bios a week. Be very good. We prefer originality. That is what jazz is all about." Borje Lindquist suggests visiting Export Music Sweden (www.exms.com): "They can help foreign artists in pursuit of making it in Sweden and getting a licensing deal." The site has a wealth of resources, including Swedish record labels and festivals. Mario Limongelli of NAR in Italy mainly licenses rock and pop. A translator helps him look for meaningful lyrics. If you want a deal in Italy, Limongelli advises, "Be a serious professional. Look for an independent label, not a major. You have more chances this way." You can learn more about the Italian music industry at www.fimi.it. (Warning: This site is in Italian.)

Jan Kubicki says Magic Records licenses club music—vocal- and artist-driven—with pop artists. He says radio and TV are supportive and assures artists, "If the music is good, it can sell itself in Poland. A lot of promotion goes into it." Kubicki advises, "Contact us first by email. I like to get an actual recording to hear the music. Then I'll ask for more." Alex Lasmarias says Discmedia works with most genres: electronic music, country, blues, alternative rock, Americana, even classical. He says they receive so many CDs it's hard to go through them all, and advises, "Send a parcel with reviews, a press kit—anything to show you are special. It is important to make us feel that you take it seriously. Press coverage from anywhere is very important. We appreciate nice artwork, a well-written biography, and photographs." They license for Spain and occasionally for Portugal.

Thomas Degn says Bonnier Amigo Music is both a record company and a distribution label: "We are the largest independent record label and distributor in Scandinavia. We are very wide-ranging in all our music and have offices all over Scandinavia (Denmark, Norway, Sweden, and Finland)." Bonnier Amigo can do a distribution deal or a record deal that works for all of Scandinavia in a broad variety of genres. They want to license artists who tour and sell CDs. Degn says, "Just email or send us a demo. It's nice to have the full package, but it's the music that really counts." If you want get into the Scandinavian market, he suggests you contact indie labels, which are easier to reach than major labels.

Iain McNay, Chairman of Cherry Red Records in the U.K., says they'd consider licensing a band with a CD but prefer to deal with labels. He agrees that a touring band that would come to the U.K. to work has the best shot. McNay says, "The attitude of the band is important: You must realize it's a partnership. It's unlikely to happen without you working very hard. You must have the ability, the talent, and the craziness as well." Classical music is different in Europe. Rob Blesma, Export Manager at Joan Records in the Netherlands, says they distribute worldwide. They own and record close to 75 percent of their own catalogue; the rest is licensed. Blesma says, "For us, the classical market is still growing. It's hard to break into classical music. You need really good material; it must be very good quality. We review material if it is interesting to us."

Germany can be friendly to American music. Michael Baur says that adult artists such as Toni Braxton are a stable market for Edel Music AG. Based in Germany, the company covers all of Europe. They operate like a major, with their own distribution and marketing. Edel is careful about newcomers and prefers to license established artists that bring a market with them. For independents, Baur says, "We must feel they know what they're doing and have a clear strategy for their product. They need to meet a minimum level of sales per release." There must be a story behind an artist, no matter how good he or she is. Baur adds:

> Our first question is, what have you done in your home territory? It's very difficult for us to break artists into our territory if they haven't been successful in theirs. A pop artist would need chart positions on more mainstream stations than college radio. A newcomer should be available to come to Europe to live for one or two months. They would definitely have to be a live artist, and be able to touch us—emotional value is very important.

Baur says that a big buzz on the Internet can show record labels that there's a good market for and interest in the artist. If you've taken steps to get buzzing in Europe, he advises, "Contact us. The first step would be to email us. Send a link to your website so that we can read about the artist. Then send a package." Andy Burhenne says Metal Blade works only with metal bands, from death metal to power metal. He adds, "It's all about the songs. Bands can have a fantastic history, but if the new songs sound like shit, we're not going to sign them." Burhenne says bands can send a demo tape, though they tend to mainly sign bands that they hear about. That's why getting media coverage is so important.

ZYX Music's main office is in Germany, but they also have offices in cities like New York, London, and Paris. Gregor Minnig says, "Many labels forget to develop artists. We continue to do it. If they come from other territories, it is hard for them to make it in the German market. It's expensive. But for specific artists, we help. The best promotion for bands is to get on tour, which you can organize by yourself." Minnig says that he prefers to be sent a package and likes press kits because they show how skilled you are at promoting yourself. He suggests getting help from a professional—a lawyer or manager—who knows what record companies need.

Australia offers licensing opportunities if you're prepared to tour there. Clive Hodson says ABC Music was set up to exploit program-related materials from their television and radio stations. They do classics, jazz, country, adult contemporary, and children's music—both compilations and albums. Hodson says that Triple J, their youth radio network, has the "Hottest 100" every year. The public votes on the best hundred songs, and ABC Music creates two compilation CDs with the winners. Hodson says, "We have a website with contact information. You can send a sound file. But it's hard to break an international artist into Australia if you haven't toured there. I look for artists with some degree of success." There are many indie labels in Australia; most of them are listed at the Association of Independent Record Labels website (www.air.org.au).

Asian markets license music, too. The Japanese in particular love American music. Yuko Suzuki licenses dance music and usually finds artists at MIDEM and Popkomm. She advises going to the Avex website and says, "It is best to email information and send stuff. You can send music files online, too. We like to get a press kit. If we like your stuff, we will contact you." I spoke to several reps from Disc Union Records, a distributor that also licenses most genres. If they get a CD they like, they'd consider making it available to stores. But Keith Cahoon doesn't think it's worthwhile to mail stuff out cold: You need to know which labels are appropriate. He suggests finding people who know the market to advise you. Japanese labels will also want info about your accomplishments. Steve McClure says, "Labels want photographs, bios, and some commitment of time."

China is now expanding into a viable market, too. Zhang Dajiang, General Manager of China Record Corporation, says he licenses all kinds of Western music. Fifty to seventy-five percent of music on the label is from other countries—major and indie artists—and they also license for compilations. Dajiang says, "A lot of foreign music is brought into China through small private companies. The Internet is used a lot."

Carl Parker, General Manager of ToCo Asia LTD in Hong Kong, says they mainly license dance music from European territories, occasionally world music and rock, too. ToCo distributes in Asia (Japan, Korea, Taiwan, etc.) and the Middle East. The music they license is distributed through EMI Asia and EMI Music Arabia. Parker says, "Oftentimes we are very keen to work with artists who are album artists as opposed to single artists because you can then develop something. We can bring them to Asia for promo tours and to work with local artists. If they're good-looking we can have them in magazines as models." He prefers artist-driven records but dance compilations sell well, too. Parker says they don't take much American music but would like to find more: "There's a huge American population in Korea and Japan. People are very interested in hip-hop and R&B." He says American companies tend to be a bit more suspicious than European companies; they always want money up front. ToCo mainly signs indies. Parker suggests, "You can approach me by email. Send MP3 files or try to arrange a conference with me."

INTERNATIONAL TOURING

Once an American artist tours internationally, they're usually hooked. Suzanne Teng says, "We love it. People are so receptive and we're treated really well. And they pay well." People in foreign markets value and respect music. Club owners treat performers well, usually providing food and a place to stay. Festivals are very popular abroad and offer exposure to large, diverse crowds. Most performers say that international touring spoils them: You're playing large clubs with good crowds that treat you like a star if they like your music.

Touring helps you break into foreign markets. Matthias Winckelman says, "Today a career is more dependent on live performances than on recordings. Live performances leave the lasting impressions. Follow that up with a good record—that's what works." Tony Talbot, former Chief Executive of the Northern Ireland Music Industry Commission, advises:

> There's only one way to find out if your music works: by playing it in front of an audience. Try it out in front of many different audiences. When you play in your local town, you get positive feedback because they come to cheer you on. When you play for audiences who don't know who you are, you quickly work out how to present what you've got in a way that makes the audience respond well.

Phil Tripp says the live music scene in Australia is more vital but brutal, too. You need to be really good to survive. They don't watch much TV, Tripp says: "We drink a lot of beer. It is an amazing live scene here because you have so many smaller venues—hundred-seaters, four-hundred-seaters—and then the larger ones too." There are many independent promoters in Australia, and you can find them in the *AustralAsian Music Industry Directory* that Tripp produces. The directory is available both online and in print, and it has all the contacts you need, with the URLs and email addresses hotlinked in the online version—a bargain at $50! If you order it, you also get an email every two weeks telling who's gone, who's come in, who's changed numbers, etc. Tripp says there are only six urban centers in Australia, mainly on the coast: "It is a great country to tour in. If you're an independent overseas band, building an audience can be easily done"—IF you have THE GOODS.

Festivals are big in Australia. For example, the Big Day Out goes from ity to city, similar to Ozfest. Tripp says outdoor festivals are very popular and many indies play at them. He advises getting in touch with the festival promoters. Australia's seasons are the opposite of the Northern Hemisphere's, so summer there is from November to March—the dead season elsewhere. You can preplan a tour online before going over. Tripp advises tapping into the primary street press in the main Australian markets: "In Sydney, it's Drum Media (www.drummedia.com.au). In Melbourne, it's In*Press or Beat (www.beat.com.au). In Brisbane, it's Time Off (www.timeoff.com.au). In Perth, it's Xpress (www.xpressmag.com.au). In Adelaide, it's Rip it Up (www.ripitup.com.au) or DB (www.dbmagazine.com.au)." Most of it is online, so you can look up who's playing where. Tripp recommends getting a hard copy of local street press to see who's playing. You can order by phone or email. Or, he suggests, fax them on nice stationary to ask for an advertiser's copy: "Say that you will be touring in Australia and would like to consider advertising in their publication. Could they please send a recent copy of the magazine, their rate card, and a media kit? Address it to the advertising manager. More than likely, they'll send it."

New Zealand is another potential place to tour. Tripp says some bands do a circuit—L.A. to Honolulu, then to Auckland and Wellington, New Zealand, then to Australia, and then to Singapore, Bangkok, or Japan. To maximize your touring potential you can get a Circle Pacific ticket, which allows you X number of stops in that area. The New Zealand music industry is included in Tripp's directory, but there's a separate directory for the New Zealand music industry, too (www.musicnz.co.nz).

Australia and New Zealand are easiest for American artists to tour because everybody speaks English, but China now brings in Western artists for their music festivals. Sun Xiangyan, General Manager of Logistix, says, "You can perform with a private company or agency, or go to a state-run company or official department. Contact the Chinese Ministry of Culture, which artists can do on the Internet." The Internet sources you're looking for may be in Chinese, but Xiangyan also suggests, "Find local agents for China on the Internet. An independent artist has a chance to come over, but not as good as a major artist."

Steve McClure says, "The concert business is healthy in Japan." Speech toured Japan many times and agrees: "The fans are very responsive. They're an educated music crowd—intuitive to the lyrics. Many speak English as a second language, and they usually understand it better." McClure advises, "Build up relationships within the music industry. If you make a buddy at a big touring company, they're very loyal. People keep coming back. For indie acts, it makes more sense to cultivate contacts in the equivalent corresponding musical community on the other side of the Pacific." Networking with foreign artists works for all nationalities! Keith Cahoon says it's tough to get a booking agent without a label deal, because a label is expected to support at least some aspects of the tour. That's hard to do if you don't know anyone. However, many Japanese artists tour or attend school in the U.S. Cahoon advises seeking them out and making friends with those who share your genre; they may be able to help you get gigs in Japan. He also says Japanese industry pros go to SXSW (www.sxsw.com), the big music conference in Austin, Texas: "It's more of a mix of major and minor labels than at MIDEM. Lots of Japanese bands play SXSW. It might serve you well to go to the Japanese showcases and go out of your way to meet people in the industry there. They can give you ideas of who you should talk to in Japan." Ezina Moore toured Japan by once again working her Rolodex®. She sent her record to a friend in Japan, who got it to clubs that sponsored her trip over. She says, "I played in Japan three times. They paid me well. You can get a big ego, because everyone gets excited and you feel like a rock star."

PROFILE

Dorothy Potter is a singer, guitarist, composer, and songwriter who began making music professionally in 1990 and became a full-time indie in 2002. She's run three bands: Her focus was originally on Latin music, but now she's turned to rock and pop with her band, B1. Potter has found a variety of venues to help pay the rent, from clubs to hospitals and even busking in the subway. In spring of 2004, she put together her first tour to Europe. She now does spring and fall tours in European markets and sells lot of CDs.

Japanese festivals book indie artists, too. McClure says, "The big summer festivals are a great chance for foreign acts to break here because there's so much buzz surrounding them. You have to plan a lot in advance." Cahoon agrees, "Summer festivals can be the best thing to happen to you. They book close to one hundred bands and can take more of a leap to try bands without much of a track record. You might be able to get signed on to Fuji Rock without a record deal and play in front of ten or twenty thousand people." As I said, make Japanese friends—especially musicians! You might meet foreign musicians online if you browse enough websites. The Japanese market is very lucrative for those who do what it takes to make the first contact.

European markets offer many possibilities for touring. If your music is good, you can book your own tour. Don't count on getting agents! You might get one after you establish your presence, but as in the U.S., they work with artists who have a story and a fan base. Matthias Winckelman says, "The few really good agents go to concerts and festivals and approach the people." If you perform, an agent might notice you. Thomas Degn says, "We have festivals all over Scandinavia and Denmark. The biggest is Roskilde. This is friendly to all kinds of music. Performers at Roskilde represent countries from all over the world." Alex Lasmarias says, "In Spain, we have many festivals and big concerts every night in larger cities. But it's harder to break in if you aren't distributed." Ricardo Ferro says they have many festivals in August in Portugal, too.

Johan Hendrickx says, "There are many possibilities in Belgium. We bring in bands from the U.K. and would do it for the U.S., too. There are plenty of festivals and concert halls." They don't pay big money, but you get to play if you're willing to go. Hendrickx books urban music, rock, pop, and rap for the festival season from June to September. Contact 2 Brains by email and send a package. If they see talent, they determine what festivals you will fit into. As Mario Limongelli advises, "Distinguish if your music is good for Italy; then try to collaborate with an Italian manager to have you over." Henri Lessing says there are opportunities to tour with a band in Holland if you create hype from the ground up: "They look at what's happening with your career abroad. If the band is not happening, it's not easy to start from nothing." Many resources for the Dutch market can be found at www.dutchsound.nl.

After lots of radio airplay in Europe, fans asked when Lisa O'Kane was coming over. Her publicist has contacts with European DJs, and O'Kane was invited to perform on VLOK Television in Holland, followed by a live radio show and a tour of Spain organized by a Spanish DJ. She performed in Holland, followed by a live radio show and a tour of Spain. She says, "The people were gracious and welcoming. I was unprepared for the effect that my music has on the fans. It was a very gratifying experience." Now

O'Kane performs in small clubs, concert halls, and large festivals in Holland, France, Spain, Switzerland, and Germany.

Little Egypt toured Poland. Visual Poet says Polish guys who ran a website based on underground hip-hop in the States bought the group's CD and broadcasted from their apartment in Manhattan to Poland. Visual and Forge developed a relationship with them. People in Poland called local radio stations after hearing Little Egypt's music. The DJ on a major radio station in Poland agreed to support the tour to bring the group over. Forge says their expenses were covered: airfare, food, lodging, and a fee per show. Jan Kubicki says, "If you want to sell records in Poland, you need to tour." Little Egypt still sells many CDs there. Speech adds, "We now go on to Eastern Europe. These are new markets for us. The hip-hop market, and Western music in general, is huge."

Networking is key in any international market! Marly Hornik played in Italy through networking. When she opened for another band, she met a promoter who does freelance consulting and asked him about Europe. He knew a band in Italy that wanted to work with someone from the States. DJ Minx goes to the Winter Music Conference in Miami every year to meet pros from around the world. She says it's great for networking. It began to pay off when she met a woman who owned a booking agency in Berlin and asked for a mixed CD—the woman loved it. Minx says, "She then asked if I'd like to travel and play my music in lots of other places."

Rachael Sage did two European tours with Eric Burden of the Animals after promoters saw her grassroots tour in Germany. Sage's grassroots tour began with networking. She hooked up with an agent (a friend of a friend) she met while performing. They put together the groundwork, and she went to Germany, Austria, and Czech Republic four times. Then she got an email asking her to do an opening spot for Burden—right away—with a full band. She was touring solo but says, "At times like that, you say yes and figure it out afterwards. I threw together a band in a week. Two weeks later we were on the road. They paid for the whole band." Sage adds:

> More than anything, I built a fan base over there, which you can't put a price on. I've learned so much by playing in small pubs in Germany. When I opened for Eric, it was really a challenge to put on a show that kind of reached the back of the house and had more projection. I had been used to performing as a folk/pop artist. I continued to be me but more intensely.

George Baum says Lost And Found goes to Germany at least once a year. Their friend, who works with youth in the Independent Lutheran

Church of Germany, helps set up their tours. These concerts aren't huge but they don't lose money. Many artists view a break-even trip to Europe as worth it. They love playing for enthusiastic audiences, seeing foreign countries, and creating fans for life. Be resourceful like Ezina Moore, who wanted to spend a month in Greece. She says she searched the Internet for names of venues in the Greek islands and called or emailed them. If they didn't speak English, she'd type in English and convert it to Greek on www.translate.com. After three months of work, she booked venues on six islands.

Booking international tours yourself is very doable, thanks to the Internet. Matt Allison lives in South Africa but focuses on building an overseas fan base, via message boards and worldwide album sales, that helps him earn a living from music. If Allison does this from Africa, you have no excuses! How does he book international tours? Allison says:

> Many late hours and countless amounts of coffee! Research played a big role—trying to find states where I had the best chance of drawing a crowd and where I knew artists whose fan base I could tap into. Often, you rely on other people. On my recent New Zealand tour, I knew nothing of the industry there and relied heavily on my distributor to book shows and make the best use of my time there to promote my new album.

Dorothy Potter's first European tour was three months in Germany, France, Denmark, and Switzerland with her songwriting partner. She says, "The Internet is full of anything you need to book a tour. All you need is a high-speed connection." She began booking her first three-month tour by searching music scenes in countries she thought were appropriate, using key words on Google to find venues in those markets.

Potter starts by booking "anchor gigs," a term she learned in a book about touring. These are gigs that pay well. She says some are obvious—really important venues—and adds:

> There are high-profile venues that will be an anchor gig no matter what they pay. I want them on my résumé, and they still pay decently. I discovered them by calling and calling from lists I created. I spend non-calling hours culling pages of venues with telephone numbers from the Internet. I sort them by "likely" or "not so likely." Book any gig you can get at the beginning. Then, try to fill in based on geography. If I have an anchor gig in Berlin on a Saturday night, I want to be in that area and try to find cheaper gigs during the week near Berlin. You plan around the big gigs to make life easier travelwise.

Potter says once she creates her list, she calls one after the other. When she calls, Potter asks first, "Do you speak English?" and then, "Is the person who books live music in?" If not, "When are they in?" She advises getting as much information as possible from whomever answers the phone: names, hours, and email addresses. She explains:

> If I get the person, I say, "I'm booking for fall and also well in advance for spring. How does your calendar look?" I don't talk about the music right away. I call as "a duo from New York," in the first thirty seconds of the conversation asking how often they have live music, how open is their calendar, and how willing they are to talk to me about it NOW. I get information about the rates they pay and the [best times to reach them by phone], to avoid making follow-up calls to people who are never there. Get all their numbers: mobile, home, email, etc. Ask about the sound system and accommodations. Always remain sensitive that these people are working—don't take too much of their time. I try to be really efficient and ask questions I need to ask. Often all the guy has seen is my website and he hasn't heard the music. But I give him a sense of confidence on the phone and say I'll do exactly what I'm told needs to be done. He needs someone to do music that will keep a pub crowd happy for three hours; I have a repertoire of two hundred songs. In most venues you're the only artist playing.

When asked how much she charges, Potter responds, "It depends on the size of your venue, how many gigs you give me, and the day of the week. How much do you usually pay?" If they give her a range for fees, she asks for the high figure, as if it's normal. Potter's cheapest gig in Europe paid 100 euro for the duo on a Wednesday night, plus a place to stay, food, drink, and tips. But they also booked them for Friday and Saturday, for much better money. She figures it's better than not working at all on Wednesday and paying for a room. Plus, they tip well in Europe. After booking weekends, Potter finds places to play on weekdays. She looks at venues that may have music during the week—either large clubs with music many nights a week, or small places like cafés, nonprofit organizations, or theaters. Why would a promoter book you? Potter explains:

> He wants to fill his calendar, too, and hasn't had time to listen to the CD. I always push to close the deal right away. The minute they have their calendar out, ask if they're ready to book dates now. Once I book a date, I ask if they're interested in a couple of more a month later? I can turn one gig into three simply by asking the right questions. That comes

from experience and a sense of security. You got a gig? Try for two or three more. Then your job is easier.

Touring Europe isn't easy. Potter hasn't used a contract yet, and she says no matter how many emails they exchanged, it's scary to arrive in a little German town for the first time wondering if the bar is really there and her posters are in the window. But she loves it enough to tour Europe several times a year now, and she expects to make more money each time. To book a tour, sound professional and confident when you call, even if you're nervous. Potter advises:

Spend time doing the research. At the beginning, it may seem like you're spending a lot of time for no results. It WILL pay off. You've got to do it! You won't get gigs the first week you do research. If you really want to be a touring musician in Europe, make a multi-year commitment to doing it. Learn a bit of German, French, Danish, and Spanish. So far, those are the best countries I've found for booking rock and pop. Don't whine or be a pussy. Just put the time in. You can do it. I can do it. Anyone can do it.

Another way to get to international markets is through the U.S. military. Find out where bases are, target clubs nearby, and promote at the base. Americans in foreign countries love to see American acts. If you know someone (or someone who knows someone) who's stationed in a foreign country, ask if they can help you book a gig, either in the nearby town or on the base, and also provide a place to stay. Or, contact the local NCO and Officers' Club yourself. Or, search for festivals in all countries—most large cities have them. Festivals often pay better than clubs and offer the opportunity to play for a larger audience.

Potter says, "We realized that making a living as a performing artist in New York City is very frustrating." She learned she can book months of gigs herself by investing serious time and discipline into finding her market and selling herself to it. Be prepared to put in a lot of very hard work. Potter says they start calling at 6:00 a.m. because of the six-hour time difference. Many musicians won't make that kind of commitment. You must!

INTERNATIONAL PROMOTION

There are many opportunities for promotion in foreign markets. Phil Tripp says, "Free music press is big in Australia. That's another way to break through. Having recognition overseas and distribution over here is important." Great music gets you further than in the U.S.: People are polite and easier to reach.

Try to spin a story around whatever small success you've had—radio play, touring, record sales, etc.—to give you an edge. You'll have a much better chance if you go to that market in person: If foreign press feels your presence, they're more likely to support you. But if your music circulates online, they may still find you.

Pete Tong says he looks for individuality in music that he plays on his very popular radio show, which is heard worldwide. Publicist Martha Moore says, "The press in Europe are fabulous—much more musically inquisitive. They want to know about the music and about you." She advises that you Google publications to find foreign publications online. Lisa O'Kane's friend sent her album to *Country Music People UK*, a European publication. She became the spotlight album and received a five-star review. Then she hired Moore, who sent the record out to European radio stations—they all loved it. Three years later, her record is still played all over Europe.

Radio can be accessible to you, depending on the country, if they love your music and you court them. Moore set up radio interviews for O'Kane prior to going to Spain. They hung out with journalists who introduced them to other journalists. When Moore and O'Kane had a booth at the Country Music Fair in Berlin, Moore emailed everyone she knew to say they'd be there. Media people came to them and introduced themselves. Since industry people tend to be friendlier and more open in overseas markets, you can work it—IF you have THE GOODS and a friendly personality. It's very different from here. Martha Moore explains:

> There are many community radio stations, but their signals aren't very big. Then there are national stations—BBC, etc. If you can befriend a DJ, you might get airplay on one. They call DJs "hosts" and "programmers" over there, and you can go to them directly. The DJs bring their own CDs to their shows. There's still a library at the station, but they can play what they want and mix it up—they are not geared to any chart. They play each track less frequently than American radio does. Doing interviews gets a great response.

Radio play brings rewards. Mary Gauthier says, "Overseas radio play does correlate to sales in the store. You need to get the radio play." Henri Lessing says, "Commercial radio has to know that you will attract a lot of listeners. National radio has to do the same, but it might be easier." National radio stations are more accessible—just like here! Borje Lindquist adds, "In Sweden, some television stations are public service, and they play a lot of independent music." Thomas Degn encourages:

If you are an independent label and want to get your music on radio, it's easy. In Scandinavia, it's not who you are, it's what music you have. National radio in Denmark and all over Scandinavia are very much out there with their ears. You don't have to come from anywhere to get music played on national radio. Sometimes we notice a great band on national radio and if they don't have a label, we sign them.

I worked my rap records in European markets. I called DJs for specialty hip-hop radio shows and asked if I could come and do an interview. I got on many many of them. Then I literally walked into the offices of magazines and my friendly personality got me press. It may not always be that easy, but if you're confident and outgoing, the media is a lot more accessible than in the U.S., and your music will speak to radio listeners. Interviews require some sort of interesting story: I was the Rappin' Teach. Figure out your angle; you need something to talk about in an interview.

Australia also offers radio opportunities. Phil Tripp says Triple J is the national youth radio network—like our public radio but for young people. It's one national broadcaster that transmits all over Australia. They play music that's not heard on mainstream radio. Tripp says, "Getting your music on Triple J is great. Submit your material to Triple J about six months prior to booking a tour here." Clive Hodson adds, "If you're from overseas and want to play in Australia, send your stuff to Triple J, say that you want to come tour here, and ask to have your stuff played. More American bands are coming here to tour because it's a really good pop circuit. Triple J is at the cutting edge of what is going to happen." He adds that it's not easy to get into the most popular radio stations, just like here. Tripp points out that if you have a video clip, there's a national TV program called "Rage," also on ABC, the national public broadcaster—send them your video.

Steve McClure says promotion is different in Asia, especially Japan. They use what are called "tie-ups": songs used for endorsing products in commercials or as themes for TV programs. There aren't many radio stations in Japan. People take trains to get around, so they listen to radio less. People learn about music through television. McClure explains:

Tie-ups remain the single most important form of music promotion in the Japanese music market. Radio and music TV are much less important than they are in North American and European markets. The problem is that if you let your song be used, often you sign away your performance royalties to the ad agency or television station for free publicity. It's a devil's bargain. In the rest of Asia, MTV and Channel V are more important.

When promoting your music internationally, make sure you coordinate getting media attention with your budget and availability. Howie Statland hired an independent radio promotion company in England but says, "I spent all my money on the promotion and didn't have any to go there and play. They actually got it on the radio. It was playing on a bunch of stations, but I was out of money to get over there and play, which would have helped." Plan carefully!

● ● ● ● **CHAPTER 20** ● ● ● ●

Some Final Advice

sincerely hope that I've gotten through to you and helped you find the confidence and direction you'll need to succeed as an independent artist. If you want a satisfying career in music, take charge! Don't wait for a label to do it. This book has presented you with many opportunities. Now, go make your own! If you have more blessings than others, share them. Never forget to lend a helping hand to those who are trying to come up behind you. As success begins to smile on you, please remember where you came from, and don't let it go to your head in that nauseating way. Remember the clubs that gave you a chance and do a show for them occasionally. Hold on to your sense of humility. You'll meet the same people on the way up as you will going down, and you may need a hand from them one day. Don't let successes get to you. We're all equal in our place in the universe. What goes around will come back to you.

I've interviewed a lot of music industry people. Often it's those with the biggest names who are the most generous and gracious with their time, while musicians who are just starting to come up in the world often act the most full of themselves. They expect special treatment and have the biggest attitudes. I've met many famous people and appreciate those who act like regular folks. Keep your ego in check. No one is better than anyone else, even if he or she is more famous. I laugh when people call about my seminar and are surprised that I answer my own phone. Why not? My friends have explicit instructions to kick my butt *hard* if success ever gets to my head. Give your friends the same instructions.

Visit the sites of all the artists in this book to see what else you can learn about how they do things. Learn from everyone you can. I do private consulting by phone if you need it. You can also find me through my website at www.daylle.com. In the meantime, following are the best pieces of advice from some of the musicians in this book. Absorb their words!

MICHELLE SHOCKED: Being in the right place at the right time is nothing more than a simple matter of doing what you believe in. If you're doing what you believe in, then you're automatically in the right place at the right time.

MARY GAUTHIER: Kidding around isn't going to make you a working musician. If you want to be a working musician, you have to be willing to do the work. I look at these things like pulling the thread on a sweater: You've got to keep going until you completely unravel your whole sweater. You have to keep pulling on it until you get a *no*. When you get a *no*, you move on to the next one. How was I to know that that one emailer from Amsterdam who wanted a free record wasn't just a wacko who wanted a free record? But I sent it, and it unfolded the whole of Europe for me. Now I've sold more in Europe than I have in the States. I could go there and pretty much make a living if I wanted to.

LISA O'KANE: You have to do what makes you comfortable. I have two children to raise, and living in southern California is expensive. I have no intention of being a starving musician. I expose myself regularly as an artist to every opportunity that arises, and good things always seem to come of it. The more exposure you have, the better.

EZINA MOORE: EXPECT to be successful. EXPECT to be able to support your family making music. The music business is not open only to a select few. It is open to all of us. If you have THE GOODS and are willing to give customers what they want, you will succeed. Have faith. Connect with other like-minded musicians who are out there and kicking ass! Band together and help each other out. Refuse to be jealous, competitive, or petty. Refuse to be offended. Refuse to procrastinate. If you have a fear of failure or success, find a good shrink to help you sort it out. Music is like love: Everybody needs it.

BARBARA TUCKER: What you put in is what you get out of it. Stop waiting for everybody to do it for you. You have to work yourself and it will work for you.

ALEX WOODARD: Take responsibility for yourself and your career. Good things will happen if you do.

HOWIE STATLAND: Don't listen to what other people tell you. Just do what you believe.

JENNIE DEVOE: Follow your heart and work hard. Be open to the opportunities that arise from working hard. Be a good songwriter.

CANJOE JOHN: Everyone in this business who survives is unique in their music, lifestyles, stories—they are cut from their own molds. Do not try to make it in this business trying to copy how someone else works or styles or lives. To succeed, start with a whole new idea and make it work—make it your own.

VISUAL POET: My best advice is to stick to it in the beginning. You really have to love your art and realize that there is going to be a time when you have to give one hundred fifty percent. To me, everything comes in levels. You reach a plateau, and then it becomes easier to book shows because you're starting to get a name. Then you do a show and somebody else will ask for you.

DAVID IPPOLITO: Show up. Woody Allen said that eighty-five percent of life is showing up. Just do it. Do it because you love it. Create your own venue; create your own music business.

EVAN R. SAFFER: There are so many steps, but it all starts with heart. You know if you've got it.

GREGORY ABBOTT: To make a living independently from your music, first make sure you have a burning desire to do this. It's not the easiest of professions, and there is no one forcing you. You have to be self-motivated. Second, do as much of it as you can. If you sing, learn to harmonize. Learn different instruments, music theory, etc. Learn to record. Learn the legal jargon. Get a real understanding of what all of this entails. You can do a lot more than you think. On the other hand, however, be realistic enough to let others handle areas where you find yourself lacking. It is a good time for independents. The important thing is to stay positive and keep creating good music. Rock on. *Namaste.*

CORKY McCLERKIN: If you are choosing to be independent, speak to both successful and unsuccessful independents and listen to what they consider their advantages and disadvantages.

ZAK MORGAN: Keep your chin up, keep a smile on your face, and be willing to work, work, work. Don't listen to people who tell you that you can't do it, because you can.

JENNIFER MARKS: Love what you do. Be creative musically as well as in business.

ADAM RICHMAN: Just do it. You can't sit around and just expect it to happen. You have to build your value on your own so that people will perceive you as having value. Try to become a better musician all the time. When your music speaks for itself, it's everything.

CHRISTINE KANE: I simply encourage you to trust in the process and to take small steps each day towards making your business happen. It is an enormous undertaking. Anytime something seems overwhelming, step away from it so you can get perspective. Ask for help.

PAT DINIZIO: No one is ever going to be as interested in what you do as you are. Assume that you have to do everything yourself. That's the problem with the major labels: They don't want you to do that. That's why there's a whole system in place. Labels are populated by people who love music, wanted to be musicians, and for whatever reason couldn't make it—and knew that the next best thing would be to work at a label and stay close to it.

DJ MINX: Nothing happens overnight. If you're a DJ, promote yourself as much as possible and get out there often. When your name is in everyone's face and you finally get your music pressed, you could be remembered for all your positivity and good work, which could help record sales. Remain optimistic!

DANIEL LEE MARTIN: It's a lot of hard work and if you don't believe in yourself, it won't happen. The money slowly rolls in. Never take *no* for an answer. Ninety-nine out of one hundred people are going to say *no*. You have to find the one who will say yes. Network and play. Let people hear you sing. Don't spend any time at home; you always have to be out there. Keep a smile on your face. Don't burn any bridges. Be careful whose feet you step on today, because you may need to kiss those feet tomorrow.

DANIELLE EGNEW: My best advice is to JUST DO IT! Don't stand on the sidewalk and wish your dreams away. Only YOU can make your own miracles happen. Dreams come true when they stop existing only in an artist's head, and manifest in the real world through good old-fashioned hard work. Be enthusiastic about what you have to offer, and follow through. There is no magic in success.

There is only hard work, and the courage to put that work into the belief in what you are designed to do. That's what separates the armchair quarterbacks from the real ones on TV. There is a lot of money to be had around music. Be creative. Be the vibe. Be your own miracle.

SUZANNE TENG: I always tell people that I'm the best at being Suzanne Teng, and nobody could do what I'm doing, better. I've created a combination of my own styles. Everyone else has that same quality—who they are and nobody can do it better. Be true to who you are. If I tried to be the best at something that wasn't me, then I couldn't do it. You have to follow your path. Let the path unfold, and follow it. Sometimes the hardest lessons are the biggest blessings.

PREECH: All that many people can think of is the money. You have to have a love for it. It's a job. You can have a hundred other rappers trying to do the same thing, but they may not be as dedicated as you are. A lot of rappers I grew up with gave up because they didn't see anything coming. I won't stop.

LORRAINE FERRO: I would love to tell you not to be afraid during all of this process, but you will be at times. So be afraid, be very afraid, but DO IT ANYWAY. It's not a matter of mastering this or that before you can do something worthwhile in this industry. It's a matter of DOING something that will make the things you do worthwhile, one way or another.

GEORGE BAUM: Stay independent if at all possible. We've known lots of bands that were doing fine until the labels got their claws into them and took all their money. The main points we emphasize if you're hoping to make a living independent of the major labels are these: Write your own songs. Record your own CDs for the purpose of selling them—avoid making pointless demos. Keep track of people who express an interest in booking you. Play as often as you can for free or for offerings, at least initially. Get a mailing list and gather as many names, postal addresses, and email addresses as possible; your mailing list can never be too large. And if someone from a label approaches you about signing a deal, run away as fast as you can—and don't look over your shoulder lest you be turned into a pillar of salt.

A record deal isn't your enemy. Not developing yourself as an artist before trying to expand your career, is. Some successful indies get deals that help them. But don't make a record deal your only goal. Instead, strive to be the best you can be, and work as hard as you can to let others know how good you are. You CAN do it. The artists in my book are proof of that. And they're just a sample of the many indies who are happily solvent. I could fill many books with all of them. Their names may not be familiar to you because they don't spend money on hype like majors do. But indie artists don't care about that since they're earning a living doing what they love. Do you love your music? Then practice, practice, practice. Don't put off until later what you can do now. Play for anyone who'll listen. Try the advice in my book, and create your own methods, too.

It's time to look at the world with a new vision! Without wishful thinking. Without "what ifs" and "if onlys." It's time to accept that your life won't change and your career won't expand unless YOU do something about it. It's time to stop waiting for someone to discover you. Get off your butt and discover yourself! It's time to stop complaining that no one comes to your gigs. Find out why and accept that you may need to improve your song-writing and/or your performance. So DO it! Your career is in YOUR hands when you're independent.

It's time to stop waiting for a manager to sign you before you can begin to make money. Managers want to rep artists who make enough money to be worth representing for their small percentage fee. Your life and your career begins and ends with YOU! When you accept the reality of your life, you can nurture yourself to a greater level of success by taking responsibility for it. I hope that you find the strength and motivation to get yourself to the next level. You're not alone! Independents are standing up and shouting that they're here to stay. Join them! Go to a mirror right now and say, "I can become successful! I don't need a record deal!" And mean it. I wish you joy and blessings in your personal declaration of independence.